Women in the Canadian

Women in the Canadian Academic Tundra

Challenging the Chill

ELENA HANNAH

LINDA JOAN PAUL

SWANI VETHAMANY-GLOBUS

McGill-Queen's University Press
Montreal & Kingston · London · Ithaca

© McGill-Queen's University Press 2002
ISBN 0-7735-2274-3 (cloth)
ISBN 0-7735-2280-8 (paper)

Legal deposit second quarter 2002
Bibliothèque nationale du Québec

"On Being Homeless: Aboriginal Experiences of
Academic Spaces" Patricia Monture-Angus
(pp 168–73) is © Patricia Monture-Angus, 1998.

Joyce Green's Chapter, pp. 85–91, was first published
in *Pushing the Margins Native and Northern Studies*, J.
Oakes, R. Riewe, M. Bennett, and B. Chisholm, eds.
(Winnipeg: Native Studies Press, 2001).

Printed in Canada on acid-free paper that is 100%
ancient forest free (100% post-consumer recycled),
processed chlorine free, and printed with vegetable-
based, low VOC inks.

McGill-Queen's University Press acknowledges the
financial support of the Government of Canada
through the Book Publishing Industry Development
Program (BPIDP) for its publishing activities. We also
acknowledge the support of the Canada Council for
the Arts for our publishing program.

**National Library of Canada Cataloguing
in Publication Data**

Main entry under title:
    Women in the Canadian academic tundra: challenging
    the chill
    Includes bibliographical references and index.
    ISBN 0-7735-2274-3 (bound) –
    ISBN 0-7735-2280-8 (pbk.)
    1. Sex discrimination in higher education – Canada.
    2. Women college teachers – Canada. 3. Women
    college administrators – Canada. I. Hannah, Elena
    II. Paul, Linda (Linda Joan) III. Vethamany-Globus,
    Swani
    LB2332.34.C3W65 2002   378'.0082'0971   C2001-903600-0

Typeset in Palatino 10/12
by Caractéra inc., Quebec City

*To our parents, who taught us to love learning,
and to all those who work to melt the tundra ice
for women academics.*

Contents

ix   Contents

Acknowledgments

We express first of all our appreciation to all the contributors for coming forward with their stories and reflections, and for their extraordinary patience in staying with us throughout the long gestation period of this project.

We specifically thank Philip Cercone, executive director, McGill-Queen's University Press, who was enthusiastic about this project from the very beginning, and whose constant encouragement and unwavering support were vital to our bringing the book to publication.

Our thanks also go to the competent staff at McGill-Queen's, in particular to Joan McGilvray, Brenda Prince, and Margaret Levey, for skillfully guiding us through the publishing process. We are indebted also to Jane McWhinney for her invaluable editorial suggestions, for the sensitivity with which she dealt with the stories and their authors, and for her patience, sense of humour, and willingness to work for consensus.

The staff members in our three universities who assisted in processing the manuscript also deserve our special thanks. We are particularly grateful to Sharon Wall, General Office, Science Building, Memorial University, who, with help from her colleagues Marilyn Hicks, Eileen Ryan, and Peggy-Ann Parsons, typed and retyped numerous versions of the manuscript as it evolved, and meticulously put together the final copy. We also express our gratitude to Kanthie Seresinhe, Faculty of Arts, University of Regina, who similarly worked to help produce the initial manuscript. Our thanks go also to Teri Rogoschewsky, University of Regina.

We gratefully acknowledge the generous financial support of McGill-Queen's University Press as well as our respective universities: namely the University of Waterloo, Waterloo, Ontario; the Publications Subvention Program of Memorial University of Newfoundland, St John's, Newfoundland; and the University of Regina, the Faculty of Arts, and Luther College, the University of Regina, Regina, Saskatchewan.

Last, but not at all least, we owe a great deal to our respective spouses and other family members. Linda Paul would like to thank her husband, Alec, also a geographer, for his continual support and encouragement throughout this project. Swani Vethamany-Globus expresses her special thanks to Morton Globus, her partner in life as well as in her profession, and to her two adult children, Julie and Brian, who provided support and life-sustaining warmth for her life in the Tundra. Elena Hannah wishes to thank her husband, Ted Hoekman, for his insightful editorial suggestions and his generous technical assistance. These and many others have cheered us on, counselled us, given much-needed help, and energized us with their enthusiasm.

Editors' Note

It has been over four years since we started collecting stories for our book. The lives and circumstances of our contributors have, in some cases, changed since they responded to our call for papers. The narratives and reports you are about to read may therefore not accurately represent current situations in all cases.

Some contributors have received important awards; others have published books, papers, and journals or have distinguished themselves in some other way. A few have decided to leave the faculty ranks and engage in other pursuits. Space constraints do not permit us to include many of these particulars.

Overall, however, the general picture regarding the lot of Canadian academic women has changed insignificantly, if at all. While our unique collection has been in preparation, other books and articles have been published that confirm what our contributors courageously reveal.

We have chosen to present the editors' names and the sequence of the articles according to alphabetical order, thinking it the most equitable way to proceed. No ranking is in any way implied. Each author is fully responsible for the content of her or his article. As co-editors, we assume responsibility or liability for no articles other than our own.

Elena Hannah
Linda Paul
Swani Vethamany-Globus

Women in the Canadian Academic Tundra

Challenging the Chill

This book is an anthology of stories of academic women in Canadian universities, told in their own voices. It is a tribute and a testimony to the persistence and resilience of such women who, against many odds, continue to contribute to the academy with energy and determination.

The tundra is a treeless, barren land, semi-frozen for much of the year, inhospitable to most forms of life. The Canadian Arctic falls into this geographical zone. We, the editors, found a parallel between the struggle it takes to survive in the Canadian tundra and the lives of the academic women who have had to face a daunting, unsupportive working environment. Life in the tundra is harsh, and it takes extraordinary tenacity, determination, and strength for creatures to eke out a living in this terrain despite its rugged beauty. The imagery struck a sympathetic chord with our Canadian academic sisters, many of whom have come forward to narrate their experiences.

We want to showcase their lives, to let them speak in their own voices about their dreams and expectations upon entering the academy, the challenges and struggles they have faced, and their successes. Many books and research papers have been written about the status of academic women, in an effort to document and correct inequities in the workplace. Many academic women continue to fight an uphill battle, as they face extraordinary resistance in practising the profession for which they trained long and hard. Some succeeded, many barely survived, and some left university life as they found the academic tundra too inhospitable. We decided to collect personal narratives to convey what data cannot: the uniqueness of each life, each soul. Through this multi-coloured tapestry of personal stories we hope to give an insight into the complexities of their survival or demise in this harsh terrain.

GETTING TOGETHER

We took up this project with the recognition that there existed a desire and need among academic women to share their stories and experiences in the academy. We came together at the Status of Women Conference of the Canadian Association of University Teachers (CAUT-SWC) held in Halifax, Nova Scotia, in October 1996. For the first time in the history of CAUT-SWC conferences, a session on part-timers at Canadian universities was included, organized by Linda Paul, a geographer from the University of Regina and a member of the Status of Women committee for CAUT. Swani Vethamany-Globus, a biologist and half-time faculty member at the University of Waterloo, was an invited speaker at this conference. Psychologist Elena Hannah, a full- and part-time lecturer for many years at Memorial University, Newfoundland, was an enthusiastic participant. We became sensitive to the frustrations of conference participants who were unable to tell their stories because of the inherent time constraints. At the suggestion of Swani Vethamany-Globus, we agreed to call for stories from academic women across Canada and to compile them into a collection of narratives documenting women's experiences.

Although we initially focused on part-timers,[1] we concluded that it was vital for all women's voices to be heard. As stories trickled in, we were touched, enraged, and at times struck by feelings of helplessness and despair, but we became all the more determined to publish. Some women were counselled by their peers not to submit their narratives for fear of reprisals. Some submitted their stories with a brave heart only to withdraw them later because of potential backlash from their universities. Some consulted their lawyers to clear the possibility of liability suits. Many toned down their words and feelings. In only a few cases do the contributors' smouldering resentment and anger sear through their veiled language. Perhaps women are too polite, too compliant, too non-confrontational. As Harriet Goldhor Lerner (1985) writes in *The Dance of Anger*, "Anger is a signal, and one worth listening to. Our anger may be a message that we are being hurt, that our rights are being violated, that our needs or wants are not being adequately met, or simply that something is not right." Since women have long been discouraged from acknowledging or expressing their anger, this collection of narratives may contain more than meets the eye.

THE LANDSCAPE

The second feminist movement, which started in North America in the 1960s, promoted change in people's attitudes, lifestyles, and workplace to a degree unimaginable even a decade before. The air was heady with possibilities for women: yes, you can have it all, young women were told – the "all" meaning, of course, both a family and a career – what men had always had (Schwartz, 1992). Through the 1970s and 1980s the number of women in faculty positions in Canadian universities increased, catalyzed by the rapid expansion of existing universities and the creation of new ones. Yet, although the absolute numbers of women in academia grew in some years, the percentage of women relative to men did not change much. In fact, there was sometimes a slight proportional drop, until the ratio steadily rose between 1973 and 1994 to reach 22.7 per cent (Ornstein, Stewart, and Drakich, 1998).

Ingrained attitudes and behaviours are resistant to change, however. Women academics discovered that change comes in many onion-like layers, and the numerical changes that had begun to take place were only the first layer. Women were often told that their salaries need not equal men's because, once they were married, they would be supported by their husbands; men's salaries needed to be larger to support their families. Affirmative action and equity programs helped, but a perusal of figures from universities across Canada shows clearly that women are still concentrated in the lower ranks and that, within the same rank, their salaries are lower than men's (Ornstein, Stewart, and Drakich, 1998). These facts raise questions: Why would these very bright women who got through graduate school in an extremely competitive, male-dominated environment not be on a par with their male colleagues? (Schwartz, 1992). Why are women represented in decreasing proportions as they progress from undergraduate to graduate studies and into faculty positions? (Schiebinger, 1999).

The basic problem is that the academic world is still quite androcentric. It is based on the model of a working man who has a stay-at-home wife, a model that frees him to work long hours and relocate when necessary or desirable. A successful career in academia demands numerous publications, which in turn lead to hefty grants, which lead to more publications in an ever-upward spiralling academic path. Success also requires networking, committee work, and informal contacts where alliances can be made. To onlookers, academics seem to lead charmed lives, strolling unhurriedly through landscaped campuses, sitting in book-lined offices removed from worldly concerns, dictating magisterial lectures to eager students, or conversing with like-minded colleagues in a congenial atmosphere. But this romanticized picture does not reflect reality. The academic world is cutthroat and competitive, and most of its members need to dedicate time and effort to establishing politically valuable relationships with peers. Moreover, a precise academic clock regulates the timing of certain achievements. The fact that women are now an integral part of the academy and yet are also the childbearers and principal caregivers (Brayfield, 1992; Devereaux, 1993) has modified neither the demands nor the clock. Worse still, since most of us buy into the fantasy that things have indeed changed, when a woman fails to follow this male-created model because of conflicting family demands, she is blamed for her failure and, even worse, she might blame herself.

Despite the trend among career women toward later parenthood and smaller families, childbearing can and does derail many women from the straight academic track. In fact, the first child causes major changes in lifestyle and economic opportunity (Spain and Bianchi, 1996), and each child thereafter contributes exponentially to the time and energy crunch so familiar to working women. In most households, women still bear the brunt of what was traditionally "women's work" (Berardo, Shehen, and Leslie, 1987). We are undergoing what Arlie Hochschild (1989) has called the "stalled revolution." Since motherhood and related responsibilities were used for years as an argument to prevent women from joining the workforce, when women saw a window of academic opportunity they entered into what Felice Schwartz (1992) calls "the conspiracy of silence." Motherhood went underground. Women felt that denial was a small price to pay for being allowed to "play with the boys" and develop their potential, to find the fulfillment they felt they deserved, in the world of work. In this conspiracy of silence, the academy seemed to be saying to women: If you pretend to have no family encumbrances, we will pretend that you are as good as a man (Schwartz, 1992). This downplaying of maternal identity is still a noticeable characteristic of the academic environment; it can lead women to burn-out or to hard choices between career and family (Hornosty, 1998).

Not all women academics jumped on the academic bandwagon. Some married women were steeped in the tradition that their husband's careers were more important and sacrificed opportunities for their own careers. Others found that after having children their deep attachments made full-time work undesirable. Yet others found that daycare nightmares, the endless merry-go-round of homemaking and career-making, and the discovery that their husbands were not prepared to shoulder half the home-related responsibilities (Brayfield,

1992; Devereaux, 1993; Douthitt, 1989) were so draining that they revised their career plans. Women's perceptions of their husbands' contributions to household and childcare do not always reflect reality. Most women attribute more helping behaviour to their partners than is warranted, so when they are tired and stressed they conclude that they are really not capable of combining career and motherhood (Hochschild, 1989). The reality is that, although men have increased their contributions to home and parenting and women have reduced theirs, there is still a wide gap between the two. "As long as men have fewer family responsibilities and women have more, the potential exists for women to choose or accept lower occupational status and earnings" (Spain and Bianchi, 1996). Women also tend to be unaware of the fact that, of all industrialized nations except the United States (Berk, 2000), Canada still has a very poor record regarding maternity leave and childcare subsidies. And when maternity leaves are available many women feel unable to take them.

Academic women in particular experience a timing crunch shared by women in few other professions. By the time they have finished their long years of education, their childbearing years are substantially reduced. The crucial first ten years when academics establish themselves, with long hours of work and networking, are precisely the years when most women also have children and enter a labour-intensive phase at home.

These personal circumstances, combined with the chilly climate and the systemic inequities of Canadian universities, determine that a sizable percentage of bright, capable, and promising academic women opt out of the standard career path. Women who take time out from academic careers pay a very high price. What is often intended to be a temporary hiatus turns out, in all too many cases, to be a permanent arrangement without recourse. Those who want to keep a toehold in their academic lives and do research or teaching on a part-time basis find that, when they are ready to rejoin their peers, they are not wanted back. Particularly in the sciences (Hornosty, 1998, Lynn and Todoroff, 1998), previous "desertions" on the part of women are seen as proof positive that they just don't have "the right stuff."

When this attitude is added to an economic climate where the word "downsizing" has become a sacred mantra, women who return to academia find themselves marginalized and stigmatized. Part-time positions may be compatible with family responsibilities, but the costs are great and long-lasting. Loss of income is not such women's only penalty: they also risk erosion of wages, loss of seniority, and, in most cases, loss or reduction of benefits, and no job security (Corcoran, Duncan and Ponza, 1984; Holden and Hanson, 1987). And the penalties include a usually irreversible derailment from the academic track with a concomitant loss of status among peers.

Many Canadian university faculties became unionized in the 1980s and 1990s to create a power-base for standing up to increasingly hostile administrations. However, unions often turned their backs on these "second class" academics, the part-timers. Because many part-time academics provide cheap labour for financially strapped universities, they are treated with scorn. Thus, part-timers are rejected by their full-time peers and have only recently been accepted by their unions (CAUT-SWC Conference, 1996). In addition, the corporatization of the academy, now progressing at various rates across Canada, is expected to increase the proportion of part-time academic staff (Tudiver, 1999; Turk, 2000).

Even full-time academic women who abided by the rules and in many cases made enormous sacrifices to nurture their careers still find that the playing field is not level. Although it looks as if there are no barriers, the career advancement of the immense majority of women academics stops below the level attained by most men (Ornstein, Stewart, and Drakich, 1998). Mason and Jewson (1992) argue that, rather than hitting a glass ceiling, women experience a stone floor to which they are shackled, since they are concentrated in the lower ranks. Stone floors are cold, adding to the discomfort of a "chilly climate." Caplan (1994) uses this term to refer to ways in which the maleness of the environment affects all women in academia. Examples include being ignored at committee meetings, having ideas taken over by male colleagues without due credit, not being invited to semi-social events where networking takes place, being patronized, belittled, passed over for promotions, being the object of sexist jokes or sexual innuendo – the list is long (Caplan, 1994; Stalker and Prentice, 1998).

A few women have managed to rise above the stone floor, break through the glass ceiling, and soar to the top echelons of university administration. They are role models and a source of inspiration. Although we invited several women in higher positions to take advantage of this opportunity, few responded. We applaud those who came forward to shed light on women's experiences in the executive suite. Among female academic administrators there are some who, having reached the top ostensibly without anyone's help, perceive less successful women as responsible for their own lack of achievement, denying that discrimination against women could exist in the university setting. Also, women who have achieved high status are still too few in number to constitute the critical mass necessary to effect change (Stalker and Prentice, 1998).

Lack of mentors is another barrier that women encounter. From the early days when students choose their major, most of them benefit enormously from finding a compatible mentor. Certainly by the time they are in graduate school, the role of their mentor is crucial to them. Mentors take students under their wing, establish a closer relationship than is usual between professor and student, enlighten students about potential land mines to avoid in their careers, and prepare them for the transition to independence, including connecting them with potential employers. Basically, a mentor goes to bat for her or his students. This mentoring relationship can make the difference between success and failure. Once one has an academic position, it is also beneficial to develop a mentoring relationship with a more established faculty member. As it turns out, very few women in academia have mentors since, with such a low proportion of faculty being women, female mentors are not always available. While men can be important mentors for women students, some male faculty can be uncomfortable with such close relationships with a female or, conversely, be eager to mentor because they are attracted to the younger female or consider her an object for their sexual advances (Laurence, 1989). In a university setting dominated by men, it is often hard for new female academic staff to find mentors among their male colleagues (Stalker and Prentice, 1998). Thus, women faculty tend to build their careers without the benefit of mentors (Caplan, 1994).

Yet another barrier that women academics experience, particularly as they move up the ladder, is their discomfort with male managerial styles. Respondents in a study of women administrators in British universities described the predominant male managerial way of relating to colleagues as aggressive, macho, competitive, and top-down. Men describe themselves as a team but are seen by women as competing with each other. This image contrasts with the consensus-seeking, caring, and involved style that women have been observed to favour. Many women academics in high administrative positions feel strain and even despair when they are caught between these clashing behaviour patterns (Kettle, 1996).

More recent data show that the panorama is not much better for younger academic women. While many male academics are fair, caring, and concerned about the welfare of their female counterparts, others are not. Discrimination has become subtle and difficult to prove (Stalker and Prentice, 1998). Though many male academics dare not make public statements that are blatantly misogynistic, there is ample latitude in academic hiring, promotions, and granting committees to allow for women to be left out in the cold without the appearance of discrimination (Caplan 1994). Most departments can be shown to have some women on their faculty, a fact that advertises that women are hired if they are good enough. The unspoken corollary is that their numbers are low in comparison to men because of inherent flaws in the pool of academic women.

As we begin the new millennium, we are witnessing a complacency in the ivory tower with regard to women's issues. True, some equity measures are in place and progress is rightfully acknowledged (Ornstein, Stewart, and Drakich, 1998). Federal programs have achieved a narrowing of the wage gap for full-time academic women. It can be argued, however, that large numbers of poorly paid part-timers are subsidizing this wage improvement. In some universities, part-timers make up one third or more of the academic staff (CAUT-SWC Conference, 1996). Moreover, at 22.7 percent, the proportion of full-time women faculty is still inappropriately low and concentrated mainly in the lower ranks. Change agents are often silenced or co-opted (Stalker and Prentice, 1998) and institutions do not offer the flexibility for women to balance careers and mothering. And, even if they have no family responsibilities, women continue to be discriminated against simply for being women.

NARRATIVE THREADS

These are the stories and findings of forty-eight contributors from across the Canadian academic tundra. The narratives weave an intricate tapestry of blended colours and intertwining themes. Some portray a central theme in bold relief. Others meander across the warp, radiating nuances of meaning and mingling with other issues of similar hue. For some women, the tundra is hostile and frigid. For others, it is a region of beauty in which their life stories have blossomed like bouquets of spring flowers in the wilderness. The warp that supports all these stories, that binds them all together, is the milieu of Canadian academe.

Some of the stories woven into this warp are bold and exciting. Others, however, carry the ugly knots of the double discrimination experienced by Aboriginal women, women of colour, immigrant women, or women caught in the treadmill of sessional, part-time, and contract work.

In introducing our authors, we start with the largest group, the huge cohorts of part-timers – the non-tenured, the sessional lecturers, and the contract workers. It is in academe's interest to keep them subjected, invisible, out of sight, out of mind. They make up a large percentage of the women in academe, yet they receive the poorest pay, the fewest benefits, and the least recognition. Without these academics, most of whom are women who work at near, and even below, poverty levels, universities would suffer considerable financial hardship. Feldberg, Shannon Gadbois, Diane Huberman-Arnold, Jody Macdonald, Denise McConney, Marianne Parsons, Stevi Stephens, Dorothy Tovell, Susan Turner, Susan Wilson, and Rochelle Yamagishi, as well as the three editors, Elena Hannah, Linda Paul, and Swani Vethamany-Globus are representatives of this group.

While most of us share the frustrations of subordination and invisibility that part-time employment entails, Dorothy Tovell and Shannon Gadbois are stimulated by the challenges of holding three simultaneous contracts and enjoy the concomitant flexibility in their lives. Tovell suggests that tandem contracts could offer a design for employment practices of the future. Wendy Feldberg and Elena Hannah spin a different thread, as their careers have wandered from tenure-track to contract and finally to sessional work. As their academic rank diminished, their validation in academe plummeted.

Cécyle Trépanier and Anne Lavack, on the other hand, bring a brighter tone of contentment and satisfaction with their positions in academe, reporting few frustrations or barriers in their career paths. Deborah Wills celebrates women in all their complexities and shapes as she writes about "Largesse." Similarly Susan Wilson, Carol Stos, and Mary Hampton with Peggy Wilson celebrate their own lives as well as those of their female colleagues and students.

Writing from the student perspective, Amy Rowat emphasizes the importance of role models for female students. Andrea O'Reilly describes the frantic pace of graduate student mothers who lack any institutional support. Student Petra Remy and her advisor Lesley Harman discuss the countless daily activities that intrude upon linear career paths, the academic clock, and the biological clock. Struggling to obtain her doctorate in a university distant from home, Rochelle Yamagishi is torn between living with her family and obtaining an education, while searching for her roots in a cross-cultural environment.

Two winners of the Canadian Association of University Teachers' Sarah Shorten award speak out. Consultant Helen Breslauer looks back on a varied academic career that offered many opportunities to observe conditions and developments related to academic women. In contrast, Diane Huberman-Arnold has found personally that academia excludes, inhibits, and in fact squashes women.

Four CAUT-Status of Women Committee chairs, past and present, also share their perspectives. To Jane Gordon, teaching within a female-dominated institution paradoxically does not bring a friendlier environment. Marilyn Taylor, presenting six themes that she considers important in working toward change for women, also suggests that considerable retrenchment on women's advances has occurred recently. Jennifer Bankier examines the costs of seeking equity in a male-dominated society, and Jeanette Lynes discusses problems women encounter when negotiating job details and contracts.

Doubly-marginalized groups, such as Aboriginal women and women of colour, often end up being labelled, but still unhelped, by equity reform. Lillian Dyck and Rochelle Yamagishi draw strength from their traditions and cultural roots. Patricia Monture-Angus, having moved from law to Native studies, finds the critical mass of Aboriginal voices important as she seeks a safe intellectual, academic home. Although discussing problems relating more to gender than to racial issues, Dyck, after being bullied by superiors, lists positive steps one can take to ensure that harassment does not continue. Fyre Jean Graveline, a Métis feminist, asks what academic freedom means as she endures stereotyping and backlash from university settings steeped in patriarchy and colonial barriers. From a different perspective, Mary Hampton and Peggy Wilson, a member of the Cree nation, recount how they used a traditional indigenous healing circle to combat the hostile, frontier mentality of a sexist environment. Denise McConney, a non-Native in a Native studies department, finds the culture stimulating but the sessional juggling of courses exhausting. Finally, Joyce Green discusses the challenges that Aboriginal and other marginalized women face as they deal with a sexist and racist academy.

Immigrants Elena Hannah from Argentina, Swani Vethamany-Globus from India, and Suzan Banoub-Baddour from Egypt recount their experience as newcomers striving to find a foothold in the cold tundra. Some question whether race has played a negative role in their efforts to achieve positions and acceptance. Few have reached secure posts in their universities. Top administrative jobs seem beyond their reach. Vethamany-Globus suggests that a steel rather than a glass ceiling exists for women of colour.

Another representative of an equity-seeking group is Susan McCorquodale. She assigns herself to a double minority, as a female with a disability in the dominantly male world of political science. Fortunately, neither characteristic was an impediment to a successful career.

Some authors initiated surveys to determine whether their personal experiences were unique or more general to the academic world. Maxine Mott interviewed women in administrative positions. An important companion to her survey is Dianne Common's perspective, which verifies that academic administration is steeped in the traditional practices of a patriarchal hierarchy. She develops a theme that contrasts female and male behaviours in governance.

Jeanette Lynes takes her experience with numerous job interviews and turns it into a question: Do women negotiate with hiring committees for better employment? Her situation was complicated by her having an academic spouse who had work requirements. Lynes found that her lack of confidence to negotiate better salary or other benefits was shared by others. Lesley Harman (and Petra Remy) conducted interviews with both female and male faculty and determined that the latter were more likely to achieve uninterrupted, upward linear career progression.

Combining parenting with a full-time career is a major obstacle for many women. Anne Morgan typifies women who eventually opt for parenting exclusively. Many others chose time off or a lighter teaching load while their children were young: Swani Vethamany-Globus, Carol Stos, Linda Paul, Elena Hannah, Jody Macdonald, Wendy Feldberg, and Susan Turner, for example, found their careers stunted or stalled as a result. Others, such as Andrea O'Reilly, Rochelle Yamagishi, and Suzan Banoub-Baddour, wrestled with their guilt while taking graduate classes or, as in Amy Rowat's case, questioned this dichotomy prior to marriage and a career. Still others struggled with a full-time career: Fyre Jean Graveline, for one, brought her child to work despite criticism, and others contended with their children's major health problems or with abnormal pregnancies. The permutations of this theme are endless. In contrasting her career to that of her academic husband, Peter Bowal, Irene Wanke notes how previously similar salaries for both sexes diverge once pregnancy and children arrive. Having children tends to stunt the career growth of women academics in the tundra far more than it affects their male counterparts.

Many of our contributors have written about the choices that are made throughout our university sojourn. Susan Wilson examines ethical and career path choices. Susan Turner, like Wilson, ultimately questions whether to leave academe, as she undergoes great oppression. The life-changing decision to follow a husband's employment opportunities such as Carol Stos, Irene Wanke, Joan Scott, and others made early in their careers, cannot be made lightly.

On a less serious note, Alison Hayford presents a tongue-in-cheek look at academe. Like Bluma Litner, Jane Gordon, and Jennifer Mather, she questions the basis on which we evaluate academic work. Should research be confined to narrow fields of study? Litner's title tells all; to her dismay, "Teaching Doesn't Count." In response to the slights of systemic discrimination, Hayford offers humorous survival tips for the academic tundra. Harriet Lyons writes a satirical, self-deprecating piece about her search to find herself, her field, and her husband! She ends by extolling "irony," a gift that can help survive any depth of permafrost. In a similar vein, enumerating the reasons why she "didn't have time to write her article," Denise McConney chronicles the pulls of daily life on sessional teachers. Carol Stos, on examining her career, concludes that while she may seem "to have it all," academe is perhaps not as women-inclusive as it appears.

The theme of patriarchy is expressed time after time in the chapters of this book: by a vice-president (Common), a former dean (Mott), a former assistant dean (Hayford), a chair (Stos), former chairs (Lyons), professors (Graveline, Litner, Mojab, Green), sessional instructors (Paul), and graduate students (O'Reilly). Women have been fighting against patriarchal hierarchy for a long time, but the glass ceilings, or steel ceilings, often unconsciously erected by men who are used to controlling, are still very low, with only scratches in the steel, hairline cracks in the glass.

Women in science, exemplified by Irene Wanke, Lillian Dyck, Jennifer Mather, Anne Morgan, Amy Rowat, Joan Scott, Dorothy Tovell, and Swani Vethamany-Globus, practise in a field strewn with obstacles. Vethamany-Globus and Morgan, for instance, worked for years without salary, using NSERC grants to fund their projects, in the hopes that they would eventually be rewarded with permanent positions. Scott highlights problems for girls who are systematically directed away from science during their school years.

When Cupid unites hearts, he seems unconcerned about the repercussions of unions between academics. As the number of women in graduate schools increases, so do the number of academic couples who share an area of expertise. Finding faculty positions within the same institution, let alone the same discipline, is very difficult. Academic wives usually face discrimination. Some couples share laboratory facilities and collaborate quite successfully, but, when motherhood becomes a factor, the woman may face the triple discrimination of being a woman, an academic wife, and a mother.

This book contains several examples of academic couples: Bowal contrasts his relatively easy ride, once past the sessional stage, to that of his wife (Wanke) in a different discipline; Morgan and Vethamany-Globus decry the fact that as members of husband-wife teams in the same discipline, their credentials, research, and job applications were often given short shrift in comparison to their husbands'. Paul and Stephens describe how hiring rules favoured their husbands when they moved together to new places of employment. Huberman-

Arnold discovers that she is frozen out, despite being in the same department as her husband. Mather's relationship has a different twist: although both she and her husband have doctorates, she holds the tenured position. When Lynes was interviewed for a job, the interviewers alluded to possible difficulties arising from her academic husband's career. When he was interviewed, her career was not mentioned.

Equity officer Shahrzad Mojab describes her formidable task in a male-dominated power structure that seemed to support her role only because of the requirements of the Federal Contractors Program. At odds with the administration were those feminists and anti-racists who supported change, as Jennifer Bankier also discovered. Marty Laurence, a self-described practising feminist change agent, has studied women who work against women.

Some articles delve into other inhospitable aspects of a very chilly environment. Ellen Facey's "No Welcome for a Woman: Desperately Seeking Colleagues in a Cold Climate" speaks for itself. Susan Turner and Diane Huberman-Arnold find their philosophical homes intolerably cold and harassing. Unfortunately, in spite of being chosen 1998 winner of the CAUT Sarah Shorten award for outstanding service to academic women, Huberman-Arnold was dislodged from her sessional position and has found employment in another institution. Turner has found a similar environment, one so frigid that the frostbite may force her to leave academe.

To fill out our tapestry, we must include the brighter colours of the narratives that some sessional lecturers bring. Shannon Gadbois's story is heartening. In the midst of two serious health problems, she twice found very supportive chairs who were concerned more for her health than with her teaching responsibilities. But she questions sessionals' lack of benefits and academe's willingness to let them flounder with little if any protection. Jody Macdonald argues for more flexibility in employment practices in her plea for university acknowledgment that some academics might want to create a "Life Vitae" by blending family, career, and community activism in a more balanced lifestyle.

The careers of Marianne Parsons and Stevi Stephens reveal broken threads in our coast-to-coast tapestry. The gaps are so obvious that in her submission, "McTeaching," Parsons describes moving six times in four years, in one year teaching seven courses at three different universities. Finding part-timers in academe so devalued, marginalized, and expendable, she equates them to employees in fast-food joints. Stephens's title, "Roads Scholars," signposts the long-distance travels to which many sessionals teaching in disjointed and detached places must resort. Wendy Feldberg adds even more colours to the weft. "Presenteeism," a newly coined term, refers to the plight of sessional teachers who, despite having submitted job applications and taught in departments previously, must still show up just to remind administrators and support staff that they are available for teaching. She also alludes to "ageism." Teaching as a sessional for years may backfire as hiring committees opt for younger applicants when full-time job openings come up. All too true is another Feldberg observation: many part-time women academics can only survive on their low salaries because their husbands or partners have more secure and highly paid jobs. The contributions of sessionals and contract workers are so seldom recognized in fair contracts that their situation seems to have faded to the invisibility of colourless threads. It is our hope that the narratives we present here will bring all the strands into a bolder relief that demands attention.

NOTE

1 We use the generic part-timers to signify non-tenure track or contractual staff. There are many combinations and permutations and the nomenclature varies across universities.

Paying the Inequity Tax

JENNIFER BANKIER

I am a strong, passionate, compassionate, fair, fifty-year-old, White, straight, middle-class, temporarily able-bodied woman. I entered Osgoode Hall Law School as part of the first big wave of women lawyers in 1971 and I have remained at the leading edge of this wave throughout my academic career as a law professor (Wayne State University: 1979–82; Dalhousie: 1982–present).

Throughout my professional life I have had to fight battles over competence and credibility. My intellectual credentials are unassailable, so the *competence* challenges have focused on my personality. They come whenever I attempt something new. First, I was "too emotional" to teach. After eleven years of successful teaching, I was "too emotional" to be a dean. The *credibility* problems are more persistent. For example, I have won a contested Dalhousie Law School committee election exactly once during sixteen years. "When I am right, no-one remembers. When I am wrong, no-one forgets." I spent a lot of time and effort trying to fix these problems. For example, I tried never to show any emotion, to the point that my students complained I was talking in a monotone. I worried constantly that every action or outcome might reinforce negative assumptions about me.

In the spring of 1990, the Dalhousie Faculty Association (DFA) asked me to serve as DFA president-elect, president, and past-president (1990–93). I did this and then served a second such term from 1993–96. I was also elected to the Canadian Association of University Teachers (CAUT) Status of Women Committee (SWC), and am now the chair of SWC and a member of the CAUT executive.

My time as DFA president was a revelation. Everyone assumed I was both competent and credible. If I did things right, I got praise and thanks. If I made a mistake, it was an ad hoc problem that could be fixed, not evidence of general incompetence. My advocacy often produced useful results in a reasonable time frame, and people, even the administration, treated me with respect. It was as if an invisible three-hundred-pound rock had rolled off my shoulders. I soon had the strong realization that my entire life would have been like this if I lived in an equitable society, or if I was a totally privileged person – that is, White upper-class male – in our society.

For a time I hoped that my demonstrated competence outside the law school might translate into credibility within, but this did not happen. It became clear that, since I am the same, competent person both at DFA and in the law school, my law school experiences had nothing to do with competence and everything to do with other people's political agendas. I had been warned as early as the 1970s that "if the reasons you are given keep changing but the result is always the same, you know that the reasons you are being given are not the real reasons".[1] Because I wish to think well of other people, it took me until the 1990s to accept the implications that the credibility and competence arguments were rationalizations designed to marginalize "upstarts" who might challenge the comfortable status quo of privileged people.

As full recognition dawned, I realized that our society imposes a variety of "inequity taxes" on people from oppressed groups that their counterparts do not pay. Energy that we must expend in coping with inequities in our lives is not available for study, work, or play.

The nature, intensity, and frequency of inequity taxes varies from group to group. I don't pay an inequity tax when I go shopping because merchants see White middle-class women as valuable customers. Many Nova Scotian Blacks, on the other hand, are hassled by merchants who view them with suspicion.

Inequity taxes are imposed in three broad contexts: group status taxes associated with mere membership in a disadvantaged group, leading edge taxes on those who are "trail-blazers" for their group in new social contexts, and equity work taxes on people who actively fight the inequities of our society.

Group status taxes are imposed on people simply because they are members of a particular disadvantaged group. Such taxes may result from stereotyping, conditioning, or imposed social roles. Merchants' discrimination on the basis of skin colour is a stereotype tax on Black Nova Scotians. For White middle-class women, "second shift" work associated with child care and household maintenance is a role tax.

Leading edge taxes are imposed upon members of equity-seeking groups who boldly go where no members of their group have gone before. Members of equity-seeking groups are at the "leading edge" when there are no senior members of their group in their educational or work environment who can provide support by explaining invisible rules, serving as role models, or resisting institutional attacks on junior members of their community. Leading edge taxes may reflect stereotypes, or alternatively, the tendency of institutions to define the norms for professional competence in terms of the characteristics, preferences, and ideologies of privileged groups (e.g. White, able-bodied straight men are the norm for professors and deans). Finally, these taxes may reflect the fact that people who blaze trails for their groups must be strong, independent, and able to think for themselves in order to ignore all the formal and informal messages that say, "Go away! We don't want you here!" Such traits are unwelcome in academic units that prefer conformity. Dalhousie Law School has such a culture; people who think for themselves are distrusted by all political networks. This was demonstrated in the 1990–91 dean search. After offers to two traditional White men had fallen through, the search committee aborted the search with three strong, independent leading edge candidates still in the pool (a Jewish man, myself, and another leading edge White woman).

Equity work taxes are imposed on people who actively work for equity, either on behalf of their own group, or as an ally to other disadvantaged people. The achievement of equity often requires challenges to the privileges or self-image of advantaged people, and the resulting backlash can be vicious.

The reference to "taxes" (plural) in the previous paragraphs reflects the fact that there are inequity sub-taxes that may be applied in varying combinations in all three contexts. And, in some cases, privileged people may receive corresponding "inequity subsidies."

The *incompetence tax* manifests itself as an (irrebuttable?) presumption that members of historically disadvantaged groups are incompetent. There is a corresponding presumption that members of advantaged groups are competent until they clearly demonstrate otherwise (a *competence subsidy*). In recent years, for example, the Nova Scotia edition of *Frank* magazine has trashed all my Black and Aboriginal colleagues and all short-listed Black and Aboriginal appointment candidates as incompetent. As a White ally to the targets of these attacks, I have been trashed in the same stories in *Frank*, but never for incompetence, since in this context I am privileged (White). Instead, I am portrayed as a political maniac.

The *credibility tax* may reflect social status or conditioning (for example, in situations where suggestions by women are first ignored, and then subsequently adopted when a man proposes them). It may also be strategic: defining speakers from an equity-seeking groups as non-credible across the board provides a convenient excuse not to listen to any of their arguments instead of making a case-by-case evaluation. There may also be a *credibility subsidy* that reflects status or power, since people yield to the powerful in self-preservation. Alternatively, there may be an earned credibility subsidy for people with a proven track record, but only if the successes in question serve the agenda of the dominant group.

The *Catch-22 tax* reflects the fact that members of equity-seeking groups can be punished both for conforming to social norms for their own group, and for meeting the norms for privileged people. For example, following the 1990–91 dean search, I was told that I had been rejected because I was too feminine, while the other female candidate was rejected because she was too masculine.

An *internalization tax* also exists. Members of equity-seeking groups who take seriously the rationalizations that are used to discredit them begin to feel inferior, retreat from action, or waste energy trying to fix non-existent problems. A drawback to having an open mind if you are a member of an equity-seeking group, is that people throw garbage in it. Until the 1990s I paid a heavy internalization tax.

A *health tax* reflects the fact that all forms of discrimination are stressful. This tax is most obvious when participants in equity struggles have to take stress leave. But the health tax can also manifest itself in physical consequences derived from stress, such as high blood pressure or diabetes. My own health illustrates this problem. In December of 1993, my doctor discovered I had high blood pressure, but tried to control it without medication. My blood pressure began dropping satisfactorily. A few months later, my dean sent me a letter reprimanding me for supporting a Black colleague in an equity dispute. I fought back successfully (the letter of reprimand was shredded) but in the middle of the crisis my doctor discovered that it had increased my blood pressure to the point where medication was needed immediately. My doctor was so angry that I had to restrain her from writing a furious letter to the dean.

The imposition of a *power tax* on members of equity-seeking groups and the corresponding grant of a *power subsidy* to privileged people reflect two factors. Many people in our society are nice to others with power (you catch more flies with honey than with vinegar) but are discourteous to or take out their frustration on less powerful people such as members of disadvantaged groups. It is also much easier to get things done with reasonable effort if you hold institutional power, but members of equity-seeking groups are often excluded from such positions, for fear that they will destabilize the status quo. As DFA President, I held a power subsidy for the first time in my life.

And then there is a *retaliation tax*, which combines elements of all the sub-taxes into a vicious, intense, personalized form of trashing. The retaliation tax is most frequently directed at people who do equity work, although it may occasionally be applied in other contexts (e.g. misogynists may punish women merely for being women, or leading-edge people may be sanctioned for being "uppity"). The retaliation tax may be applied in three ways: formally, through mechanisms such as discipline, withholding merit increments, denial of (re)appointment, tenure, or promotion; informally, through ostracism, personal attacks (face-to-face or behind the target's back), and day-to-day harassment; and public attacks through the media (e.g., *Frank*). The retaliation tax also serves as a deterrent to future action. Other members of target groups may be silenced by fear of similar trashing.

There may be many other inequity taxes or subsidies: develop your own list!

This analytical framework explains much of my life. In the law school I have paid all three taxes heavily – group status, leading edge, and equity work taxes – in varying combinations over time. By contrast, neither DFA nor CAUT has ever penalized me merely because I am a woman or because I have leading-edge traits. Indeed, such traits may be essential in a successful DFA president, since she or he must be strong and brave enough to tell powerful administrators things they do not want to hear. Both DFA and CAUT have subjected me to equity work taxes, however, demonstrating that equity work is unpopular even in otherwise benign environments.

Those of us who choose to pay equity work taxes do so in the hope that we can ultimately eliminate all inequity taxes, so that everyone in our society will be able to direct all their energy toward constructive goals. We need the equity equivalent of a tax revolt, the political equivalent of the Boston Tea Party. Let's start by throwing the internalization tax overboard!

NOTE

1 Personal communication.

A Nurse Educator's Experience in Academia

SUZAN BANOUB-BADDOUR[1]

I joined the School of Nursing at the University of Alexandria after graduating from high school. I had the unique experience of being taught by well-prepared and highly skilled Egyptian as well as Canadian and American nurse educators. Being the recipient of scholarships throughout my program, I was able to travel twice to the south of France where I worked as a summer relief nurse, gaining a different perspective of the health care system. When I graduated with a Bachelor in Nursing Sciences *summa cum laude*, I received the highest award of the university for undergraduate students, the golden medal of excellence. I immediately got a position as a nursing supervisor in a large hospital and did so well that, a year later, I was offered the opportunity to fill the position of director of nursing services. Feeling honoured yet overwhelmed, I preferred instead to secure a job as a clinical instructor in the same university school from which I had graduated. Little did I know then that I would end up teaching in a Canadian University more than a decade later!

In the meantime, I got married and had my first child. Despite my full-time teaching position and motherhood role, it became quite clear that I needed to pursue my graduate nursing education if I were to remain in academia. At the time, I didn't see any other choice, since I could not afford to stay home and there were no part-time job alternatives.

Only through the love, care, and support of my family and my arduous but fruitful labour, was I able to make it. My husband, himself a university teacher and also engaged in graduate studies, consistently facilitated my work as a mother, teacher, and student. My parents and mother-in-law also provided tremendous support.

I will always remember a particular incident that left me feeling guilty and frustrated. Just two weeks after my second child was born, I had to resume my graduate courses and complete a clinical nursing practicum. I was breastfeeding at the time and had to express my milk throughout the day. There were no facilities for such an activity, and I felt misplaced and sad. On the eve of the exams, I had to breastfeed my baby, holding my infant with one hand and a textbook with the other! Despite that tremendous pressure magnified by my return to work, I passed my exams, obtained a scholarship, completed my Master's thesis, and graduated with distinction.

I then spent more than three years in England where my husband was studying. I was able to obtain a leave of absence from work and concentrate on my doctoral dissertation, which partly focused on the topic of breastfeeding and infant health. In Egypt, as in other parts of the world, traditional breastfeeding practices were rapidly being eroded. At that time, great efforts were being exerted in the scientific realm and in the British media to sensitize health professionals and the general public to the dangers caused by infant formulas, especially in developing countries.

Upon my return, I introduced the content of breastfeeding in the undergraduate and graduate pediatric nursing curricula at the University of Alexandria School of Nursing. Soon, I was among the first graduating class of doctoral students in Nursing Sciences from the University of Alexandria. My academic career proceeded more or less smoothly and I was promoted to the rank of Assistant Professor. As for my life journey, it went on with its daily struggles and successes until it took me from Egypt to Canada where I joined the Memorial University of Newfoundland School of Nursing, in St John's. I taught at both the undergraduate and graduate levels, more specifically in the first Master of Nursing program to be offered in that province. Again, I introduced the content of breastfeeding in that Master's program. Since Newfoundland had the lowest breastfeeding rate in Canada, that content was much needed in order to sensitize and teach the graduating future nurse leaders.

It has been my intention to highlight the successes of my academic journey. Yet, despite these accomplishments, my professional life has not been easy, as will be seen later on. Let me first present some of my other less visible triumphs, particularly in regard to my relationships with my students and my adaptation to a new university culture.

Whether in Egypt or in Canada, I always felt that students had a good, harmonious rapport with me. They frequently commented on my enthusiasm, sound preparation, and genuine interest in their educational achievement and progress.

I always strove to teach my students more than content in a course. My aim has invariably been to be a guide, a role model, and a friend. Throughout my life in academe, students have confided in me, seeking support or guidance. I have actively encouraged them to deal with the stresses they faced as young novice nurses, sharing my personal approaches to prevent back pain for instance, or cope with a child's death or a family's grief. Informing my students about my research interests, projects, publications, and other achievements such as conferences attended and textbooks or journals read or reviewed is another strategy.

Adapting to a different work environment and university culture is a challenge I had to face and overcome. In one university, faculty members who teach in the same course share a large office. Although interfering at times with concentration and work, such physical closeness enhances collegiality and generates a sense of community in which friendship and mutual support flourish and knowledge and information are exchanged.

On the other hand, in the other university, faculty members' work was mostly confined to their own offices. Meetings and coffee breaks were usually the only times for exchanging information. Intense competition for research funds and for getting individual credit seem to be typical of this university culture. Yet one learns to adapt to the different environment, create new networks, and function optimally within and even outside the university boundaries, acting as consultant, associate-editor, or journal reviewer.

I also encountered hardships in academe. Among the problems I had to struggle with were inequities in status, intellectual acknowledgment, and collegial relationships.

Equity concerns. According to Astin (1985), schools of nursing are often considered relatively "low-status schools." What accounts for the relatively low status is that the nursing profession has traditionally been occupied by women. Is it a repercussion of that social situation that doctorally prepared nurse educators are still addressed, especially by male colleagues, by our first name or as "Ms," "Mrs," and hardly ever as "Doctor"?

Is it another consequence of the "low-status school," or is it due to some other form of discrimination, that I had to start in a university on a lower-than-deserved position and salary? Only through a formal complaint was I able to get my salary partially adjusted. As for my deserved position and title, a committee had to deliberate my case before it could eventually be resolved.

Intellectual property and credit. Popularity among peers is often an indicator of success and prestige at work. Standing up for issues that one believes to be right and well-founded may interfere, however, with access to such favourable status. An example of such issues deals with the subject of intellectual property and academic authorship. The concept of academic freedom often blurs the significance of and appropriate attribution of credit. A variety of standards frequently exists within schools in the same university. In some places, recognizing the primary source of ideas is considered a "trivial" problem, despite – or possibly because of – the fact that innovative, authentic productivity is greatly prized in academia.

Competitiveness. Since scholars usually compete for limited resources, whether for teaching or research, ethical questions arise and conflicts do occur. Outsiders would expect that in an academic milieu staffed almost exclusively by women, an ambiance of harmonious collaboration and *esprit de corps* would prevail. However, my experience indicates that even in an all-female academic environment, women adopt "male" values of competitiveness. But are these the indicators of success in the academic world that we wish to pass on to future generations?

For some time, it was my desire to write about my experience as a woman academic working primarily among women colleagues. It is a theme that is interwoven through my many joyful experiences of watching students grow, and contributing to a patient's recovery, or completing a research project or a publication. It is also a theme about feeling a sense of loss. Being uprooted from one place to another, from one university to another, experiencing disappointments and frustrations such as denied credit, and struggles with different values are all forms of goodbyes I have experienced in the academic tundra. Eventually, I learned to accept a life that may be unfair at times. As Rupp (1988) wisely concluded, we need to change in order to grow and to let go before we can move on.

NOTE

1 Although this author has worked in two different universities, the situations depicted in this chapter are composites drawn from several incidents and circumstances occurring there. No reference to any single individual or university is intended.

Women in Canadian Universities: An Insider's View from Outside; an Outsider's View from Inside

HELEN J. BRESLAUER

Everyone has a unique perspective on their own situation and the situation of others. Some of us have the good fortune to be situated in such a way that we have the opportunity to broaden that perspective. I am one of those fortunate ones. In 1992 the Canadian Association of University Teachers (CAUT) presented me with the Sarah Shorten Award "in recognition of an outstanding contribution to the advancement of the status of women in Canadian universities." It was a very proud moment for me. I had worked with Sarah Shorten, had admired her, had been delighted that the award had been created to honour her, and was touched to be its second recipient.

I was exposed to the experiences of hundreds of women in the higher education community in Canada during my sixteen years as senior research officer for the Ontario Confederation of University Faculty Associations (OCUFA). I served as staff support person to the OCUFA Status of Women Committee during its first ten years and was involved as well in the structures that led to its creation. I was the OCUFA observer on the CAUT Status of Women Committee from the time it was reconstituted in 1981 until 1995. I liaised both inside and outside universities with women's groups such as the Ontario Employment and Educational Equity Network, the Status of Women Committee of the Council of Ontario Universities, the Ontario Women's Directorate, the Pay Equity Office of the Ontario government, and the Women's Committee of the Ontario Federation of Labour. I was "grandmothered" into the Senior Women Academic Administrators of Canada (SWAAC), a group to which I still belong.

And my perspective during all of this time was informed and enhanced by my experiences as an academic woman as a member of the Department of Sociology at the Erindale Campus of University of Toronto from 1970 to 1977. During most of that time I was also associated with the University's Centre for Urban and Community Studies, with which I continue to have a nominal affiliation. Many of the situations I encountered in those years also resonated back to my days as a student – as an undergraduate at Antioch College in Ohio, as a graduate at Rutgers University in New Jersey, which included time as a research assistant, and as a predoctoral research fellow [sic] and as an instructor.

During the second half of my years with OCUFA, I also did some consulting work on university issues concerned with equity matters and, in particular, with women's issues. Since leaving OCUFA in 1995, I have been working full time as a consultant on similar matters, primarily for universities and groups associated with universities.

During the past twenty years, then, my work, although not necessarily *in* the university, has been almost entirely *of* the university. I have maintained some links to academic work as well, presenting papers and publishing articles on women in universities. So I have been steeped in women's issues, and especially those of concern to academic women, and this experience has taught me the necessity and the value of combining theory and practice, the academic and the applied, rhetoric and action. And I have learned for myself that the personal is political and for me the political is also personal. My new life as a full-time freelancer has allowed me the freedom to run for office, which I did (unsuccessfully) in the federal election of 1997. That experience added a new dimension to my education, both personally and politically.[1]

There is no doubt that there have been improvements with respect to the representation of women in Canadian universities over the last twenty to thirty years. Our numbers among the faculty have increased and we have come up through the ranks. Among students, more than 50 percent are female and even in areas such as engineering where representation has always been very low, the number of female students and faculty has increased some. By and large, however, the proportion of the women in Canadian universities who are visible minorities, Aboriginal people, or people with disabilities remains very low.

Pay equity legislation in a number of provinces has put somewhat more money into the pockets of women faculty and women staff in universities. Mentoring programs have helped provide role models – as well as savvy advice – to women starting out in a male-dominated profession. As I look back on my experiences working with women's groups and individual women, and on my own experiences, I recall a number of landmark moments, deciding issues. Four of these – gender-neutral language, employment equity, chilly climate, and violence against women, stand out.

Gender-neutral language. Among my earliest memories and experiences in the women's movement were the tortuous, often acrimonious, debates over language, such as the use of Ms or other titles; the terms chairmen, chairpersons, chairs; and the application of the term girls as opposed to women.

During my teaching years in the early 70s, I remember receiving memos addressed to "Ms Breslauer" from those making their best efforts to be conscious of changes in the language, when all my male colleagues received memos addressed to "Professor." And I remember how stunned (and grateful) I felt when Lorna Marsden became chair of my department and wrote memos using the female pronoun as generic.

During the 1980s many universities developed policy about gender-neutral language. A very early effort stands out: a booklet published in 1981 by Wendy Katz on behalf of the Status of Women Committee of the Nova Scotia Confederation of University Faculty Associations (NSCUFA) entitled *Her and His: Language of Equal Value.* Today it has become more and more common to hear male professors speak of chairpersons as a matter of course, even when referring to a male. Yet I know the work is not complete, either inside or outside the university. At a recent ceremony at Toronto City Hall celebrating the forty-ninth anniversary of the Universal Declaration of Human Rights, keynote speaker Roberta Jamieson, Ombudsman [sic] of Ontario, observed that it will require an act of the Legislature to make her title gender-neutral, and she has been unable to get one to date.

Employment equity. Another decisive moment was the introduction of ways to deal with underrepresentation, and it began with another kind of language conundrum surrounding policy formation, first at CAUT and then at OCUFA. Or perhaps one should say first in the Royal Commission on Equality in Employment (known as the Abella Commission because it was chaired by Rosalie Abella). It was Abella who coined the term "employment equity" to distinguish that process from the American term "affirmative action." The American term came with a lot of baggage, including the notion of quotas. Discussion of quotas in turn raised a number of spectres including the loss of civil liberties by some and the abandonment of excellence

for all. Employment equity, with its premise of ensuring that qualified individuals have the opportunity to compete, was a much more
saleable and palatable concept in Canada.

When CAUT set out to devise a policy to address the issue of the
underrepresentation of women in university faculties and our "over-
representation," such as it was, in the lowest ranks of faculty, as well
as our near absence in a number of fields, the dilemma presented itself:
what would such a policy be called? I remember lengthy discussions
in the CAUT Status of Women Committee on this matter that resulted
in a policy called: "Positive Action to Improve the Status of Women."
When the OCUFA Status of Women committee subsequently tackled an
extension of the CAUT policy in Ontario, it called its policy: "Employment Equity for Women Academics: a positive action strategy."

With the application of the Federal Contractors Program to Canadian universities in particular, employment equity was applied to
four groups designated by the Federal Government: women, Aboriginal people, visible minorities, and persons with disabilities. When
OCUFA and CAUT wrote their policies to include all four groups, they
both used the term "employment equity."

Those who follow these matters will know that affirmative action
has fallen on hard times in the United States. Although employment
equity is still alive in Canadian universities, the confluence of funding cuts from the federal and provincial governments, and the
increase in "backlash,"[2] have caused it to take a backseat to issues
viewed as "more pressing." The early arguments about quotas and
preserving excellence have been dragged out again. I think, and I
hope, that these things are cyclical; gains have been made and there
are more of us inside now to argue against those who would turn
back the clock.

Chilly climate. Attempts to warm up the "chilly climate" resulted in
another stunning series of moments in the history of women in Canadian universities. (Let us hope that the word "tundra" in the title of
this book does not visit similar thunderbolts on its editors.) I believe
the term originated (or at least reached prominence) in the United
States as a result of the work of Bernice Sandler and Roberta Hall
when they were associated with the Project on the Status and Education of Women of the Association of American Colleges. During
that time they wrote a number of excellent pieces about the chilly
climate for women in universities, inside and outside the classroom.

But the term virtually exploded on the scene in Canada with Connie
Backhouse's paper documenting the historical evolution of the chilly
climate at the University of Western Ontario. Several years later there

was a sequel to that paper that reported the results of a contemporary study done by Backhouse, et al. of the continuing chilly climate at that institution. Some years after that, the report of the "Chilly Climate Committee" in the Political Science Department at the University of Victoria caused a virtual firestorm, and there was the University of British Columbia, and the University of Manitoba ... the list could go on. Learned societies such as the Canadian Sociology and Anthropology Association passed resolutions asking CAUT for assistance in dealing with the extraordinary reactions to these studies.

In most cases those reactions were similar: the integrity of the work was called into question; the scholarly credentials of the authors were challenged; and the issue itself was transformed from one of a collective systemic problem to one of individual civil liberties. At the time I ended my close association with OCUFA and CAUT, the best advice that could be given to women in Canadian universities was to be very careful indeed in using the study of chilly climate as a tool for change. To the best of my knowledge, both the problems of the chilly climate and the reaction to any study of it remain problematic to this day.

Violence against women. Many women in universities remember exactly where they were on 6 December 1989 when they heard the news about the Montreal Massacre, the slaughter of fourteen young women, thirteen of them engineering students, at the École Polytechnique at the Université de Montréal, by a man who yelled "You are all a bunch of feminists." The news came over the television as I was walking into my bedroom, and I froze and began to cry. Oh my God, what have we done, I thought. Is this the price to be paid for seeking equality in the university?

In the subsequent days, a shocked university community and nation argued about whether it had been the random act of a madman or an act that needed to be understood in the context of systemic bias towards women in our society. Feminists working in the academy for change knew it was the latter.

That tragedy led to some improvements, both in the universities and outside. Work has been done by faculties of engineering to change the culture that made them such woman-unfriendly places. Policies and practices changed in individual institutions, and the National Science and Engineering Research Council set up fellowships [sic] for women in engineering and a chair and national committee for women in engineering.

Among the other responses the came with increased awareness in universities and outside were resources for safety in public places, anti-harassment policies including anti-sexual harassment, and rape crisis centres. Universities and governments drew attention to violence against women by mounting campaigns against date rape and domestic abuse. Gun control legislation was passed. Jean Golden, a member of the OCUFA Status of Women Committee at that time, and I collaborated on an article, "Violence and the University," which was first published in OCUFA's newsletter *Forum* and subsequently reprinted in *Society/Societé*, the newsletter of the CSAA.

On an initiative by Dawn Black, MP, December 6 was declared a National Day of Remembrance. I have observed that day in one way or another since 1989, primarily in the context of the university. On 5 December 1997, I attended a very moving memorial service in Hart House of the University of Toronto. The Warden of Hart House, Margaret Hancock, pointed out in her address that it was appropriate that this ceremony be held in Hart House, because it was the twenty-fifth anniversary of Hart House being open to women. It wasn't when I arrived at the University of Toronto in 1970, and stories (perhaps apocryphal, perhaps not) abounded at that time of how important meetings could be held in Hart House and women could not participate in them. To this day a small tingle goes up my spine each time I enter the building.

And this was the year that I also became more aware of the many anti-violence initiatives going on outside the university in commemoration of December 6. I attended a fund-raising dinner for the December 6 Fund in Toronto, which raises money in order to assist women who have left abusive situations in paying for low-cost housing when they leave shelters. One of the guest speakers was Francine Pelletier, a journalist who had been one of the feminists on the list of the Montreal killer. She described (and I use my own words because I cannot reconstruct hers) a reaction very similar to mine among Montreal feminists when they heard the news of the massacre: What might we have done that could lead to this?

Perhaps the lesson to be learned from all this is that women inside the university must come together with women outside it and work for change; that the world inside the university mirrors the world outside and that sisterhood can only be powerful when it crosses through the campus gates and embraces women of all races, ethnic groups, creeds, abilities, and sexual orientation.

NOTES

1 There are undoubtedly those who would observe that working on behalf of faculty associations and working on behalf of women in the

university were not always comfortable or compatible objectives.
I would concede that it was often a delicate balancing act to conscien-
tiously discharge my responsibilities as a staff person and also do the
work I did on behalf of women. These are interesting matters that
should be examined in some detail in some other forum. It should be
kept in mind, however, that the work I did originated in and was
supported by faculty associations.

2 We should be mindful of Janice Newson's cautions about the use of the
term "backlash" as expressed in her paper "Backlash against feminism:
a disempowering metaphor," first presented at the Learned Societies
meetings in 1991. Newson prefers the term "neo-sexism" and, by
extension, I would assume would prefer "neo-racism" and "neo-ablism"
as well.

"Bend and You Will Be Whole": Women in Canadian University Executive Suites

DIANNE L. COMMON

I borrowed the title for this essay about women in senior university administration in Canada from the teachings of Lao Tzu, one of the earliest master teachers of Ancient China. Although he was writing about men and for men over 2000 years ago, his ideas have inspired me in my work. Let me introduce one of his poems to you, with the pronouns, of course, carefully changed:

> Bend and you will be whole.
> Curl and you will be straight.
> Keep empty and you will be filled.
> Grow old and you will be renewed.
> Have little and you will gain.
> Have much and you will be confused.
> Therefore, the Sage embraces the One,
> And becomes a Pattern to all under Heaven.
> She does not make a show of herself,
> Hence she shines;
> Does not justify herself,
> Hence she becomes known;
> Does not boast of her ability,
> Hence she gets her credit;
> Does not brandish her success,
> Hence she endures;
> Does not compete with anyone,
> Hence no one can compete with her.

Indeed, the ancient saying: "Bend and
You will remain whole" is no idle word.
Nay, if you have really attained wholeness,
Everything will flock to you.

Some women, not many, a few, make it to senior university administrative positions. These few women in the executive suites of our
universities today are exemplars of the "brave women" that Gloria
Steinem described in 1972: "I have met brave women who are exploring the outer edge of human possibility, with no history to guide
them, and with a courage to make themselves vulnerable that I find
moving beyond words."[1] One such woman, Diane Lee, vice-provost
for student academic affairs at the University of Maryland (Baltimore
Country), says her daily struggle is to establish "voice" and to maintain "visibility." For her the critical question is "How to get things
done while holding on to the values and ways of being that we
treasure as women?"

I also have struggled to make sense of and to seek explanations
for the problems that I and many of my other female colleagues in
administration in Canada have encountered. While I remain hesitant
to suggest that I have found answers, I hope that answers may be
unearthed in the experiential ground I will till in this essay. My purpose is to expose and examine the characteristics of the culture of the
executive suite of senior administration as my experience allows.
From there, I will ask how well women are prepared to survive,
perhaps to thrive, in the universities of the new millennium. In order
to do so, I will reflect on my fourteen years in university academic
administration, with almost ten of them in the senior executive suite.
In about half of these years I have been part of various administrative
teams that have struggled valiantly to create a culture that nurtures
the success of women; during the other years I was a member of
teams that resisted such struggle. In their resistance, cultures were
reinforced that were at best paternalistic about, and at worst hostile
towards, the successes of women. All these teams were dominated
numerically by men who, for much of their careers in the academy,
had not worked in teams with women of comparable authority. The
women they did interact with were, or had been, in subordinate roles
such as student, secretary, or junior professor. In all situations, the
rhetoric about the advancement of women clearly punctuated the
talk about equity. In all situations, policies and procedures were in
place to protect women from the ills of harassment, guarantee maternity leave, recognize interrupted career paths, and provide some day
care. Yet all these teams were beset by tensions that clearly were the

result of differences in approaches to university administration as practised by men and by women. Some teams reconciled, were even energized by these tensions; others were not able to do so.

In my observation, these tensions within the senior administrative culture arise because it is a culture shaped by academic men and acted upon by academic women. I choose these two verbs representing the actions of the men and of women deliberately. What men shape in the executive culture they rarely need to subject to careful analysis. It is a product of their socialization to the academy as an organization; it is a culture that they protect instinctively because it has enabled their success. Because women have not had a history of shaping this culture, they need to examine it in order to survive in it. Such examination tends to distance women from the culture and forces them into a type of engagement with the culture that is initially and primarily intellectual. This engagement is of a different kind than that of men, whose engagement is initially and primarily emotional. Given all the crises and challenges facing those who reside in the executive suites of Canada's universities, men are fortunate to enter the culture there feeling comfortable with the established norms, the values, the language, and the patterns of individual and collective behaviour. Such emotional culture they find succouring and restoring. The culture is close to them because it was engendered by them. For women, however, the culture offers little such comfort.

This contrast between the emotional engagement and the intellectual one produces an initial state of tension between women and men. This state of tension is exacerbated by two contrasting sets of behaviours, which consist of four particular behaviours of men and four of women. These two sets of behaviours I have tried to portray in Figure 1. On the left side of the ledger, as it were, are four types of behaviour that men typically practise as they engage in institutional governance. On the right are four types of behaviour of women administrators. I contend that each type of behaviour practised by men has a "counterpoint" in the practice of women. So, the practice of didactic speech by men is contrasted to that of interactive talk by women. The practice of definitive action by men is countered by reflective inquiry by women; public display on the part of men by private engagement on the part of women; and finally, the practice of dependency by men is countered by the practice of independence by women. It is within the contradictions between the counterpoints that the initial state of tension escalates and acquires the potential to render the working relationships between men and women dysfunctional.

The four typical behaviours of male executives shape the culture of the executive suite. These are the behaviours that women examine

Figure 1
The Ledger
Two Sets of Behaviours as Counterpoint

Behavioural Practices of Men Administrators	Behavioural Practices of Women Administrators
Didactic Speech	Interactive Talk
Definitive Action	Reflective Inquiry
Public Display	Private Engagement
Dependency	Independence

and respond to in an intellectual way. The tension resides not in the counterpoint itself; it resides rather in the ways the behaviours are inconsistent with each other; in the ways behaviours entail different consequences.

So let me begin with the first of these counterpoints: the practice of didactic speech and that of interactive talk. Much has been written about the differing conversational styles of men and women and the misunderstandings, social dislocations, and political inequities that result. These two styles compete in the executive suite. Men tend to enact decision-driven agendas with precise or closed time frames, and to employ discourse that is problem-centred. Women tend to establish issue-driven agendas with indeterminate but not unending time frames, and to engage in discourse that is more context-centred. Men perceive the discourse of women to lack the precision that they value highly. On the other hand, women tend to feel that talk is too rushed and only partially informed if the context, as well as the issue, is not examined.

Women's discourse has a character of interrupted speech. Women build on the ideas of others. They shape these ideas around others' emotional responses to these ideas. They frequently examine the feelings of the people creating the conversation: Do they feel included? Do they feel free to risk a novel, perhaps outrageous idea? In meetings, for example, women tend to pick up threads of ideas laid down previously, often by others, and then to offer only partial arguments in order to invite response. Men often see such partial argument as an incomplete argument grounded in partial ideas. Men make statements of declaration, often mini-speeches on the problem at hand. Women tend to react to the mini-speeches as if they invoke closure to the conversation. Women find the affirmative tags that men often add to the end of their speeches distancing. The following example, on the issue of the denial of a further appointment of an administrator, illustrates the points: "Well, you are the person to whom he reports. Do you think you should talk to him? Given that he believes there is tension between you two, I should probably do it. Right? OK, I'll talk to him." The superordinate male administrator made this mini-speech to the subordinate female administrator following a meeting of the executive team in which the performance of the administrator under review was discussed. At the meeting, all members of the executive team agreed on two things; first, that unsatisfactory performance was the issue, and second, that there was no evidence to warrant the claim of bias and unfair treatment on the part of the woman administrator toward the administrator under question. Nonetheless, the judgment was rendered, and the woman administrator was effectively removed from the situation.

The second counterpoint is the practice of definitive action in contrast to the practice of reflective inquiry. Sometimes administrative decisions require extensive mental worrying. Often they require revisiting time and again. This rumination quite naturally produces some anxiety for all involved. Women tend to be quite comfortable with the stress that accompanies the uncertainties and possible reconsideration of decisions or solutions to problems. Men are not. Women tend not to be concerned about being decisive or appearing decisive. They have a different sense of timing and do not seem to be as enamoured of the big, bold decision. As a result, women can be regarded by men as being indecisive or waffling. Men are tempted to define themselves by decisive acts. The sports and military metaphors of decision-making to enable winning or losing, victory or defeat, which shape the talk of academic men, do not enable their understanding of reflective inquiry as practised by women. Consider this situation:

After a number of years of collegial but tense debate, a decision that was eventually made by a woman administrator to integrate two academic units was not, in the end, implemented. During the period of debate, the members of the two units were required to meet, and in so doing, worked out some new and more productive patterns of cooperative behaviour. Also, a new head of one of the units changed the social dynamic sufficiently to suggest that the new pattern of behaviour would be sustained. In effect, the old problem that the solution of integration was designed to solve no longer existed. While the woman administrator was pleased with the new working relationships and spoke of a new era of cooperation, the head and some members of one of the units, who had opposed the initial proposal for integration, spoke publicly, inside and outside of the academy, about beating the central administration, employing the metaphors of winning the war, and coming back from the brink, and the inability of women in particular to make reasonable, effective decisions.

This short vignette nicely leads to the third example of counterpoint between men and women in the executive suite: the behaviour of public display versus that of private engagement. The academy, for all of its virtues, is notorious for the vice of destructive talk. Theses defense hearings are replete with stories of the demolition of arguments carrying down with them the hearts and souls of suffering students. Academic senates are too often the battleground for a contest of wills rather than a constructive debate. This type of public performance is a central characteristic of men in administration in particular, and the academy in general. It is an intriguing version of show and tell, or better still show and complain, that often plays out in writing, most often in the form of the memo, copied to numerous others, sometimes to others outside the academy. The memo typically lists accomplishments, real or imagined, complaints, real or imagined, about lack of recognition, unfair treatment, and the dire consequences if redress is not immediate. The memo is formally sent up the organization and copied latterly around the organization. The blind copy is ubiquitous. The memo, and other forms of public performance, are used to personalize issues in such a way as to suspend or delay future, anticipated administrative decisions. As an example:

A female vice-president and a male dean had a series of three meetings concerning the outcomes of external reviews of two of his programs. The objective was to determine which of the many recommendations would be carried forward to the president. It was expected and assumed by the vice-president that the dean was discussing the substance of each of the meetings with his program heads. The dean indicated that the recommendations could enable changes of considerable value to his program areas, one of which was in some difficulty. Once agreement was reached, the vice-president would meet with the president who would accept or reject the recommendations and then communicate back to the dean. This was a new step in the review process and had not yet occurred with previous reviews. This meeting, the vice-president explained, would not occur for at least three weeks because of her international travel plans and those of the president. At the meeting of the academic senate two weeks following, and in the absence of the vice-president, the dean publicly challenged the unsuspecting associate vice-president, who was explaining some of the progressive new and generally accepted policy and procedural changes for academic reviews, about what he and his colleagues believed were problems in the formulation of final recommendations. The challenge went unanswered in the public forum.

Women prefer private engagement to address and solve problems that have been reduced to the levels of personalities or, that is, personalized. Private conversations about issues that are weighted with emotion come easily to women. Women are more willing to be open in such meetings and to consider broad continuums of issues at hand as they try to find the context that offers the interpretation, and from the interpretation, a possibly novel solution of compromise. These conversations in the private engagement have much to compare them (quite well) to politically negotiated orders as opposed to orders that are hammered out in the fires of confrontational debate. When men refuse to accept the private engagement and to activate the specific behaviours of public display, they often claim that their behaviour is justified in terms of academic freedom and the processes of collegiality. Women administrators tend not to engage in the public response side of the debate. What was put in writing or captured in minutes of meetings remains therefore undisputed in the print and digital archives of the university.

The fourth counterpoint between men and women administrators is perhaps the reason women find it difficult to understand how to address the other three behaviours of men: the practice of dependency versus that of independence. When men are newly appointed to senior administrative teams, they are invited into what we call the network. Again, while much has been written about the proverbial "old boys' club," there is a fascinating dimension of dependence within it that often escapes women. The established men quickly work to make the new man dependent on them. A brief vignette will drive this point home:

The university president, a man, was relatively new to the organization. The directors were a robust group, the majority of whom were deeply devoted to the university. After a particularly feisty meeting, the president was informed by the men in his senior administrative staff that the directors were riled and frustrated. Fortunately for him, his staff knew the directors well and he could depend on them to keep him informed and head off trouble before it landed on his desk. Very quickly the president became dependent on a select group of individuals who he had come to believe were keeping him aware, defended, and protected.

While much of this dynamic has to do with securing one's place in the organization, in particular the executive suite, the behaviour is typically paternal, although it is not well recognized as such, because the objective is to make "the boss" dependent on those surrounding him. This is a dependency up the organization.

Women who reside in the senior executive suite have made it there because of a very strong streak of independence. They have had to overcome many obstacles without the benefit of established networks and emotional safety-nets. Their journey is a lonely one. As their journey

Figure 2
The Ledger: The Contradiction in Women's Behaviours

Behaviours: Men Administrators	Behaviours: Women Administrators
Didactic Speech	Interactive Talk
Definitive Action	Reflective Inquiry
Public Display	Private Engagement
Dependency	
	↕ ↕ ↕
	Independence

carries them higher in the organization, the loneliness becomes at
times overbearing. Rarely is there even a small group of women,
never mind a critical mass, to facilitate their development of more
effective skills of interdependence as they mature as administrators.
Not only is dependency foreign to their understanding, it is foreign
to their skill set and emotional resolve. They rarely know how to make
their bosses dependent on them in ways that really matter. Their independence is often perceived by their male counterparts as an inability
to work effectively in teams. This independence disposes them to
engage problems alone, a move that often leaves them exposed in the
organization, subject to the penchant of the men in the academy for
critical attack through public display. At this point, the sets of practices that have enabled women to progress so far and be so successful
as teachers and as heads of academic programs – the ability to engage
in interactive talk, reflective inquiry, or private engagement – are most
often inappropriate. Their established independence from the senior
team, and their inability and disinclination to create the conditions of
dependency that could invite the senior team of men to rally, fails
them and ultimately the university they were trying to serve.[2]

From my discussions with other women in senior university
administration, there are many who understand much of what I have
written. They have understood the tensions that these counterpoints
entail and have developed a skill set on both sides of the ledger. And
they, as do I, perceive a contradiction in the behaviour of women that
exacerbates the existing tensions. It is a contradiction that confuses
men and women both.

Simply put, there is an inconsistency between the set of behaviours
of interactive talk, reflective inquiry, and private engagement, and
that of independence. The first three in the set of behaviours that
women bring to their administrative practice are conditioned in the
ways women are socialized generally; the fourth is not. I have tried
to represent this in Figure 2. This contradiction unsettles women and

confuses men as they struggle to engage in administrative work. Independent women can be fiercely so. And the behaviours of independence that they exhibit must be extremely confusing to men in administration who keenly observe the discrepancies in their behaviours and are uncertain how to engage their women colleagues who doggedly forge a path alone.

AFTER ALL THAT STRUGGLE ...
THE SEARCH FOR HOPE

Nancy Adler of McGill University and Charles Hampden-Turner of Cambridge University strongly believe that women and the values our Western society terms feminine are essential to the competitive success of Western companies in the new century. As Hampden-Turner put it in 1993: "The ultra-masculine corporate values system (in such countries as the United States) has been losing touch progressively with the wider world. It needs a change of values, desperately, or it will continue to under-perform, continue to lose touch with the values systems of people from the rest of the world, which ironically are much closer to the values in which American women are raised."[3]

Hampden-Turner argues for the critical importance of including people from different backgrounds in management or leadership teams in an effort to learn to use the inherent diversity to build stronger systems. He calls them culturally synergistic systems. Success in the new century will come to those who know best how to use the complementarity of opposites. And Adler, focusing on the specific question of the contribution of women and underscoring the importance of the different management styles of women, argues that their styles will be essential in the development of governance appropriate to the new society of the new millennium.

I believe that Anna Yeatman, who has studied equity-oriented change in universities, would strongly underscore both the arguments and the hopes of Hampden-Turner and Adler. She advocates for the centrality of women as equity change agents within all organizations, universities in particular. From this position as change agent, women should be able to exercise a considerable capacity for effecting reform within the new politics and practices of organizational restructuring. "Because of their positioned lack of loyalty to the established way of doing things (and to the established masculine elite of the institute) those of them who show management and policy talent [will] become highly valued managers for change in the new environment."

Kathy Marasco, a principal consultant with PricewaterhouseCoopers, makes it clear that companies that do not take pains to promote and retain their women of exceptional ability will continue to feel the absence of women at higher levels in the future, when all of the talent will be scarcer. The best and the brightest will have many opportunities and they will not be attracted to companies that have advanced few women. They will be drawn to those that have already demonstrated they value women. She offers a gloomy portent for companies less attractive to women. They will eventually fall by the wayside, crushed by their inability to attract new talent and their inevitable falling out of favour with their customers. And the fate of company leaders who failed to effect a corporate culture change? They will either retire or "be retired," perhaps much sooner than they had planned. It will happen, Marasco warns, perhaps not soon enough for some of us, but the time will come.

There is a strong consensus emerging in the literature on the experiences of women in the corporate world about the development and implementation of policies that enable their advancement. Beginning with an acknowledgement of the fundamental difference between men and women, the biological fact of maternity, organizations then must provide flexibility for women, and men, who want it. Organizations must enable women who have an interest in administration or who have demonstrated leadership potential to develop the management expertise essential to high levels of performance. Organizations must improve the corporate environment by removing barriers that exist for women but not for men.[4]

According to The Conference Board of Canada's 1997 study "Closing the Gap: Women's Advancement in Corporate and Professional Canada,"[10] women claim that male stereotyping of their abilities is the biggest barrier to advancement, while the chief executives in the study perceive the barrier to reside in women's lack of line experience. Chief executives are almost three times as likely as women to identify "not being in the pipeline long enough" as the hurdle. Women are three times more likely to attribute "exclusion from information networks" as the bar. According to the CEOs, the three most critical areas of skill and experience required by all to advance to the senior executive level are leadership, networking, and the ability to demonstrate results. A total of 36 percent of Canada's CEOs believe that women lack these skills. There is another particularly disturbing outcome of the Conference Board's study. While 75 percent of CEOs believe that opportunities for women have improved "greatly" or "somewhat" in the past five years, only 56 percent of the senior corporate and professional women agree.

Executive women in corporate Canada identified two strategies that had contributed to their successes thus far: consistently exceeding performance expectations; and developing a style that enables male managers to feel comfortable. Other essential strategies, while of lesser importance, are: gaining line-management experience; seeking out difficult or highly visible assignments; and having an influential mentor. The initiative to change the culture of the corporate world to make it receptive and enabling to the advancement of women must come from the top; from the leaders of the organizations. And what must these corporate leaders do? According to Kathy Marasco:

1 They must make a visible and credible commitment to strategically developing and promoting women in their organizations;
2 They must equip all employees with the tools and processes to address career planning, training, sponsorship and mentoring;
3 They must develop techniques and processes to measure their progress;
4 Finally, and this may be the most effective way of getting the attention of those who are somewhat hesitant to jump into the initiative, the compensation and reward system of the organization must incorporate metrics that gauge efforts to promote and develop women. Not just how many lofty speeches they have made in a given year, but real statistics, like how many promotions and appointments they have approved for women in their span of control.

Canada's universities have come a long way in the three decades since Pauline Jewett was appointed president at Simon Fraser University. Until recently, the trends indicated that there were more and more women in senior university administration. Until recently, the trends also indicated more and more women in the executive suites of corporate Canada.

After all of the struggle, it is frightening to embrace a new reality. Women in the junior to middle level technical and line positions in the United States are leaving their organizations in droves. This exodus is not just an American condition. It mirrors exactly corporate Canada.[6] Sheila O'Brien, senior vice-president, Human Resources and Public Affairs, NOVA Corporation, put a very sharp edge on the image in the mirror. At the conference, Maximizing Women's Talent: Organizational Strategies for Success in Toronto on 10 December 1997, she said, "The pipeline is not only full of women, it's backed up and that sucker has sprung a leak. Women are entering the pipeline, but they're leaving."[7] From the recent experiences of executive search consultants for Canada's institutions of higher education, the situation is repeated in our universities and colleges. Women are either leaving the executive suites or are disinclined to move into them.

There never has been a more significant time to reflect on what we have learned about women in senior university administration. It is often said that the dawning of the information age rendered universities more important than ever before in their long history. This great potential, however, depends so much upon the visionary leadership of the men and women who administer them. Never before has the place of women in the executive suite been as critical to the future of our universities as it is today.

The modern university is our institutionalized version of learning communities that have served the public's interest since the close of World War II. For decades, this public interest was defined primarily in terms of the scholarly advancement of knowledge and the education of undergraduates across a variety of academic disciplines and professional fields. This definition of the public's interest did not challenge the work of professors as they built organizational structures around the discrete scholarly fields. Scholars of economics built economics departments; scholars of civil engineering built schools of civil engineering. These organizational constructs have proven to be more enduring than the disciplines and fields they were designed to contain, maintain, and sustain. As bodies of scholarly knowledge have evolved, some, such as computer science, exceedingly rapidly, existing organizational structures have often hindered as much as enabled their development. As the many problems of modern society, whether they be the depletion of the ozone layer in our atmosphere or the decay of the inner cities, become better understood, it is profoundly apparent that their solution will require the integration and application of diverse bodies of knowledge. Neither our established organizational structures nor our traditional approaches to the advancement of knowledge through research easily promote the cooperation of professors, students, and ideas in our universities in tackling these critically pressing problems.

And yet, this coming together is so very much in the public's interest and in the public's expectations for our universities. We have little choice. The rapidly changing environment both inside and outside the university is forcing the organization of the academy to reconsider and to reinvent the way it engages in governance. Everything that I have written about the type of management required for the coming century underscores one vital point. The skills of interactive talk, reflective inquiry, and private engagement are essential to the repertoire of tomorrow's university administrators, men and women. I believe that the practices of didactic speech, definitive action, and public display also have an essential role, but each must be tempered by and serve its counterpoint. In other words, didactic speech can be a means of achieving the larger goal of interactive talk; definitive action can lead to an outcome of reflective inquiry; public display can become a complement to private engagement. And all must, when practised by men and women, precipitate a culture not of dependency, nor of independence, but rather of interdependency. The interactive talk, reflective inquiry, and private engagement of women ideally position them to engage the university community of the future in the construction of interdependent ways of governance. Men must learn to integrate these behaviours, which are learned, into their administrative practices. Through their implementation, women and men gain the potential to create new forms of learning communities. And a community of learning clearly is premised on interdependence. Bend and we will be whole.

Many universities in Canada are in the midst of this reinvention today. It is my deepest hope that they will be guided by a clearer understanding of the contributions of women, and the particular behaviours of administration they practise, so as to foster the creation of learning communities for the purposes of institutional governance. Perhaps this hope is shared by Jayne M. Hodder, president and vice-chancellor of Bishop's University, who said:

The problem I see today is that women's progress in our institutions and even in our political life is too often impeded by the pressure to see career or personal success through the lens of a leadership and power model. It is as though women's successes had to be predicated on the adoption of a world view which in many ways does not seem coherent with our experience of life – our need to shift priorities to meet changing circumstance, our efforts to integrate our personal and professional identities, our need to see our contribution as leading to community success and not only to personal achievement ... I am arguing for the peaceful coexistence of more than one model of leadership, more than one language for power. It seems to me that in an increasingly complex and pluralistic society, we need to accept the wealth created by having competing world views. Maybe then we could have useful conversation about balancing competitiveness and increased consumption with the need to create and nurture just human communities."[8]

NOTES

1 Quoted in Richard Ivey School of Business, *Women in Management*, vol. 8, no. 2, Dec./Jan., 1998, 5.
2 If we consider how women and men rise to prominence in the wide world of sports, something instructive emerges. The vast majority of our

male sports stars are from teams. In contrast, almost all of our female sports heroes are individual performers. The curler Sandra Schmirler clearly made her Olympic Gold Medal mark as part of an incredible team, but of course, it is a team of women. At the risk of over-generalizing from this situation, I believe it is germane to conclude that although women tend to be the better team players when measured against a wide range of indicators, men seem to know better how to make an individual mark within a team. Women, it seems, have to leave the team to acquire sports stardom, and that is, media stardom. The role of the media in starmaking is a factor here, but if we assume that the media reflect somewhat well the society they report and interpret, then there is something here of relevance to the larger point I am making about women in administration.

3 As quoted in Nancy J. Adler, Global leaders: A dialogue with future history, *Management International*, 1997, vol. 1, no. 2, 21–33.

4 See, for a further development of this argument, Felice N. Schwartz and Jean Zimmerman, *Breaking with Tradition: Women and Work, The New Facts of Life*, New York: Warner Books, 1992.

5 The Conference Board of Canada, *Closing the Gap: Women's Advancement in Corporate and Professional Canada*, 1997. The study was based on a survey of over 400 high-level women, approximately 200 CEOs in Canada's largest corporations and professional firms, and in-depth interviews with selected senior women and chief executives. The average woman participant was 40–44 years of age, and earned between $100,000 and $200,000. 35% have earned professional degrees and 87% provide half or more of their family's income.

6 The following appeared in the June/July 1998 issue of the Richard Ivey School of Business, Women in Management (vol. 8, no. 4), 5:
   · surveys suggest that more than 2/3 of women executives were contemplating leaving their jobs;
   · women are leaving the armed forces combat positions at an annual rate of 42%;
   · women are opting not to apply to the judiciary;
   · women are opting not to run for elected federal office: in 1993, 472 women ran; in 1997, only 408 ran;
   · women are opting for self-employment. According to Statistics Canada, over the past 5 years, the number of self-employed men increased by 29%, but the number of self-employed women increased by 62%.

7 Quoted in The Conference Board of Canada, *The Inside Edge*, January 1998, vol. 2, no. 3, 10.

8 Excerpt from a speech delivered at the "Women and Work Symposium" hosted by the Faculty of Commerce and Administration of Concordia University and reported in Richard Ivey School of Business, *Women in Higher Education*, vol. 8, no. 4, June/July 1998, 6–7.

Dare to Be Brave:
Stand Up for Yourself

I have always loved working in a lab and figuring out the results of experiments but at times the politics of the workplace have troubled me to the point that I almost gave up and decided to quit. It seems as if the more experienced and independent I became, the more excluded and the less accepted I became. While no one in my workplace has been openly racist towards me, sexism abounds. When I became Dr. Dyck, I expected to be valued as an equal by my peers and by decision-makers. I thought that since they were educated they would be unbiased, fair-minded individuals. But this has not been my experience with some of my colleagues.

My worst workplace experiences occurred several years ago when I was told to give a passing grade to a student who had extensively plagiarized in a major term paper. I refused. This led to an intense period of bullying aimed at making me change my mind. Over an eight-week period, I was subjected to nine sessions of overpowering verbal barrages. The first two took place within a couple of days of my refusal to assign the passing grade. I felt like a deer caught in the headlights of an oncoming car – not sure what was coming at me, what was happening, or how to get out of harm's way.

I was accused of having personality characteristics that I did not think I possessed – of being rigid, dictatorial, bureaucratic, unbending, dogmatic, inflexible, too emotional, too close to the students to be impartial, manipulative. Phrases such as, "You're alone in this; no one is on your side; you're out on a limb; no one will believe you" were peppered throughout the barrage. Threats of punitive action against me were implied by comments like "I haven't done to you what I could have done; you now have space that you can't justify; it's too bad that this had to end on a sour note, otherwise you would have done a good job of teaching."

At one meeting, I was given a gag order and told not to tell anyone from outside what was going on with respect to the grading of students. Shortly afterwards, I was told that although I perhaps had been given the impression that I was under a gag order, that was not so. At subsequent meetings with people from outside, I could express the consensual view of the group but not my own personal viewpoint.

I remember breaking down and crying during one verbal barrage. The barrage continued, but fortunately it was interrupted when another person arrived, and I had a chance to escape. Back then, I did not have enough sense of self-preservation to leave when I was being harassed. Some of my colleagues saw me crying but they did and said nothing, and when I asked a couple of them for help, I was turned down. I really did feel alone. The only people who offered me any support at that time were the secretaries, a technician, and the janitor.

In retrospect I realize I was traumatized by the verbal barrages and the lack of support but didn't know it at the time. When I came to work after a week of these strange, unnerving incidents, I could not enter the building. My legs were shaking. I went home and stayed there for three days while I tried to figure out what to do. I was ostensibly on vacation leave.

I consulted the Sexual Harassment Officer. While she was empathetic and that was a relief to me, there was no solution that seemed feasible at the time. Basically I would have had to prove that I had been discriminated against on the basis of my gender, but I was too shaken to do that. Who would believe me? It would be his word against mine. I felt like a nobody compared to him. When I objected to what was happening to me, my harasser denied that he had harassed me. He replied that I was being treated no differently than my colleagues and that in fact I had been been treated well, favored, pushed ahead, and promoted. This certainly did not match my perceptions. Of course, most of my harassment occurred without witnesses, and when witnesses were present, they seemed to be too afraid to do or say anything.

I remember walking home from work one day with tears streaming down my face. I was demoralized, feeling helpless, frightened, betrayed, abandoned, confused, uncertain whom to trust or where to get help. Then, just when I was at my lowest point, feeling completely hopeless and overwhelmed, a thought flashed into my brain like lightning out of the blue. If my mother, who had been a Cree woman, could overcome the hardships of racism in her short lifetime, then I'd be damned if I was going to let some man push me out of my job just because I was a woman. My inner strengthening began at that moment. Though I was subjected to many other incidents of inappropriate behaviour over the next few years, I got stronger and stronger as I undertook what seemed like risky actions of standing up for myself. The more risks I've taken, the better things have gotten for me.

Oddly enough, the greatest deterrent to further harassment occurred accidentally. I had received a memo from one of my harassers claiming that I had behaved badly in my interactions with a senior administrator on campus. The memo clearly was intended to bad-mouth me. I took what seemed like a big risk and responded to this in writing. I was worried that the harasser would subsequently get angry, come to my office and verbally harangue me. My new office had only one door; if he shut the door as he came in, I would be trapped and no one would know if I was in trouble and needed help. I called Security Services on campus to find out how to increase my safety. There was no answer. I called again. Still no answer. This lack of response made me feel even more vulnerable. It triggered a panic attack in me as I seemed to re-experience the feelings of vulnerability and fear from my worst times years before. I called the Employment Assistance Program (EAP) for help. Later I found out that the phones in Security had been down. An investigator was sent out to interview me. She understood the dynamics of my situation. I didn't file a complaint but a report was filed. I was told by my harasser that I had no right to call Security. I said I did and I walked out of the office calmly, while he continued to argue his viewpoint forcefully. Since then, I no longer have been subjected to accusations, veiled threats, angry outbursts, or other inappropriate behaviour. The threats that I worried about either dissipated or backfired. In all likelihood, they were empty threats meant to make me feel powerless and scare me into silence or submission.

Bullies have two faces. To people whom the bully doesn't bother, the bully seems perfectly normal and perhaps even charming. A bully may even be a feminist female. The bully side of him or her seems out of character and unbelievable to those who have seen only their nice side. They can engage in angry outbursts and afterwards act as if nothing has happened, and they can be quite charming and avuncular to those they have bullied. When they have lost control of something in their life, they seem to try to make up for it by "kicking the dog," telling you that your productivity is down, that you are on the verge of being fired, that you should only work part time – all unjustified comments. Bullies are masters at finding your most vulnerable spot and they keep poking at it until you feel weak or anxious. I did for a time bend to their will, but this only offered a temporary respite from further bullying. With hindsight, I think that the wisest things I did were:

· to report my problems with harassment and implied threats to someone with greater authority than the bullies;
· to continue to do so if necessary;
· to get insight and group support from feminist groups on campus;
· to get help from counselling services, such as EAP;
· to obtain a greater understanding of who I am by seeking out Elders;
· to develop self-confidence, belief in myself and my core beliefs. As Shakespeare said, "This above all; to thine own self be true."

I am still not accepted as an equal in my workplace. I never will be by some people. I cannot change their opinion of me, but I can change how I react to them. I no longer allow their attitudes to poison my opinion of myself and I take pride in what I have been able to accomplish despite being born female, poor, of mixed racial background coupled with the sometimes hostile, non-supportive environments within which I have worked. If I don't get special salary increases and other perks, so what? I have my integrity. It cannot be bought. I have become an alchemist, transmuting the toxins in my environment into fuel for my internal spiritual strength.

Now I am able to look at myself in the mirror with a sense of pride and know that I can trust my inner instincts despite what others may try to pressure me into believing or doing. Developing this sense of my inner self has meant taking the risk of standing up for myself time and time again. In return I have found my inner courage and my pride in who I am – my mother's daughter and daddy's "little girl," who grew up to be not only a scientist but also a Woman who Can Walk Tall, Walk Strong, Walk Respectfully and Walk in Beauty.[1]

NOTE

1 This paper is dedicated to my parents, Eva Muriel Quan (McNab) (1920–1956) from the Gordon's Reserve in Saskatchewan and Yok Leen Quan (1898–1962), who came to Canada from China in 1912. "I have seen, for their dead eyes, the fruits of their labors. I would tell them they can now close their eyes in sleep." (Denise Chong, *The Concubine's Children*).

No Welcome for a Woman: Seeking Colleagues in a Cold Climate

ELLEN E. FACEY

First, a cautionary tale about collegiality from my first years as a working professional. Then, a discussion of the road to tenure in a socially and intellectually cold climate. I have chosen for the purpose of this paper to focus on the personal aspect of my experience of working as an academic in two Canadian universities. A completely different story might be recounted if I were to concentrate on my research career or on my contractual status in a time of retrenchment.

I have included a small number of concrete cases or events but omitted names and other means of identifying particular persons or places. What I bring forward, however, are only a few indicative examples out of many. It is not possible here to depict fully the accumulation of ten years, let alone assess the emotional impact of what I think the reader will agree is a pattern of casually abusive treatment.

I completed my PhD in Australia in 1982 and returned home to Canada in the midst of a major recession. There can scarcely have been a worse time to join the Canadian academic labour market with a fresh, and foreign, PhD. A twelve-month appointment was the best one could hope for; and, that year, I returned too late in the year to obtain even sessional work. I spent the year waiting for final word from the assessors on my dissertation, house-sitting for friends, and doing small research assistant jobs.

The next year's job market looked equally bleak. It was with some misgivings that I accepted an offer to re-enter, this time as junior faculty, the department I had left as an undergraduate a few years previously at "Mondo University." I learned a lot that first year about how to manage a class and to be more relaxed and therefore teach more effectively. Support in this and in other things came exclusively from female colleagues. Among my male colleagues, there was only one junior faculty member who ever showed the slightest concern for how I was managing.

In general, when I think back to those male colleagues, I remember only coldness and indifference, and their attempts to make me carry an excessive load, indeed, sometimes do their work for them. On one occasion that has always stuck in my mind, a male, tenured, senior faculty member asked me whether I would take over his class one day, as he was not feeling well. When I discovered that it was in only three hours time and was a senior theory class that met only once a week, I asked with great concern what the topic was. His reply was, "Oh, it doesn't matter; just go in and shoot a few baskets." What total disregard for the students as well as for me.

In my second year there, I decided that I had to take the initiative in creating positive collegial relationships, especially with my closest specialist colleagues. I knew they frequently socialized, although they had never invited me to join them. In the same week in which I first tried to open an informal social dialogue with one of them by dropping in on him in his office to discuss an upcoming conference, the other colleague held a party to which he invited scholars in our field from two nearby universities. I heard about it only later, when one of those scholars, normally friendly toward me, confronted me with why I couldn't be bothered to attend a dinner when all the specialists from other universities were coming? I replied that it would have been bad manners to attend without having been invited.

At the end of one of my contracts at Mondo, I was informed that I would have to provide a public lecture as part of my application for another contract. Even though this had not been necessary the previous year, I agreed without quibble. After having delivered the lecture, however, I was told that I would have to provide a second public lecture (on a different subject, of course) because one of the senior male faculty members had been unable to attend my first lecture and he insisted that he have the opportunity to hear me lecture. Again, I agreed, suppressing my annoyance that one individual could exert this kind of power and that I was powerless to prevent it. My feelings went far beyond annoyance, however, when I delivered the second lecture only to find that, having demanded that I give it, this same person had failed to attend this lecture as well. He neither sent his regrets nor ever apologized for his absence.

After five years at Mondo, three on one-year contracts, plus two on a postdoctoral fellowship, I was told that there was no position available, although I was offered teaching on a course by course basis. In other words, I could do the same work for half the pay and no benefits. I declined, knowing that even if a full-time contract offer elsewhere did not present itself that year, unemployment would be a more lucrative and less demoralizing option.

I did find work that next year. In that case, moreover, I was not replacing someone on leave, as had been the case with each of my three appointments at Mondo. This time I was told very explicitly by the department chair at "Micro University" that the Department's intention was to convert this to a tenure-track position as soon as possible and that I had been hired with that in mind. This sounded good!

The department was composed of three men, and my position was repeatedly referred to as that of "the fourth man." I was rather slow to object to this sexist phrase, feeling wary of being pegged as ungrateful or, heaven forbid, shrill. But I finally reacted: when the position of the "fourth man" was mentioned, I began referring to my colleagues as "the other women." They failed to see the humour, although the irony at last penetrated their thinking – "Oh, does that bother you?" – and they began to use the phrase "the fourth position," in my hearing at least.

For five years, both the department and the university were a social and intellectual wasteland for me. On his "bad" days, one of my colleagues used to snort when greeted with a pleasant "Good Morning." Although I was alone in town, I was invited to each of my colleague's homes precisely once, in each case at the beginning of the semester, by whoever was chair that year – a duty invitation, no more.

Every year I taught six courses per year and had time for minimal research activity. In my final year at Micro, I taught 215 students in one course alone, so my total for the year was close to 400 students, twice others' loads. The average for introductory classes was 75 to 100. For assistance with this load, the department provided the princely sum of $90, precisely fifteen hours' worth of marking by an undergraduate student assistant. There was no other assistance, so I had to do the bulk of the marking as well as managing all student contact, advising, proctoring of exams, and so on.

In terms of social relations, again, I think I went half-way. I hosted departmental events. I asked my colleagues one day whether they would like to go to lunch. (They went off together regularly in my presence.) They looked at me in amazement and asked, "Why?" I said that I thought it might be nice to do something social together and that we had never had lunch together. They replied that they had never invited me because they thought I didn't want to go with them. I responded, "How could that be so, as they had never asked me?" And their answer? "Yes, we did ... No? ... Oh. Well, that must have been _X_," the female sessional who had preceded me in the department for one year. I guess they just could not tell us apart. It is hard to describe the depth of alienation that that conversation produced, or perhaps just confirmed, in me.

At the end of my second year at Micro, the Faculty Association refused to give their permission to the administration when the latter proposed to offer me a three-year contract in lieu of a tenure-track appointment. Although I took this as a hopeful sign of future commitment on the university's part, and accordingly told the Faculty Association executive that I wanted the three-year offer, the executive refused. Ever watchful for heinous tricks on the part of the administration which would create dangerous precedents for the membership, my own union thereby denied me relief, at least for two years, from my annual time and energy-consuming job search.

Partway through that contract, I was offered the opportunity to apply for promotion. I did so and it was granted at the end of that year. At the same time, however, I was again offered a one-year contract, and I found myself thinking that the only thing worse than not getting tenure at Micro would be getting it. I would then be consigned to spending the rest of my career in a department where there had never been any social or intellectual welcome for me and where I had been betrayed by both management and my own union. Although I had always enjoyed the students, the city and the area, I knew that would not be enough for me in the long term.

I now work in a primarily administrative position in northern British Columbia. Winters here are as frigid as in the east and, with only one staff member, I work based out of the regional campus that I pioneered. Like doing field research or teaching in a hostile academic environment, it is an isolating experience; however, this is a matter of climate and geography, not of social and sexual barriers. Since my initial interview, I have felt valued and respected by my immediate superior (male) and likewise, later, by my fellow admin staff (male and female), most of whom also work in regional offices far from the main campus.

My situation is remote from such events as faculty squabbles and the main campus space wars, so there are compensations. But, while my colleagues in administration are supportive and appreciative of one another, I still yearn sometimes to have a set of academic colleagues close at hand, working together as a team and sharing friendship and intellectual interests. But maybe that's just a woman's pipe dream. After twenty years I may yet have to abandon academia in order to find what I'm looking for. Based on my experiences, I am in awe of the few women who are able to make a life, not just a living, in academia.

The reader may wonder whether these same experiences might have been the lot of a male, if placed in the same circumstances. I could not answer that in regard to such matters as the contractual problems I have mentioned. From the experiential point of view, however, while I cannot imagine a hypothetical male's experience, there is no question that the lack of welcome I experienced as a colleague would not have been that offered to most male faculty in the same circumstances. Many of the comments and expectations that I encountered were inarguably gender-based.

In my view, the value of this collection as a whole is for the reader to be able to compare individual women's experiences and see whether there are trends and patterns and, if so, what they are. Only then will any of us be in a position to draw general conclusions about "women's experience" in academia in Canada. I am not attempting here to analyse why my experience was as it was. My goal has simply been to offer grist to the mill, one story among many.

Part-time Language Teachers in the Academic Tundra

WENDY FELDBERG

Equity is a faint hope for women who, like me, are part-time language teachers at my university. As inhabitants of a ghetto within a ghetto, we endure systemic evils that deny us equality of job opportunity, equal pay for work of equal value, pay parity, fair hiring procedures, and adequate protection for our academic freedoms and intellectual property. We have lost much of the equity we once gained, even as we face new equity issues related to computer-assisted learning, intellectual property, and university revenue-creation schemes. Among the tools of systematic abuse (management structure, hiring policies, for example), discourse is the most powerful. The term "part-time language teacher" now serves only to exclude and disinherit us; among no other group of academics is the term "part-time professor" so inequitably applied and so flagrantly abused.

My department, a second-language teaching institute, is an academic service unit within our bilingual university and is staffed mostly by language teachers whose work is governed by exclusive "ghetto" articles in the collective agreements of both full-time and part-time professors. Our department structures and practices have thus evolved in patterns unlike those of traditional university departments. Ninety percent of career language teachers, full-time and part-time, are women. The department's thirty-year policy has been to depend heavily on part-time, hourly paid teachers to deliver its core courses, not merely to take up slack or inject new blood; now, part-timers assume responsibility for over 50 percent of the department's instruction and student-contact hours, and this percentage continues to grow. Over the years, a caste-like course delivery structure has entrenched itself, with a teaching hierarchy arranged in three tiers. Unionized full-time language teachers and a few regular professors occupy the first tier; hourly rate, part-time language teachers with some union protection occupy the second tier; and a growing number of educational workers on non-unionized contracts occupies the third tier. Some part-time language teachers, pilgrims like myself, shuttle between tiers. Many part-timers have been in the department long-term, most for more than 10 years, and some for well over twenty years. Many carry the equivalent of a full-time load, their commitment "part-paid," not "part-time." The management structure is two-tiered, with language teachers occupying middle management posts, and a regular professor in the chair's post. Middle managers act as conduits, insulators, translators, and lightning rods between the chair and the language teachers, who thus have no direct access to senior management. For part-timers, the hierarchy is actually three-tiered, for office support staff (mostly female) regularly assume functions that official management neglects or delegates. Leadership roles have gone to a disproportionate number of males, and new posts are usually assumed by men. Often the same man will occupy a job several times or trade posts with the other men. Male senior managers have been parachuted in from other departments to assume vacant posts. On three occasions, sinecures were created expressly for males whose careers had died in other departments; when these men eventually retired, their "tombstone" jobs either expired, or went to female support staff, but never to female career academics. A language teacher had never been chosen to head our department until July 1998, when a male language teacher was appointed. Women have regularly occupied middle management posts, but our only female chair was a regular professor, not a language teacher.

I have worked in this part of the academic tundra for most of my professional life, seventeen years as a full-time, tenure-track language teacher, and the past eleven years as a part-time teacher. I left full-time teaching after the birth of my third child, deeply regretting that there were no creative employment options for mothers who were career academics. To be home with my small children, I had taken several leaves without pay, but this couldn't go on: "If you don't want the job, others do," my (female) manager said. So I left full-time teaching for family, and worked part-time on non-teaching non-unionnized contracts just to keep my hand in, and to remain close to the peers whose lives I had shared professionally and personally for so long. One year after my resignation, my husband (just turned fifty) was laid off by his company, and suddenly we were starting over. I managed to obtain a half-time contract to share a full-time job with another colleague; but the job-sharing experiment was fleeting, for when the female senior manager who introduced the job-sharing concept was succeeded by a male, job-sharing was replaced by hourly rate contracts. By then, though, my husband could afford to support me in hourly rate university teaching, and so I decided to return, despite the conditions, but with some tough new equity questions: To what extent was my part-time university job viable only because my husband was willing to underwrite it? What was the dollar value of our joint volunteer contributions to the university?

Working on part-time, hourly rate teaching contracts brought me to experience in earnest the rotten core of marginalization: disrespect for my time, intellectual property, academic freedoms, qualifications, experience, and professional aspirations. On my first day as a part-time professor, my middle manager, my former peer, dealt a knock-out blow to my career aspirations: "You are no different from someone who has walked in off the street." To the university, my seventeen-year service as a full-time professor in my department was a liability, as was my motherhood. Furthermore, the part-time union was unreceptive to a former full-timer: "You can't just parachute in here, you know." Lack of seniority in the part-time union had stripped me of my whole work equity. Eventually, after creating and teaching a new course on a non-unionized contract, I obtained enough seniority to parachute me into the union. (Even now, I still cannot call my parachute my own, for in a mockery of equitable job-sharing, the management has often split my course hours in half and required that I "team-teach" with another professor for half the pay and half the seniority.)

From my "Upstairs-Downstairs" perspective, I can attest to the discrimination that governs teaching "Downstairs." Teaching supports such as office space, photocopying, library access, and computer access are no longer tools indispensable for a professor's job, but privileges to be conferred and withdrawn, rewards for compliant behaviour, or bones thrown across the bargaining table. Contracts are often signed after courses begin, pay delayed for six weeks or more, jobs are routinely posted without notice or only forty-eight hours before classes begin, and job offers (along with ultimatums) are left on answering machines. "Presenteeism," a new word in my dictionary, describes an unwritten tradition here: Make sure you are around, "showing your face"; forget the forms you have filled out describing your availability, for support staff (stewards of department inequities) might stop your mail, inform you that you no longer work there, or directly communicate others' low opinions: "You think

you're so special?" Research projects proposed by full-time professors need the co-operation of part-timers; when you ask about pay
for this activity, incredulity and outrage greet you: "You want a consulting fee? It's only a few minutes of your time!" A revenue-producing
ESL programme staffed by part-timers only funds travel expenses to
conferences, but for full-timers only. Full-time professors work in
non-credit ESL programs for non-teaching purposes on full salary,
while part-time professors receive no compensation for their non-
teaching contributions to the same programs. No official teaching
evaluations are carried out in non-credit courses taught by part-timers.
No annual report of teaching and research activities is required of
part-timers, even though they frequently carry the equivalent of a
full-time teaching load and are engaged in scholarly and community
activities besides.

In the profession of university language teaching, these marginal-
izing employment patterns remain steadfastly entrenched despite
significant equity gains made by both full-time and part-time language
teachers. Two categories of full-time jobs created in the seventies have
been abolished; the work is available now only as separate tasks on
hourly rate contracts. Only classroom teaching contracts, and not
even all of these, are regulated by the collective agreement. All other
critical teaching functions carried out by part-time professors in the
regular discharge of their duties are considered non-union work,
and, if paid for as contract work, can only be obtained by private
negotiation with all the inequities implied by that arrangement. The
work can include: curriculum development, language test development, grading of entrance and language proficiency exams, second-
language acquisition research projects, computer-assisted learning
projects, language advising, mentoring and advising students, planning in a team, training junior teachers, planning and attending cultural activities, assembling teaching and testing materials, gathering
and processing data to aid second language acquisition research,
serving on university committees, and engaging in scholarly publishing, presentations, and research. These essential functions are
simply regarded as volunteer work when carried out by part-time
professors, and are largely unpaid and unattributed. Part-timers'
work is squeezed from below as well as from above. A recent reor-
ganization of one language program quadrupled class size to over
eighty students and wiped out all unionized part-time jobs. Time
with language-learning software replaced classroom contact hours
with unionized professors. A third class of workers (temporary,
lower-paid and misleadingly classified as "teaching assistants")
replaced unionized part-timers. Some veteran part-timers accepted

these non-unionized jobs at two-thirds less pay, rather than have no job at all. A non-unionized, temporary worker even received a patronage appointment as a manager, while career part-time professors were passed over. The part-time union failed to challenge these abuses.

Not the least source of equity deficit for language teachers is the university's deliberate policy of obtaining cheap, non-unionized labour from language teachers through anti-equity employment schemes. Part-timers, notably ESL teachers, have now become the favoured target of the parasitic, revenue-creating policies of a greedy Higher Education Industry in search of revenues it cannot otherwise generate. Part-time language teachers are pressured to deliver cash-earning English language (ESL) courses to international students who pay high fees for intensive language courses. But the course profits have *never* been reinvested in intensive language programs or in their human capital; instead, the money goes elsewhere in the university. The university continues to try to get part-timers to work in similar programs without a collective agreement, for pay well below union rates, and without protections for intellectual property or academic freedoms. Senior university administration defends its approach with a business argument: "You language teachers are not competitive." Despite a fifteen-year history of member protest, the part-time professors' union has continued to buy this same argument, for part-time language teachers continue to be paid a rate officially set at 25 percent less than other professors. The changing face of university teaching thus is challenging the entire higher education industry to learn ethical methods of managing the sale of language teaching services so as to avoid employment abuses and conflicts of interest. Language teachers also need protection from private language teaching business interests with university connections, which stand to benefit from the availability of a pool of highly qualified but vulnerable professionals.

Language teachers' early equity issues were more easily discerned and defended, and during the seventies and eighties, both full-time and part-time language teachers in turn made significant strides in basic employment equity. Full-timers obtained their first collective agreement in 1976, when I researched, wrote, and presented the first employment equity brief in collaboration with a few of my female colleagues. Despite our department's old boys' club, the all-male university negotiating team, and the exclusively male university administration, we made landmark gains. We obtained four full-time job categories: two tenure-track categories that accommodated traditional university research, and two extended-contract categories that recognized commitment to classroom practice and curriculum. We also obtained a full slate of benefits, though maternity leave was at first a contentious issue and was finally resolved by arguments bearing on female professors' roles as producers of future students for our male colleagues' classrooms. Further landmark equity gains were made when part-time language teachers unionized in the early eighties and set up a seniority system that redressed many of the inequities caused by patronage appointments, cronyism, and secret contract negotiations. Part-time language teachers, to their great credit, led the rest of the part-time professoriate into a union.

Alas, these gains from the seventies and eighties have not borne the expected fruit to date, as the recently published history of our part-time union (1998) notes, for even as old injustices return in new garb, urgent new equity issues emerge. One key new concern is the intellectual property rights of language teachers who are frequently involved in collaborative teaching. The limits of personal, collective, or institutional ownership of the intellectual property generated by collaboration among part-time language teachers are only minimally established in our current collective agreement. Language teachers' tradition of sharing ideas and materials has nurtured a culture of generosity and a healthy interdependence. Sadly, this sharing tradition has also nurtured a parasitic counter-culture of exploitation that takes such generosity for granted. Colleagues have used the sharing tradition to justify presenting other colleagues' work at conferences. One professor secretly negotiated with the male senior manager to obtain a higher salary for work he did in collaboration with a female colleague. Part-time professors who team-teach must share their materials with their partners as a tacit condition of employment, and without benefit of non-disclosure agreements. All part-timers have been asked at one time or another to contribute materials to the department's collection. And off-shore contracts proposed to part-time English Language (ESL) teachers have stipulated that their teaching materials would become the exclusive property of the foreign institution.

What does it take to reform an anti-equity culture that crosses management and labour boundaries? Dissident voices are easily silenced in a culture of workplace bullying that applies to union and management alike. Who can endure for long being ignored at meetings (part-timers' contributions frequently go unrecorded in the minutes); not receiving replies to memos or phone calls; the silent treatment; the selective distribution of mail or information; insults, intimidating gestures, dirty looks; ostracization? A few part-timers recently got up the courage to present their list of equity abuses to both management and full-time professors. A senior manager responded by simultaneously trivializing and catastrophizing their proposed reforms:

"This is shocking," he said. "Yes, and it's all true," the spokesperson said. "No, I mean your punctuation and sentence structure," the manager said. "Though if what you say is true, the department should be closed down." Co-workers offered suffocating advice: "Be nice; you're too strident." Management agreed, and forbade me to speak again at meetings, then reassigned my course to others. The union duly noted the grievances, but advised awaiting a more favourable negotiating climate.

My final view of the equity landscape concerns age and employment. Recently, I applied for a non-teaching job at my university. I didn't get the job, but later, I asked one of the interviewers from the all-male panel if he could tell me who had been hired. "Oh," he answered, "we hired a young woman who ..." He caught himself. It was I who glossed over his involuntary revelation, and changed the subject to the state of his health.

Sickness, Health, and Contract Employment

SHANNON A. GADBOIS

I moved to my current home in what many would say was a typical move for a professional woman – because my husband had a permanent job here. My husband and I had agreed before we were married that we would move wherever I found full-time employment. Prior to our marriage, he sought employment in my province while I was still a student. He did not find it and neither did I. So, I moved to his home province where he was well-established and in a permanent position. I have never regretted the move and have been grateful for the change in quality of life it has afforded me. In fact, in these last few months I have begun to wonder if all this fresh air and newness was fated me in order that I might deal with two major events that I have endured during the last two years. These events have shaped my current thoughts regarding my employment situation and have caused me to develop strong concerns for issues in contract employment, particularly with regard to my health, my commitment to work, and my colleagues' commitment to me.

Two years ago, in the summer of 1996, I was hired to teach courses in the psychology department where I have been sessionally employed since I finished school. I signed the contracts and began the dubious task of teaching two half-credit courses over the span of six weeks. The six-week time constraint was a problem in itself, but the students and I set out to tackle this task. We were doing quite well at it, too, until I began to play recreational soccer midway through my teaching stint. I had never had a major injury in fifteen years of playing the sport competitively but, as fate would have it, as soon as I was in the middle of contracts, things changed. While playing soccer one night, I was tackled from behind and ended up lying on the ground with my foot hanging backwards.

My husband arrived at the hospital just as I was being dragged from the ambulance and at the same time as my in-laws were capturing this momentous occasion on film. Amidst doctors asking for repeated descriptions of the incident, and while listening to medical opinions ranging from "you'll need surgery" to "it would certainly take a great deal of force to break *and* dislocate your ankle," I realized my greatest concern: I had to get word to the chair of the psychology department that this had happened. My husband made the necessary phone calls and returned to tell me that my chair's worry, to my astonishment, was for my health and recovery and not with my responsibilities as an instructor. It is important to understand that my surprise was not a reflection of my colleague's compassion but of my own warped sense of the matter.

Unfortunately, at the moment, there was nothing I could do, so arrangements were made that I should "forget" about my work while someone else "pitched in" to teach my class until I could return. I felt uncomfortable about these arrangements and so prepared to return to the classroom. After three and a half days in the hospital and three days in the early stages of a painful recovery, I was back in the classroom a week after my accident. What my colleagues seemed to believe was beyond the call of duty, I believed was necessary. Since I had to keep my leg elevated during the first few weeks of my recovery, I taught the remainder of my course in a wheelchair. Although it was hot in May and June to be teaching in a wheelchair, I knew this is what I had to do to honour my commitment.

Things went smoothly for about a year. My contracts were steady and my health was good. When the summer of 1997 arrived and again I was teaching summer school, I decided to be cautious and coach rather than play soccer. But my efforts to avoid ill health were short-lived; one week into my courses another health problem arose.

While lying down one day I noticed a large lump in my lower abdomen. My doctor's diagnosis was that I probably had a cyst and would need surgery. Although he reassured me that the cyst was not likely cancerous, the fact that it had developed quickly signaled potential malignancy. We spent the weekend in fear and anticipation waiting for my appointment with the specialist early the next week. Following that appointment, we went straight to the university knowing that I had to somehow get through my class while struggling with the realization that I might have cancer. From that point, the details fell slowly into place. At the same time as my students learned about conditioning, memory, language, and psychological testing, my husband and I learned about ultrasounds, uterine cysts, hysterectomies, and hormone replacement therapy.

During my second last week of teaching, we were referred to an oncologist who my specialist thought might offer some hope. I finished the last week of my course knowing that my surgery would take place twelve days later and that only after I came out of surgery would we know if I had cancer. With these specifics now available, I approached my department head, for the second time in two years, regarding my health. Again, oddly enough to my mind, she was not worried that I might not be able to begin fulfilling my upcoming commitments right away; she was more concerned about my health. I also had another concern. I had had a job interview for another contract position at the local community college. Before I went into surgery I knew that I was one of three final candidates for the position, and that the position would begin shortly. The hiring committee knew nothing about my condition and I was not prepared to tell them unless necessary.

At the end of August, for the second time in two years, for the second time in my entire life, I was preparing to undergo surgery. Although I knew the likelihood was slim that I had cancer, I was still worried about the outcome and the possibility of experiencing menopause twenty years prematurely. I went into surgery believing that, whatever the result, we could deal with it; I came out of surgery with a four-inch incision but only minus a non-malignant, "larger-than-grapefruit-sized" cyst.

Three hours out of surgery and having regained consciousness, I was relieved – we were both relieved – at our good fortune, but I was also anxious to assure my chair that I could start back to work on time. Again, she saw that as the least of my concerns. I was also anxious to know the outcome of the job competition in which I was involved. I called and spoke to the head of the hiring committee. She had no way of knowing that I was calling from a hospital bed on an eight-week road to recovery.

It is two months since this last episode in my life and I am currently working, on a part-time, contractual basis, at both the university and the community college. Although my health problems have been tough on both me and my family, I am struck above all by the irony that these problems began only after I started my career as a contract employee. I now realize that uppermost in my mind were my contract commitments and not my health.

Through these experiences I have come to some realizations that I suspect mirror common concerns for most contract employees. First,

I believe that these incidents showed me that I am as committed to my work as any of my colleagues. In contrast to what one recent text in human relations says, I am not less committed because of the nature of my position and because I have personal health issues with which to deal. I believe that the reality for contract employees is that they must put aside their personal issues and demonstrate their commitment because there is only a short time during which an impact can be made and this impact is often crucial for further employment.

Second, I have found that although the institutions have not made long-term commitments to me in the form of health benefits or "job security," my colleagues have shown their support and willingness to accommodate the uniqueness of my situation. Although some people would say that contract employees are at the mercy of their colleagues and supervisors and so are not guaranteed to experience such support as I have, it has been my experience that colleagues will commit to you when you show commitment to your work.

Finally, I believe that compassion of the kind that I encountered must be drawn upon to motivate thorough examination of the state of contract employment in universities, particularly where issues of health are concerned. The safeguards for contract employees are limited at best, and union membership offers little benefit. Perhaps exposure to stories such as mine will clarify the realities experienced by this new generation of faculty and promote change for the better.

Despite these drawbacks, I have felt involved and satisfied in my professional life to this point. I have encountered strong support for my work and, in particular, I have met many women from whom I can learn and who can relate to my experiences. The variety associated with contract employment has ensured that I "do something each day that I have never done before" as Gloria Steinem encouraged her audience to do when I heard her speak some years ago. I am currently enjoying work in three contracts and enjoy the unique balance I can establish from meeting the challenges of each of them.

Perspectives from a Woman's Place

JANE GORDON

I teach at a university founded to educate women. It prides itself on a continuing commitment to the education of women. For most of the years of its existence, the teaching faculty was almost exclusively women, and women still constitute the majority of its professors. Well over half of the senior administration are women, and there has never been a male president. The majority of students are women. At conferences and other academic venues, I meet women who suggest that I am fortunate to work where I do. The assumption is, generally, that since I work in a setting where women are the majority, my work environment is "friendlier" than that of other universities. I would like to provide some perspective on this assumption and on the larger question of university standards.

Does an institution with a historical mission to women create a more "women friendly" working environment? My first approach to this question, the more "objective" approach, will use data drawn from my research. To this I add my personal observation and experience from many years of involvement in the university and in status-of-women issues for faculty at the provincial and national level. Finally, I will look at the reasons why things are as they are and discuss the issue of (primarily) single-sex educational settings.

Using only public information drawn from the university calendar, consider the question of gender and rank at my university. (I used public information because I was unable to obtain any other kind of data.) I took the 1975–76 academic year as a baseline, and looked at

Table 1
Gender Distribution according to Rank 1975–76

Rank	Number Males	Percent of Male Faculty	Percent of Rank	Number Females	Percent of Female Faculty	Percent of Rank
Below Lecturer	0	0	0	13	21%	100%
Lecturer	8	20%	40%	12	10%	60%
Assistant	17	43%	40%	26	42%	60%
Associate	14	35%	61%	9	15%	39%
Full	1	3%	33%	2	3%	67%
TOTAL	40		39% ALL faculty	62		61% ALL faculty

Gender Distribution according to Rank 1985–86

Rank	Number Males	Percent of Male Faculty	Percent of Rank	Number Females	Percent of Female Faculty	Percent of Rank
Below Lecturer	4	6%	13%	28	20%	88%
Lecturer	11	15%	22%	40	28%	78%
Assistant	23	32%	33%	46	33%	67%
Associate	24	34%	53%	21	15%	47%
Full	9	13%	60%	6	4%	40%
TOTAL	71		34% ALL faculty	141		66% ALL faculty

Gender Distribution according to Rank 1996–97

Rank	Number Males	Percent of Male Faculty	Percent of Rank	Number Females	Percent of Female Faculty	Percent of Rank
Lecturer	20	20%	26%	57	33%	74%
Assistant	22	22%	29%	55	32%	71%
Associate	35	36%	45%	43	25%	55%
Full	16	16%	67%	8	5%	33%
TOTAL	98		36% ALL faculty	173		64% ALL faculty

faculty at decade intervals. The tables above present numerical and percentage information on the rank distribution.

All three tables show the same interesting phenomenon. The percentage of men and women on the faculty has remained relatively constant over the last twenty years, but the distribution of women across academic ranks differs from the distribution of men. A higher percentage of women than men is found in the lower ranks. And, except for 1975–76 when the number of full professors is small, men make up a higher percentage of the two most senior ranks than they do of the faculty as a whole. This is more evident in the two later periods than in earlier years. (The rank breakdown also hides the impact on salaries because ceilings exist at all rank levels).

Why does this imbalance happen? A number of possible explanations exist. Formal and informal discussion at academic conferences suggests that women believe they do the lion's share of the unrecognized work in academic departments, including advising and mentoring students. Research corroborates that women's achievements have been less well recognized and regarded than that of their male counterparts, that women see themselves as teachers rather than scholars, and that their work is ignored or marginalized. Women are also disadvantaged by lacking support for success, their misunderstanding the real rules of the professions, or being hindered by the double day.

Summarized, these various explanations suggest that "the rules" of academic life work against women. My case study suggests that changing the gender composition of the academic work force without changing the rules or the understanding of what lies behind the rules will continue to keep women in the lowest levels of the academic establishment. The rules of what constitutes academic work are, after all, legacies of a male-dominated university system. It is a system that reflects the lives and experiences of the men who developed it and were its first students. Those are the rules that need to change. They have changed in the past, and are under considerable pressure to change in the future. Although some women accept the legitimacy of the expectations and respond with careers that parallel male careers, their "success" within the old rules does not challenge the nature of the rules. Even feminist scholarship, which has served to create new theories and methodologies as well as changing the content of academic research, has largely accepted the conventional patterns and measures of dissemination of knowledge.

In my university, which has always had a woman president and women in the majority of its senior academic and administrative positions, the procedures and standards by which we operate reflect traditional and conservative academic practices. We evaluate faculty for hiring, contract renewal, tenure, and promotion by the same criteria that are used elsewhere, although our collective agreement uses the feminine pronoun. More and more, over the last twenty years, as we have tried to promote our legitimacy as a university, we have pointed to conventional measures of faculty success: publications, publishing venue, and external grants. The substance of faculty scholarship may be different, but the legitimate forms of its dissemination and evaluation remain the same. Although we laud our unique role in the education of women and the unique character of our institution, we measure ourselves by the same criteria as other institutions do. Different people, same rules.

Some years ago I applied for a promotion to the rank of full professor. My collective agreement describes the various criteria, including teaching, research or professional activity (without distinguishing between faculty by discipline or department), and service. I spent many years extensively involved in professional work in regard to status of women issues in universities, including a term as chair of the Status of Women Committee of CAUT. In my application I pointed to what I considered ten major accomplishments during my term, acknowledging that I did not do these things alone but that I was heavily involved in these activities, and, I felt, instrumental in some of them. Among the items I included in my file were a major CAUT brief that I had written on child care, which was passed by CAUT Council, and stories I had published in the CAUT *Bulletin*. My file also contained conventional academic publications and conference papers, and material documenting my teaching and service activities.

My department was devastating to my file. All of my professional work (and what our collective agreement defines as criteria for professional work) was redefined as service. This included the substantial CAUT work described above, and comparable work at the provincial level, as well as activities in women's communities. For example, I was one of five mothers of young children who served as community representatives in planning a maternity hospital, an undertaking that lasted over five years and resulted in academic presentations and publications, community newsletters and briefs, meetings with numerous groups of women with particular concerns, conferences, representation to the provincial and national government, and other forms of outreach. All of these activities were undertaken as a result of my academic understanding of systemic barriers facing women in the labour force, in academic life in particular, and as a consequence of women's double burden of career and family responsibilities. All this work drew on my discipline and used my skills at research, writing, negotiation, education, and working with people. My research on its own was considered insufficient for promotion. In fact, the committee argued that since I was in an academic department, my professional work shouldn't count in any case. Members of my department were very familiar with the collective agreement, having served the faculty association in negotiation, grievance work, and, in one case, as president. Although the dean supported my application, the university promotion committee did not, and I was turned down.

My story illustrates the reasons behind the data in the tables. The rules of the university have crystallized out of a view of the creation and dissemination of knowledge that is not mine, and has not been developed by women. They are rules that have valued the individual creation of knowledge, no matter how esoteric or obscure. They are rules that do not value collaboration outside the academy or work which is oriented toward social change. I believe there is place in the academy for both traditional research and the action-oriented community-based work done by many women; many of my colleagues do not. Publications are valued and counted, but teaching is less important. The mentoring and support of non-traditional students, whether mature women, first-generation university students, or members of minority communities, is both time-consuming and invisible, and is essential for social change.

My commitment to changing the academic workplace for women grows out of my academic understanding of the systemic problems that women experience in non-traditional workplaces. My involvement in advocacy work for women draws on my academic expertise and represents another way to communicate knowledge. It also represents the link between knowledge and action so frequently spoken of in new feminist scholarship. However, instead of supporting me in this direction and arguing the validity of this approach, my institution dismissed my work.

Ironically, and, I would argue, because we are a university where there are so many women, we do not have many of the support structures I hear colleagues describe elsewhere: no brown bag lunches for women faculty, no women's caucus in the faculty association, no university status of women committee. We believe that because we have a large number of women on faculty, gender is not an issue that we need to examine. We assume our policies and practices are supportive of women. And we do not challenge the rules by which universities operate. Even in a university setting peopled largely by women, the conventional rules apply. It is not sufficient to get more women in the university; we also have to change the ways in which people are assessed. Until we do, we will continue to hear too many stories like mine.

Everyday Discrimination:
We Know How and When,
but Never Why

FYRE JEAN GRAVELINE

This narrative is a collection of experiences throughout my life as a student and faculty member in different institutions across time and space.

How do I know
upon what Grounds
I am Discriminated against?
I am a Woman,
a Métis Traditional healer and teacher
a Single Mother
I am a Feminist, Anti-racist, Social Activist
from Subsistence Northern Bush Roots
I am now Transplanted
into a Eurocentric, patriarchal, classist,
industrial, bureaucratic, institutional setting.

As a Woman I Know
If a male Sexually Assaults me
it has to do with My Female-ness.
As a Métis woman I Know
he may hold Stereotypic Views
of the women of My Community
that have Long Roots
Deeply embedded in Colonial Relations
on This Continent.

As a Two-Spirited Feminist I know
My existence
Challenges his Expectations of
Ownership and Sexual Servitude.

As a Métis Feminist, Two-Spirited Traditionalist, Activist, Scholar
Do I know WHY the obstacles and barriers I face
Each Minute, Hour, Day, Week, Month, Year, Lifetime
are Erected and Maintained?
I DON'T!

But I know HOW.
I know WHEN.
These Barriers are Very Visible to Me
Yet Invisible to Others.
They are Flattening Forces
Caging Me
Reducing Me
Denying Me.
Hating My existence
My Woman-ness
My Native-ness
My Two-Spirited-ness
My Existence Within
Eurocentric, Patriarchal, Heterosexist Systems
Which Never ever,
Never Ever
Meant to Include Me
Me or "My Kind."
Systems I have Had to Survive ·
learn to Thrive Within.
through Immense Effort
Blood ... Sweat ... Tears.
I know How the System works
And for Whom.
Not for Me
Me or "My Kind."

So, What do I Do
when Native and Black Sisters
are Harassed
and have No Place to Go?
No Place to Go!

They Come to see Me
  "Help us Please,"
    They Say
I Must Help.
I am Obliged by my Community ethics.
My Elders Teach:
Give Back to your Community
ALWAYS Do Whatever you Can for Others.
My Mother, My Father, Role Model.
All my Life
Raised to Recognize Injustice.
Speak Out about It.
and I Do.

  "Unfair Treatment,"
    I say
  "Discrimination."
  "Prove it,"
    They say.
  "Hussshhhhh. Don't Get Involved.
  Don't be So Critical.
  You don't want to be Uncollegial, Do You?"
  Eyebrows raised, They ask.

Don't! Don't! Don't!
Be Aware of Disciplinary Action,
I am Warned in a Letter.
Beware of Backlash,
Whispers my inner Guide,
Singing of past experiences.
Power oozes from Their pores
Smell it on Their Breath.
Their Tongues are like silver Forks
Buffy would sing ... Windego.

  "Help!"
    I Cry to Union.
  "Why is this happening to Me?
  Unfair treatment?"
    I question.
I am innocent, Innocent of Wrong Doing.
My mind races.
I was only trying to Help

to Help other Community Members.
How can that be a Problem?
I am Puzzled, and Worried.
Past Experience has taught me
Justice Means Just-Us
Just the powerful ones Win.

"Discrimination?"
   They respond
"Can you Prove it?
Why do you say that?
It could happen to Anyone
Any One of your Colleagues could be Disciplined."
Disciplined I muse
My Heart Beats Faster.
   "You have to Learn
   to get along Better
   with your Colleagues
   If you Want to Stay Here.
   Just be More Collegial!"
      I am Advised.

Be More Collegial
IF I want to Stay Here,
I ponder, More puzzled than ever.
Fear raises the Hairs on the Back of my Neck.
So much for Security.
   My mortgage
   My daughter
   My unemployed partner
   Our large, poor, extended family.

Be Nice! Be Nice! Be Nice!
Must become my constant Mantra
I Practise
Smiling with my Lips.
Eyes and Soul Hollow
Heart Closed in wire mesh.
   "It could be Worse, it could be Worse."
      Grand'mère always used to Say
   "It can Always be Worse."
But then, Oh No!
Through No effort of my Own

It got Worse.
Much worse
Much, Much, Worse.
I was Spied upon, Investigated
My life Interrogated.
My Being
Who I Am
Judged.
Found Inferior.
Unacceptable.
Not one of Us
One of "Them."
"You People."

Others Who would Listen Heard:
   "No one else brings their Children to the Office
  To class, to faculty functions.
    Where's her husband?"
I am judged Unfit
Unable to Commit as much to my Job as Childless ones?
Why are we Forced
to work/teach/learn Separate
from our Children, Partners, Elders, Community Members?
I Want to Include My Family/Community in my life/work.
Why are women
  Especially Native women and poor women
    Judged by self-proclaimed Feminists and others
     for raising our Children without husbands?
     For Juggling motherhood And an academic career?
I want to Love my Child
Be supported in my Motherwork.

  "She doesn't Drink, She doesn't Smoke
  What does she do?"
    They joke.
I am "the Outsider."
Why do I have to drink Alcohol
to be part of the Faculty Club?
I want to feel Pride in my Sobriety
Be supported in my Recovery.

  "Who stole my Knife? Who Stole my Knife?
   Did You?"

Face in my Face,
Voice a High-Pitched Scream.
"Did you?"
I am "the Accused."
"Thieving Indian" slur Rang
Clear as a Bell
in My mind that day.
"They didn't Know what They were Saying"
Someone attempts to console.
But I Know the Pain it caused Me.
Impact not Intent
The Law says.
No Law there to Witness
Her word against Mine, now.
I want to be Protected from Abuse.

"What's that Smell?
What's She doing in There
Smells like Marijuana or something."
They whisper and giggle like youth in the Hall.
"She's weird."
I am labelled "the weirdo."
"I came here to Study, Not to smell Sweetgrass."
I have been Told.
"If I can't recite the Lord's prayer, you can't burn a Smudge"
They have argued.
"There will be No Burning of Substances on School grounds,"
Authorities Decree.
I am the Ancestors
Persecuted for practising Our Spiritual Traditions
Again made Illegal Here.
Enforcing with Ultimate Clarity
Who's *Land* we are on Now.
The Stink of power
Makes me Hold my Nose.

"She puts a Negative Spin on Everything"
They say.
"We didn't have These problems Until *She* Came.
She's just a Troublemaker
Trouble-Maker"
I become "a Troublemaking Métis."
I now wear a Familiar Label

Like Many Generations of Métis Ancestors Before me.
Riel once Hung for being a "Traitor."
Now monuments are Erected
Celebrations are Held
To Honor him as a State Leader.
I am in Good Company
But I Am in Danger.

"Why is She so Angry?"
   Some Demand in Loud Voices
   Grinding Their Teeth
   Pounding Their Clenched Fists.
Me, angry? I wonder calmly.
I Remember when I was an angry Youth
Waking Up to social Justice
Wanting Retribution for the Crimes of Colonization.
Now I consider myself Moderate, Peace-seeking
Living in Balance, a Healer.
I seek advice from my Elders.
   "Why should You take on Their Projected Anger?
            Who is Really angry here?"
            A Wise One Queries.

"She needs Therapy!!!"
   A Challenged
   and Angry-about-it Student
   Once Proclaimed.
"You have fifteen years as a Healer.
You are a Ceremonial Leader.
You Have Done your Own Work.
      Has She?"
            My Elder quietly asks?
Grey Cloudiness shrouding my Brain
Momentarily lifts.
This is a Stressed-Out student
Not wanting to Wake Up to
Their Privilege,
   I Realize.

"You have received Bad Reviews
From Students and Colleagues"
   I am Informed in an Official letter.
I am Stunned.

"Your Evals have been the Highest in the Department."
   I had recently been Informed.
"Come to My office"
   Authorities Demand
   In a Most Official Tone.
"Help!"
   I say.
"Union help me!"
"Don't go,"
   They say
      "Without an Officer."
"You have No Right to Union help,"
   Authorities Decree
      "Come Alone or Not At All."

Meanwhile They Strategize
   "We'll Withhold her Increment"
      "We'll Meet with her Together,
         Lay Down the Law.
      She Will Comply."

So They did.
So We did.
Authorities, Union and me.
   "You Did This and That
                  This and That"
                  They Accused
On and On
I Heard
   "You are Wrong, Wrong, Wrong."
On and On
On and On
They went
taking turns.
   "You are Wrong, Wrong, Wrong."
   "We are The 'Pioneers' in Affirmative Action"
      They Boast.
         We Know what is Best
            For You
               For You and Your Kind.
               Jumps into My Mind.
Time Ticks loudly by.
Each Second an Eternity.

Finally, my head Feels so Heavy,
It could Fall
like a Lead Balloon
to the Hard oak table.
Heavy Head, Heavy Heart.
Oppressed.

  "Hey you"
    I finally Hear –
      "What do You have to Say for Yourself?"
I Open my Mouth
No words Emerge.
I have been Silenced
Experience tongueless-ness.
"I can now say no more forever."
My mind Sings Robbie Robertson
in honor of Chief Seattle.
A Metal Band Tightens round my Throat.
Don't Speak your Truth.
Don't Live your Truth.
Smile and be Nice.
Be Nice, Nice, Nice
and Get Over It.

  "I can't Believe you Really Think
    They are Out to Get You."
    I am Told
      By So-Called Innocent Bystanders.
        I do Not Wonder
        I Know.
Getting me was Bad
but it only got Worse.
Much Worse
Backlash Started on Others.
Others I had Helped
Who had Supported Me.
  "You can Not Graduate
  You were ill-advised."
    They wrongfully accused.

        Backlash!
"Your supervisors are Not Qualified."
  New rules illegally imposed.
        Backlash!

"No One here to Hear Us.
No One here Cares about Our issues."
   Native and Black students State
   in a Letter to the Authorities.
No One!
I Shriek Inside.
In my Silence
I have Become "No One."
I am Sick.
I am Sorry.
   "Why would I apply for Reappointment?"
      I rhetorically Reply
      When Casually asked by a Colleague
      At my Door.
Tears Trapped
Behind My Stoic Mask.
I hear No answer.
   "She is Not Reapplying"
      The Official memo
      Circulated the Next Day
      Callously states.

So I Will Not Fight Anymore.
I am Relieved
of the Oppressive Weight
of this Struggle
to be Me in this Cage,
this Narrow Confined space
called Academic Freedom.
   "I can't Believe
      They put it in Writing"
         Union says
   "You Should Stay and Fight."
So I Reapply
They Deny.

   "We can't Believe you're Leaving,
   You should Stay and Fight"
      They say.
Stay and Fight.
Stay and Fight, Fight, Fight.
Fight for Whom
Fight for What?
What Rights do I have?

Academic Freedom for Whom?
What Rights will I ever have
in these Systems
Systems meant to Confine
Confuse
Conform Me
Me and My Kind.

You want to Make me Fight
For all the Wrong Reasons
Sucking my Energy
My Life Blood
My Desire to Work
For/With My Communities.
To Leave the Fight
Is a Conscious Act
Self-Determination
Self-Preservation.

A warrior must Know
How to Survive a Skirmish
Save Energy for the Battle.
Rested Now
Revitalized through Ceremony
I Continue to Fight.
I have Learned my Lessons Well.
Remember
We Each Know
Inside Our Selves
When we are Oppressed.
When we have Taken
All that we Can.
When we have Done
All that we are Able.

Self-Determination means
Being Empowered to Say:
    "NO
      I will Not Fight Today
      Today I Will Live
      Love
      Laugh.
      Maybe Tomorrow

I will be Ready
To Die for a Cause."
Remember
Your Causes
are Not necessarily Mine.
Self-Determination means
I Pick My battles.
I Recognize My enemies.
I Embrace My friends.
Respect me.
You Can Not
and Should Not
Try to Influence Me
Question My Reality
Try to Make Me
Accept Your Version
of My Truth.

Through Systems
Inside and Out
Those Intended to Help
I have Experienced Abuse
Silence
Denial
Defensiveness
Minimization
Ignorance.
Please
Do Not Help Me.
Help your Selves.
Learn from My Pain.
We All make Mistakes.
Learn from Mine
and Yours.
Who Are You
In this Trickster Tale?

This is the Way
I understand these Experiences to Be.
Others might Understand it to be Different.
These stories are Mine.
My Voice
I've told them True.

True to Me.
True to what I Know.
I Experienced it
Reflected on it
Told it
to You Today.

Thanks for Listening
Megwetch

Transforming at the Margins of the Academy[1]

JOYCE GREEN

The often-conflicted academic experience of Aboriginal women has been my reality as well as my intellectual interest.[2] My heritage includes both settler and Aboriginal peoples, and so my personal, social, familial, and political context includes all of the tensions that I will address here. This context is both a social location and an experience of an unequal dialectic of conflict, configured by dual racisms, colonialism, sexism, and marginalization. For me and my familial cohort, our history, psyche, and analysis are indelibly marked by this dialectic. We share a condition common to many non-culturally located Métis, and not coincidentally, to women of all sorts in universities: it's called Never Fitting In. My experience and my analysis are grounded in the following observations.

The category of Aboriginal academics is very small and predominately located first, in Native studies programs and departments; second, in designated Native focus components of other programs; and third, scattered across disciplines and professions depending on interest and ability. But statistically, it is virtually insignificant in relation to the universe of academics, and it is further reduced by controlling for sex.

Why is this so? It is my view that institutions, even those that promote equity hiring, are somehow managing not to hire, retain, and promote Aboriginal academics; they are not doing well in recruiting Aboriginal scholars into graduate programs; they do not see this as a deficiency except in the designated schools, programs, and discipline of Native studies.[3]

It's worth noting here that even in the arena into which aboriginal scholars are expected to flow – Native studies – it is difficult to impossible to get a PhD as there are very few places in Canada that offer such a degree. Graduate applicants with Native studies majors must requalify in another discipline (this is how I wound up in political science) and then contend with professors and students who, too often, expect them to be Indian experts on all the contentious matters in that meta-category.

And, Native studies programs are often poorly integrated into the university: they suffer from underfunding or survive on soft funding. That is, universities show weak commitment to Native studies as well as to Native scholars. Both the discipline and its practitioners tend to be ignored by related disciplines and scholars: for example, political science, sociology, economics, law, and philosophy.

Further, Native studies is ignored by the preponderance of the student body, which fails to see this study as a vital part of their education. Few will encounter the minuscule numbers of Aboriginal women academics not located in designated corners of universities, and so they neither get the benefit of our scholarship nor do they get to see us as Aboriginal, in academic positions. This reduces our role modelling capacity. Even where institutional support does exist for inclusion of Aboriginal scholars, there is weak commitment to the programs and poor visibility of the faculty.

For Aboriginal academics in the "regular" disciplines, institutional and collegial support is substantially lessened, and visibility is lower than in Native studies. At the same time, Aboriginal sociologists, political scientists, and biologists are expected to be "Indian experts" regardless of their research focuses.

Finally, the combination of low numbers of women academics combined with the dynamics of academic politics and institutional racism, as well as the lower numbers of other women and Aboriginal male academics with whom to build solidarity, results in a lonely, isolating, and implicitly hostile workplace.

I will describe the structures that shape our inclusion while they perpetuate our subordination, and then I will talk about our radical transformative potential. Many Aboriginal academics (and many female academics, and academics from other minorities) find themselves in the curious position of being marginal and tokenized at the same time as we seek space in the academy for our physical presence, our intellectual freedom, and our political and pedagogical perspectives.[4] These stances are often informed by our experiences and analyses of oppression: they exemplify that "the personal is political." They are often viewed as illegitimate, radical, unacademic, or threatening to colleagues, students, and administrative processes; to the notion of meritocratic tenure in the academy; and to disciplinary canons.

Here, three things happen to Aboriginal women and marginalized others in the academy. First, we embody difference from the dominant institutional norm, which is thoroughly constructed for male, colour, and class privilege. (In this context we should consider sexuality and disability as well.) This physical representation of difference exists regardless of our personal, intellectual, or political pursuits! This results in the Never Fitting In phenomenon, or in its counterpart, the phenomenon of self-annihilation: fitting in by rejecting one's particularity and the analysis I present here in favour of conformity with the existing institution. This is manifest in women who are as patriarchal as men; in marginalized others who deny the existence of or their personal experience with racism; and in beliefs that there is a neutral meritocracy which recognizes a scholastic excellence that may be equally pursued by all.

Second, assuming that we make our way through social and institutional filters into the student or faculty body, we are sometimes explicitly and sometimes implicitly expected to serve as representatives of those whose attributes we share. Thus, our markers of difference (which is different from consciousness of the political significance of difference) become an asset for the institution, which too often overloads us as individuals with committees and courses designed to benefit from our tokenistic appointment, sometimes with no regard for the unrelated nature of our scholarship! But while the institution tokenizes us in this fashion, it is much less willing to endorse the different pedagogical, methodological, and theoretical practices that we bring with us. For those of us who teach and study critical, anticolonial, and feminist theory and practice, there are continual challenges to our centrality to curriculum and to particular disciplines, and to our scholarly significance.

Third, we are always asked to bear too many burdens that mainstream, malestream scholars need not bear: representation, voice, mentorship, and so on, as Aboriginal and as female. That is, we are asked to legitimate the oppressive academy as inclusive; we are asked to explain the Other to the privileged; we are asked to recruit and promote Our Own, while simultaneously being asked to conform to the not-so-neutral academic career path, disciplinary curriculum, and institutional practices. Some of this is chosen by us, but much of it is imposed by institutions and colleagues who choose not to change. Educating the ineducable about gender and Aboriginal questions exhausts and enrages at least some of us (LaRocque, 1999).

Resistance to marginalized others within the academy comes from two primary factors. The first is the intuitive reaction by those who are dominant against the inclusion as equals of those who have been subordinate by definition. In other words, the historic, cultural and intellectual foundation of the academy is deeply imbued with patriarchal, racist, and colonial assumptions and practices. The conditions of intellectual life are circumscribed by these assumptions and practices. The components of what it means to be excellent rest on these assumptions and practices. It is no surprise, then, when our inclusion in the academy draws a visceral reaction, particularly from those who have not investigated their own assumptions. Let me rephrase this: we (all women, Aboriginal peoples, and marginalized others) are "always, already"[5] suspect to those whose privilege and knowledge rest on our subordination.[6]

The second factor is a logical consequence of the implications of our inclusion: power relations, life expectations, forms of knowledge, and so on will be challenged and there will be change. Notice: here I suggest that despite our marginal and suspect status, we are potentially transformative. The operation of this second factor destabilizes everything the beneficiaries of the existing academy have been led to believe about excellence, the process of knowledge production, and the recruitment of students and colleagues. Most of all, it threatens their own sense of entitlement on the basis of what they have learned to be the criteria for advancement.

These two factors trigger the reactive, hostile counterarguments to our inclusion known as "the backlash," accompanied by calls for freedom from "political correctness."[7] In this formulation, those of us who name and object to our oppression, or who stand in solidarity with marginalized others, are transformed by our stance into the oppressors of those whose privilege we challenge. The backlash and the dismissive label "political correctness" construct marginal, subordinated people as dominating oppressors. At the same time, the accompanying hostility produces what many of us have experienced: the Chilly Climate. Institutional intransigence and colleagues' hostility and derision freeze many of us out of the academy.

The exclusionary Western canon that is taught in the core disciplines reproduces the kinds of scholarship that affirm the existing relations of dominance and subordination. Theory and practice that dispute this and produce alternative accounts of reality are subversive and are barely tolerated by the academy. To the extent that the academy is grounded in race, sex, and class privilege, it reproduces these relations and the legitimations of them. And it has limited toleration of women's studies, Aboriginal studies, and class analysis. This exclusion ranges from the low numbers of academics who are marginal by definition – women, racialized people, "out" gays and lesbians – and by their exclusion as subjects from the canon.

How does all of this play out for Aboriginal women? First, it means that those who are able to gain access to the academy are excellent by definition. We have had to persevere in the face of implicit and explicit challenges to our inherent legitimacy. We have had to endure and learn core curricula that ignore, exclude, racialize, or sexualize, our histories, cultures, and persons. Then, many of us, after meeting the institutional requirements on this score, and despite the lack of financial and institutional support, have gone on to pursue scholarship that challenges precisely these kinds of exclusions and generates a more complete knowledge. We know we are good scholars.

We also know, from simple observation, that the existing not-so-neutral system of recruitment and promotion in the academy is in fact an affirmative action program for mediocre white men.[8] This is not an allegation that all white males are mediocre: many are excellent. But the presence of substantial numbers of mediocre colleagues suggests that the primary criteria are maleness and race. How otherwise to explain the homogeneous character of the academy? Inclusion of others fosters real measures of merit by requiring demonstrated excellence, not just sex and race privilege.

Second, we are transformative. From the fact of our presence and the original and radical nature of our work, we challenge the academy to confront its particular forms of privilege and its bases of exclusion. This process is conditional, continual, and far from over. Mary Daly, a feminist philosopher, observed that we hold the most transformative power when we are engaged in "creative existence on the boundary" of dominating (patriarchal, colonial) institutions (Daly, 1973). And our work is fraught with complications and contradictions, for we must negotiate not only the racist, sexist relations within the academy but also the politics and strategies of divergent Aboriginal communities and organizations. This subjects us to serious political pressure if we obtain any profile, and if our analysis or work does not suit particular individuals or organizations. Feminist Aboriginal women, and women who have contested existing power relations, have ample evidence of this repressive impulse, and it is injurious and incompatible with our work as academics. In sum, Aboriginal women academics negotiate multiple and contradictory considerations in which we are never, ever, allowed to be neutral.

Third, we are mentors: Aboriginal and many female students find some solidarity in our existence, and sometimes in our scholarship, inspiration, and enlightenment. These students become part of the transformative yeast in the academy and in their own communities.

Fourth, we are colleagues, and some of our non-Aboriginal and male colleagues resist us. Others are curious. Some are in solidarity with us. Again, to the extent that we contest what knowledge is, how it is evaluated, and what the power relations are that configure it, we instigate academic excellence and social transformation.

All this happens at some expense. It's hard, painful, and dangerous to take on consolidated power relations. Some of us are eliminated. In my own discipline, political science, many departments are considered to have Chilly Climates. But some of us are here, and we demonstrate that we are not homogeneous; we can be subversive of existing power relations; we are excellent; we are controversial; we are in solidarity with many others; and we are your colleagues. We contribute through teaching, through research, and through critique. To uphold the best elements of scholarly excellence, both administrations and individual scholars must confront the academy's racist and sexist foundations and assumptions. Further, they must incorporate those who critique these foundations, without demanding an assimilative conformity.

NOTES

1 Based on a presentation of the conference "Equity in the New Millennium," CAUT/SWC, 1–4 October 1998, Regina, Saskatchewan.
2 For a good discussion of the centrality of personal experience to theory and analysis, see Christine Overall, *A Feminist I: Reflections from Academia*. Peterborough: Broadview Press, 1998, 173–197.
3 Even apparently ameliorative measures do not remedy this: consider, for example, the University of Alberta's "Opening Doors" policy designed to improve representation of designated groups. Under the policy, representation of designated groups actually dropped in all categories. However, the existence of the policy produced a furor among some on campus, who charged that principles of merit would be violated, as worthy (implicitly White male) candidates were trumped by (implicitly unworthy) candidates who fit the designated groups.
4 See Kelly (1998), LaRocque (1996), Ng (1999), Razack (1998), Stalker and Prentice (1998).
5 The "always, already" formulation has been used by some scholars to capture the process of the racist gaze upon those constructed as "other,"

who are marked by their physical particularity as always, already subordinate.

6 This reaction was demonstrated at a plenary session of the Canadian Political Science Association at Brock University in 1996, where eminent political scientists Reg Whittaker and Philip Resnick fulminated about the evils of feminist and other critical contestations of the canon and the discipline as inherently unmeritorious and coercive "political correctness."

7 For a good discussion of the reactionary force of "political correctness," see Christine Overall, *A Feminist I: Reflections from Academia*, Peterborough: Broadview Press, 1998, 44–52.

8 Aldea Landry, a cabinet minister in Frank McKenna's 1989–91 Liberal government in New Brunswick, put it this way: "Women haven't [yet] earned the right to be mediocre." Don Desserud, Women in New Brunswick politics: Waiting for the third wave, *In the Presence of Women* (Jane Arscott and Linda Trimble, eds.), Harcourt Brace Canada, 1997, 270.

The Wandering Wombs:
Women Faculty Empower
Themselves through Friendship

MARY RUCKLOS HAMPTON
AND PEGGY WILSON

We met while teaching at the University of Alaska in the chilliest of climates – inside and outside the university. Now we are both teaching in Canadian universities. But what we learned for the first time in Alaska has come with us and allowed us to survive and thrive in academia today. We learned the power of women's friendships.

Although the University of Alaska is an American University, it is geographically and culturally close to its Canadian neighbours. The extreme environment of the far north, and its racial mix of Native, Caucasian and other ethnic backgrounds, makes for a unique culture that is reflected in its institutions. As in most post-secondary institutions in the United States, women faculty were hired as a result of affirmative action laws, yet once we were on staff, the institutions didn't know what to do with us. In fact, in our faculty, there was an outright hostile "frontier" mentality toward women faculty members.

Experiencing on a daily basis the frustrations, degradation, and demoralization that academic sexism engendered, we joined a group of eight women faculty members who came together to try to create an atmosphere where women's strengths could be acknowledged and validated. What were considered our vulnerabilities and used against us, we wanted to experience as our own unique strengths as individuals and as women. We wanted to support these strengths within an environment where cooperation and profound interpersonal communication sharing were valued. What emerged was a support base founded on the value of friendship within a small group. The results of the emerging empowerment of these women were felt throughout the entire college.

Formation of the group. A chain of specific events had precipitated the need for support for female faculty at the University of Alaska. While 25 percent of the faculty were then female, there was only one tenured woman in our College. There had been an old boys' network for a long time. The dean of the college was male, as were all the department chairs. With the hiring of new female faculty, the established power structure seemed to be threatened. Women were being told in a variety of ways that their presence was not welcome.

When a minority faculty member, through affirmative-action hiring policies, was being considered for a tenure-track position, she was told by her department chair, "Don't take it personally, but we just can't allow any more of these minorities [sic] to get in through the back door." Although the implication of this remark was that she was not qualified for this position, she later discovered that her qualifications were equal to, if not superior to, those of the person who had made the statement. Two other female faculty members were threatened by tenured male faculty with statements such as, "You're only here because we hired you. We can fire you, too."

Still other examples of gender inequity existed in expense account allocations. Male faculty were often given a budget and were allowed to travel to off-campus sites with no questions asked, while female faculty in similar positions were questioned closely about their travel. A male faculty member who coordinated a program was given release time to develop his program, while a female faculty member of equal status coordinating a similar program was expected to teach a full course load while developing her program. Another female faculty member served as acting co-ordinator of a program for one year without receiving monetary compensation or release time for the additional work. When the co-ordinator position was finally filled, by a male, he was given release time to become familiar with the program while she received not even a letter of appreciation for her work.

Other comments and actions were even more blatant. Physical improvements to the working environment, proposed by female faculty, were met with comments like, "It looks like a bordello." One woman was invited to a department meeting with the comment, "We need someone attractive there." Students were threatened by male faculty members if they enrolled in women's studies courses. At faculty meetings, women listened to put-downs and innuendos about their competence.

These injustices are only a sampling of the experiences that women faced as they carried out their faculty assignments each day. Out of this frustration, one woman from the faculty sought the help of an American-Indian woman friend who followed traditional teachings. As part of their discussion the friend said, "It is time now for you to find a way to put your shawl around the younger women." In response to that advice, with the support of the counselling and group skills of the members involved, a call to join a "healing circle" went out to all women employees, faculty, and support staff. Only eight women chose to become a part of this group; not surprisingly we were a mixed group. In addition to being marginalized on the basis of gender, the group included women who were Alaska Native, American Indian, lesbian, divorced, and representatives of other potentially disenfranchised positions. We needed support.

The healing circle. For centuries, Indigenous peoples, particularly of the west-coast region, have used the healing circle to help deal with personal and emotional matters. Typically, group members sit in a circle. The symbolism of the circle itself is important in that it represents the holism of Mother Earth, the equality of all its members. Traditionally, an eagle feather or a similar sacred object is passed around the circle. The holder of the sacred object speaks from the heart expressing whatever emerges as important at the time. The role of those present is to listen non-judgmentally and in silence until the speaker has completely finished. There is no attempt to rush in and solve the problem, to defuse the issue, or in any way to diminish the moments of contact for the one speaking. When the speaker has finished, she passes the object to the next person following the direction of the sun. Each member gets a chance to talk and to be heard.

Once a month, on a Saturday afternoon, our group of women met in this "talking circle." Of the eight women who took part, one was an associate professor, six were assistant professors, and one was a lecturer. The average age of the women was forty-one, and each woman in the group came from a different cultural and ethnic background.

What we all discovered from sharing our honest feelings from our hearts was a relief from our isolation. Most of us had internalized a sense of shame about our strengths as women and had been pressured to conform to patriarchal standards or get out. The treasures we could have given to our students and colleagues had been buried. In opening up to each other, we threw off the shame from deep inside and met each other with unconditional acceptance. We found we could use power *for* each other rather than *over* anybody else. One of our surprises was that by finding our personal power within a synergistic circle, the forces that had been dragging us down no longer could get inside us.

We found ourselves using our renewed energy for creative projects. Each of us had access to interesting resources such as teaching methods and materials, books, journals, and ideas that we had been afraid to use openly. Not only did we give each other permission to be as creative as possible but we valued our sources. As teachers, all of the women wanted to stimulate discussion in classes and to use experiential teaching methods. We had interpersonal skills that would allow us to do this and we believed in the value of shared experience. One of the group members stated, "I used to be afraid to try different things in class, but when I heard you say you got inside the podium and lectured from there, or gathered the class together in a rope, or had small groups compare the number of slang words for 'vagina' and 'penis,' I began to have courage." We discussed pedagogy and ways to help students learn.

If one of the members encountered political difficulty or wanted to present a radical proposal at a department meeting, we met to discuss strategy and gather positive energy. We began to develop an old girls' network that was based on values of cooperation and empowerment. There were moments when the academic traditions of competition may have turned us into rivals for scarce resources, but the healing circle brought us back each time into the circle of friendship. The support given to members reached into all aspects of the women's lives. Babysitting was generously offered as each member, in a sense, adopted the others' children as her own. Renewing weekends to a nearby hot spring were held. After one particularly adventurous excursion crossing the Arctic Circle in early spring (eight women packed in a little car), we named ourselves "The Wandering Wombs." One woman had T-shirts made up for all of us with WANDERING WOMBS in big letters, complete with a soaring eagle and beautiful mountains. We felt we had experienced a new paradigm in a renewal of our traditions.

As we found an avenue for expression of our concerns and support for our endeavours, we began to reach beyond the small group to touch the lives of other faculty members, drawing colleagues into social activities on the campus. We hosted celebrations for special days. Together, we made Christmas stockings for every faculty member with their names individually decorated on them, and hung them on their office doors. We organized a Christmas tree decorating party. We converted a storage area into a faculty and student lounge, a place to welcome visitors to the college. We hung quilts made by female faculty and students on the college walls and changed them monthly. We produced a college newsletter listing the accomplishments of the female faculty and staff as well as descriptions of the women's studies courses being offered. All eight women initiated a weekly lunch meeting that quickly expanded to include other male and female faculty. During these lunches, teaching and research ideas were shared so that we all could become more empowered to use innovative methods in our academic work.

One member of the initial support group said, "The coping skills that I have learned in this group of women make me feel so much less victimized." As we women began to feel less victimized, we felt more able to assist others. And as we reached out to others, a wonderful result was that the feelings of cooperation became contagious. A staff member said, for example, "Something has happened, and now that good feeling is spreading. Faculty are even starting to thank the support staff, bringing them flowers. Male faculty, also." Students commented on the changed atmosphere by saying things like, "There is a lot more experiential learning and teaching going on now. We like it." Remarks were noticed in the newly created lounge such as, "There's laughter in the department now that I never heard before," and "There's a friendlier atmosphere this year." Male faculty too began to notice change, "Things have really changed (in the department) and it's affecting the men, also. There's a gentler atmosphere."

The group's primary commitment and concern as we met on a regular basis was to ward off feelings of inequality and to go forward in teaching and learning, knowing that the offerings that we made were first-rate. We women created a culture with and for each other in our attempt to think in new ways about our intellectual lives. We began to think about ourselves not as disempowered women, but rather as women full of potential and power both collectively and individually. Just as important, as we grew, we remembered to put our shawls around others, so that they too could feel the warmth. Even when the academic environment is at its most chilly, we can call on each other for warmth.

As of this writing, all of the eight women are in improved academic situations, some at the same university, others at different institutions. Two of us have tenure and have advanced to full professorships, one is a dean, one has advanced to associate professor status, and the remainder continue to proceed toward advancement. All of us remain in close contact, even though we're separated by miles. The bond of friendship has empowered us from within and given us the ability to continue to develop our own uniquely creative gifts. As a result of our new-found empowerment, we have been able to create new networks of friends at our new institutions.[1]

NOTE

1 The authors share in this writing with our sisters Jill Baker, Dauna Browne, Germaine Kinunwa, Laurie Marum, Val Montoya, Pat Nelson, and Karen Noordhoff.

Doing the Tango in the Canadian Academic Tundra: Keep Those Feet Moving Fast

ELENA R. HANNAH

In my twenty-eight years as a faculty member in the Psychology Department of Memorial University, I have held a full-time, tenure-track position (eight years), a part-time, per course position (eight years), a full-time, non-tenure-track, contractual position (ten years), and a full-time, sessional position (two years). Apart from a few months' maternity and sick leave, and a year when I followed my then husband for his sabbatical in another province (where I also taught two full terms), I have always taught here. However, despite my twenty-eight years as an academic member of this university, I have no job security, a below poverty level income, no health insurance, no vacation pay – no benefits at all. I never know, from one term to the next, what my income will be or if, indeed, I will have one. I teach some of the largest courses on campus (around 300 students) and I am available for student consultations several hours a day. I could be asked to teach, often with short notice, any one, two, or three of ten courses in which I have expertise. Textbooks are changed often, forcing me to revise lecture notes, exams, and course syllabi without much control on my part. Conversely, I have had the experience of building up a course over several years only to have it taken away from me because a full-time faculty member chose to teach it by correspondence for extra income. I have no access to grants, travel funds, or similar resources that are taken for granted by full-time faculty.

How did I manage to end up, only six years short of retirement age, in such a precarious position? The simple answer is that I chose to stay home with my three children during their early years, and this decision derailed me from what could have been an ordinary academic path. As I run from one large class to another, along these oh-so-well-known corridors that feel like my second home, I ask myself over and over if I made the right decision, though I now know that such decisions are never made in a vacuum, and that powerful social forces within and outside the academy shaped what felt, erroneously, like a completely free choice. There are no simple answers.

I grew up in Buenos Aires, Argentina. I was temporarily living in New York City when a military coup in my native country and the ensuing dictatorship influenced me to stay in the United States to do graduate work. Upon receiving my MA in 1970, I followed my fellow graduate student and fiancé on an adventure. We had both managed to get academic jobs in this, for me, remote, unknown island, seemingly lost in the Atlantic near the North Pole. The idea was to spend two years in this "exotic" part of Canada and then move back to civilization. Finding myself with a position in a university that was growing by leaps and bounds, joining a friendly academic community, setting up house and learning a new culture and almost a new language (Newfoundland English was very different from American English!) were exciting events indeed. Despite the extra effort involved in dealing with so much newness, I felt that all my dreams were coming true. My biological clock started to tick loudly, and I was sure that I could really have it all. Yes, I would do the tango in this beautiful, new land.

Delighted as I was with my first pregnancy, I had never considered staying home with my new baby. I planned to find a good babysitter and return to work, as I did not have built-in cultural expectations that, once a baby arrived, I would prove myself a "good" mother by dropping work and dedicating myself to its care. But something absolutely marvellous and totally unexpected happened when I first held my newborn daughter in my arms, barely out of my body: I fell head over heels in love with her! Since this was a planned pregnancy, I had the summer months to be home with her. As our relationship developed, I sat in the rocking chair nursing her, gazing into her eyes, and dreading the day I would have to leave her for many hours a day.

My practical, sensible plans suddenly seemed demented. How could anybody be trusted to look after my treasure? How could we be so many hours away from each other? The university, my colleagues, my former routines, even my passion for psychology, receded into a distant background. At the last minute, I requested a semester's unpaid leave, thinking that by the time my daughter was ten months old, surely I'd be ready to leave her for part of the day. Yet, when that day came, I felt I was being torn apart limb by limb. My life became a constant tension: when I was home I felt neglectful of my academic duties, and when I was at the university I longed to be with my daughter. This dilemma worsened when my second and then my third babies were born in quick succession. I gradually abandoned research, which seemed a luxury at that time, and concentrated on teaching, hoping to last until the children were in school. I didn't. After maternity leave, I never felt comfortable when it was time to return to work. Rightly or wrongly, I became convinced that nobody could replace me while my children were so young. The constant stress of baby-sitters who didn't show up or quit without much notice, and the absence of relatives to fall back on under such circumstances added to a growing feeling that mothering and a career were incompatible. I resigned from my full-time academic appointment, convinced that, as soon as my youngest was in school full-time, I would pick up where I had left off.

Alas, it wasn't that simple. Observing those around me, I decided I wouldn't be happy with the hectic family pace that ensues when both parents work full time. I felt that this lifestyle was too high a price to pay for the privilege of academic work and a modicum of financial reward. I decided to wait to return to work full time. Meanwhile, I continued to teach on a per course basis two nights a week and felt that I had a very well-balanced life. I had enough time for my family, yet I was not cut off from my field. Through teaching, I kept current, waiting for the day when it would feel right to apply for a full-time position again. I also dedicated several hours a day, from my home mostly, to two organizations that were dear to my heart: the La Leche League, helping breastfeeding mothers, and the Childbirth Education Association. These activities were extremely rewarding and tied in with mothering far better than academic psychology.

As the academy became more competitive in the 1980s, I realized that I'd have to finish my PhD (abandoned upon moving from New York to Newfoundland) if I wanted to ensure my chances of being accepted back by my colleagues. This posed a whole new set of problems, as I no longer felt free to go wherever I could find the most suitable advisor.

Just when I was ready to go into a PhD program at Memorial upon our return from a year's sabbatical leave, fate intervened in the form of Crohn's disease, an inflammatory bowel disease that is chronic, incurable. Although my husband was a sufferer, it was not then known that there is a genetic component. When my daughter was diagnosed, I could not even fantasize about graduate work. She needed me at home (or in the hospital, where she spent many months) on a full-time basis. Her disease was far more intense than her dad's and it had hit her at a very vulnerable age, just starting adolescence. I became her nurse and teacher, running to her school every few days to get the lessons she had missed and tutoring her at home so she would not lose the year academically.

As my daughter stabilized, I was offered a contractual, one-year appointment in the Psychology Department to teach the three psychology courses required by the city hospital-based nursing programs. Our finances were so depleted, and the schedule was so appealing, that I decided to give it a try. However, the improvement to my daughter's health was transitory. I found myself teaching nine hours a week as well as dedicating much time and energy to her care.

Although my new position had its advantages, I was cut off from the Memorial campus and my colleagues, out of the loop for vital information that could have been beneficial to my career. I started at the rank of lecturer and continued as such, on one-year contracts that were renewed at the last minute, for ten years. My previous sixteen years of service were erased from my record. The promised long-term contract never materialized. When psychology was eliminated from the nursing curriculum, I was relegated to poorly paid sessional status.

During those ten years there were many dramatic, painful changes in my personal life. My only sister died of cancer in Argentina. My father and then my mother developed dementia, starting with the grief over my sister's death, and died within four years of each other. My daughter's health, both physical and emotional, deteriorated to the point where I feared for her life. My husband and I went through a very hurtful, destructive divorce that had devastating repercussions on my two adolescent sons. One of my sons was also diagnosed with Crohn's and spent the better part of a year in hospital. All of these events sapped my energy and capacity to fight for my rights. Although I continued to teach and, in fact, had to increase my teaching load to make ends meet, as I was for a while the sole financial support for my children, I had no energy left to argue for better contracts, or look for sympathetic allies, or start a research program. Although I started a PhD program, my teaching load of three semesters per year was incompatible with graduate work. This tango was tough to do on an icy, slippery surface.

Gradually, some parts of my life were rebuilt. I remarried (help me, another academic!). I retained my office despite becoming a lowly sessional instructor, and became more involved in departmental and university affairs. I continued with some of my extra-curricular activities (aerobics, jogging, choir) which give me strength and sustenance.

And I met two special women at a CAUT Status of Women Conference, with whom I embarked on this book project.

So, what now? I acknowledge that my approach to the rearing of my three children and the events that followed were not conducive to a full-time academic career. I was willing to accept the penalty of a stunted career, without reaching the higher ranks or garnering the accolades of a well-known researcher; I don't expect to be at the same level as my peers who kept to the regular academic path. However, if they wish to increase the representation of women, the academy must realize that many of us prefer to be involved in our children's rearing to a greater extent than is now allowed. Women are also the caregivers of choice in any family crisis. A more flexible academic clock and a greater acceptance of women's values would go a long way toward achieving a truly proportional representation of women in universities.

What I find discouraging and patently unfair is that there is a whole army of us in academe who, for various reasons, have not moved in lockstep with our peers but are nevertheless contributing enormously to the smooth running of the university without receiving proper compensation or recognition. We are assigned courses at the last minute, necessitating new and often unexpected preparations, review of textbooks, setting up syllabi, conferring with colleagues in that area and reading massively, all before the term starts, on our own time and without adequate financial compensation. Most don't have an office, or a telephone. None of us is listed in the university phone book or calendar, in itself an experience in isolation and invisibility. I am ineligible to apply for grants or travel funds to conferences even if I present a paper; or to be a member of a committee, or to cast my ballot in faculty council votes or any votes at all involving election of department or university officers. I have had to be very assertive to continue receiving departmental notices and minutes of meetings. I am the same person I always was, teach even more students than before, put in the same number of hours of work and retain the same interest in departmental and university affairs as when I worked full time. However, in many respects, I have ceased to exist at the university. I am now doing the tango barefoot on the ice.

It is difficult to quantify the stress, the lost creativity, and the stifled energies that result from working under these circumstances. Only when I meet my students, see their freshness, idealism, curiosity, and thirst for knowledge, when it's just them and me in the classroom and every other concern fades away, that I feel I am doing something I love. Alone with my books and journals I still get that old thrill, the feverish enthusiasm of intellectual pursuit; thus, when I meet my students I am still able to transmit a fresh excitement. Engaging young minds is a privilege that I refuse to give up. I enjoy being in a place where the commodity of exchange is knowledge. At those times, the tango flows sweet and mellow and moss cushions my steps in the tundra.

Hopefully, one day the academy will realize that it can only be enriched by a variety of approaches, styles, and career schedules. This realization will mean the end of the exploitation to which so many of us are subjected, often with the collusion of faculty unions. Students, the raison d'être of universities, will be much better served. Then, we will have a true *universitas*.

When Life Gets in the Way of Life: Work/Family Conflicts among Academic Women and Men

LESLEY D. HARMAN
AND PETRA REMY

"An academic career interferes in life" (female, 49, divorced, adult children).

As I sit watching the cursor blink on my monitor, the clock reads 3:15 a.m. The house is quiet, the housework is done, and in my head I hear the echoes of my children saying "I love you, Mummy" as they drift off to sleep. At the end of the day I am grateful for the gifts of my children and my career, for the opportunity to be both a mother and a full-time scholar.

I wonder what has happened to the past week. I am a lone parent and this week I did the majority of the child care of my three children. My three-year-old was up for hours each night with a cold. I kept her home for two of the five days that I was supposed to be working on this article. Then one of my eight-year-old twin sons had to be home for another two of those days. Then there was the school play, the violin lesson, the hockey practice, and somewhere in there the Christmas shopping. My car broke down in the middle of rush hour traffic. A book that I needed could not be found ...

When life gets in the way of life ... The countless little things that crop up on a daily basis for academics trying to combine family and career are constant reminders of how little control we really have over our lives. The irony of putting together this article under such conditions is hard to escape.

Control is a big part of the life of an academic. The achievement of the degrees, teaching experience, and publications necessary to land a secure university job is facilitated and enhanced by a firm sense of control over time, space, and finances. Sociologists sometimes use the term "linear career path" to refer to the pattern of uninterrupted education leading to a job, steady full-time employment, and increasing status and rewards. While academics experience a considerable delay in terms of age before job stability kicks in (virtually guaranteed by a tenure-track position), once a stable job is attained it is broadly assumed that the academic career will follow a linear path. It is expected that scholars will devote full-time energy to teaching and research, that they will become more and more productive and well-known, bringing in money in the form of research grants, and recognition in the form of publications, to their institution. Caplan (1994) uses the term "academic clock" to refer to the linear career path within the university. The academic clock involves "the most fundamental aspects of ... maleness and heterosexism [which include] the schedule of achievements that faculty are expected to follow in order to be hired, to have one's contract renewed, to be promoted, and to receive tenure".

In 1993 we distributed 1672 questionnaires to faculty in an Ontario university which would access both qualitative and quantitative data in the academic and family lives of faculty members.[1] We found that full-time pursuit of these goals involves, for many, an intensity and focus that allows little time or energy for competing activities such as relationships and family:

"Even without children I do not have enough time to do a good job both of teaching *and* research" (male, 62, married, no children).

"I can't imagine having been able to get to where I am with the financial and temporal strain caused by infants and young children! As it is, I am *still* in debt *without* children and I live frugally!" (male, 41, single, no children).

"No time to find a partner" (male, 46, single, no children).

"I put relationships on back burner for career. Pilot light sputtering" (male, 32 single, no children).

Full-time dedication to one's career as an academic is assumed, as in any other career. But what is the definition of full-time? The frequently made distinction between "public" (work) and "private" (home) realms does not hold up for academics, who must regularly work at home during their evenings, weekends, and "holidays" in order to keep up an aggressive publishing schedule. As one respondent remarked, "I am considered a workaholic since I generally work about twelve hours per day, seven days a week. Much of the 'extra time' is devoted to my research. I do it because I like it ... As I fill out this questionnaire, it is 10:20 on a Friday evening and I'm in my office" (male, 61, married, adult children).

If this is the standard by which full-time dedication is measured, then those who choose to or have to devote less time, for family or other reasons, will invariably have to bear the brunt of comparison. The words of these professors in many ways define the prevailing attitudes of the academy towards its workers:

"To presuppose that faculty deciding to reproduce should not be penalized in career progress ... is unfair to those who place career over reproduction. Anyone choosing to reduce job responsibilities in favour of family should expect fewer job rewards" (male, 51, married, school-aged children).

"I'm sure you will find people who say having a family adversely affected their careers, that there should be more consideration given to leave for childrearing etc. Unfortunately the world is not ideal. To keep abreast of academic developments is a full-time job. If you are not prepared to do it full-time, in most cases two elements suffer, the students being taught and the discipline/subject involved. Of course families affect one's life, and that includes one's work, but singles' bar-hopping could also do so" (male, 50, married, teenaged/adult children).

"With so many people looking for meaningful jobs, we academics are in a relatively comfortable and privileged position – and academic life itself offers considerable personal flexibility – for women as well as men. Though more is always nice in the way of personal time for women, compared to other occupations, women professors have a fair deal. Of course few people will say [so] since it's considered heresy not to moan about one's lot as a suffering servant" (female, 53, married, adult children).

The career path of an academic is intense, lengthy, and uncertain. It is based on the anticipated consequences of years of unpaid, unrewarded scholarly work leading to a doctorate (which, along with teaching and publishing experience, is the entry-level qualification in most Canadian institutions today). An interrupted doctoral program may lead to years and years of part-time instruction, which in itself is a vicious circle. The more money one needs, the more courses one must teach. The more courses one teaches, the less time one has to pursue the degree. The less time one has to pursue the degree, the longer it will take and therefore the greater the long-term debt to be paid off before eventual financial stability.

"I am very far from financially secure, having had to increase my mortgage and debt level repeatedly in order to make ends meet – in effect, borrowing periodically against future earnings" (male, 45, married, school-aged children).

"I could not afford to undertake PhD studies because of needing to support my family" (male, 51, married, adult children).

Ultimately, some postpone the doctorate for so long that the value of achieving it is lost somewhere along the way.

"I wanted to spend time with the children, therefore held off full-time limited-term until the second child was in grade one. School-age children are busy, therefore have influenced my decision for PhD. Now at 42 I sometimes think, is the PhD worth it?" (female, 42, married, school-aged children).

Control over one's life and career is considered a desirable masculine trait within patriarchal society. Indeed, the "linear" career path and the "academic" clock were patterned at a time when gender roles were far more clear-cut for both men and women than they are today. Males were raised to pursue breadwinner roles in the "public" sphere while females were raised to have ambitions toward motherhood and homemaking. This "traditional" gendered division of labour meant, and still means, that the linear career path can most successfully be achieved by males who do not combine family and career or have a partner or employee whose full-time job it is to do so. Having a family confers an element of status within the traditional masculine gender role, but being a significant participant in the reproductive process does not.

"My family responsibilities I consider shelter, food, security, etc. My time is spent with family out of love, affection and companionship for and with them" (male, 50, married, teenaged/grown children).

"My spouse gave up her teaching career to allow me to continue my career. She is now returning to teaching. That is her decision and mine jointly. Thankfully her education and degrees were completed before we had children. The right spouse has made my career aspirations possible!" (male, 54, married, teenaged/adult children).

Women have always been "potentially pregnant bodies," with their lives ruled in many ways by their biological clocks (Eisenstein, 1988). There is an inherent conflict between women's biological clocks and the academic clock. Whereas control is a major component of the academic clock, many women experience "being controlled" by their biological clocks. This is true in at least two ways. On the one hand, having children is a process over which we have limited control. Accidental pregnancies or the inability to time pregnancies for when they are most convenient, affordable, or desirable were frequently cited by female faculty as life events that interfered with their ability to succeed at their academic careers. On the other hand, the childbearing biological clock runs out at menopause.

The limited ability to "control" the biological clock affects academic women particularly because the most crucial time in an academic's life, the moment between earning the doctoral degree and achieving tenure, most often coincides with a woman's peak childbearing years. Conflicts between the biological clock and the academic clock lead to "tough decisions." Female academics' career and family patterns tend to fall into one of the following patterns: (1) delay of childbearing, (2) delay of degree or career, (3) combining both career and family, or (4) decision of career over children.

(1) Delaying childbearing until securing a permanent position, which is increasingly possible with contemporary technology, enables women to pursue the "academic clock" in a relatively controlled, unimpeded fashion, other factors remaining equal. The shadow hanging over women who choose this option is the approach of menopause. As the age of forty approaches, women may feel rising pressure to make decisions about having children. "I have been waiting to settle down into a tenure-track position before starting a family. But as years after the PhD go by, I am rethinking this decision" (female, 34, married, no children).

The despair of possibly having to opt for an abortion is heard in the following woman's voice: "I just found out today that I am pregnant and I will most likely have to abort my first (and only?) child. No support system, salary *way* lower at age 38 than it should be, given my c.v. Impossible to do this job and be a single parent. I am untenured. I feel as if, if I have to abort this baby, I will also have to leave my university position. I cannot imagine how I will feel about an environment which virtually forces you to choose a career *or* a life" (female, 38, single, no children).

(2) Delaying the completion of the doctorate or taking a full-time academic job in favour of having children while young and devoting much of one's energy to childrearing is a pattern that is more typical of older female academics, for whom the option to delay or control pregnancy was perhaps more limited. By favouring the biological clock, the academic clock is "set back," sometimes permanently. "I did not work outside the home until (the children) were in grade school … It has held me back. I "lost" 9 years due to childraising and returned to graduate school very late in life … I wish I'd established my career more firmly prior to having children" (female, 56, married,

adult children). The academic clock would have women make the choice of career over family, or reproduce in a highly controlled, predictable manner, preferably giving birth during summer or sabbatical.

(3) Combining parenting and an academic career is, for both women and men, an attractive goal but an exhausting, stressful project. It is attractive because it signals an opportunity to break free of the more rigid gendered division of labour of the past. That fathers and mothers, together or on their own, in traditional or non-traditional relationships, may do both is certainly idealized by those who see the traditional gendered division of labour as harmful and limiting to women and men alike. The rewards – that one may achieve the goals of having both a career and family – are potentially great, as one enthusiastic female professor exclaimed: "I love my career and my family – I think I'm getting the best of both and therefore can give my best to both. It's a bit of an upward as opposed to a downward spiral. [This is] primarily because [our] nanny is a 'super-woman' – she takes fantastic care of our daughter and of us (she takes care of *all* housework)" (female, 35, married, preschool child).

The costs can also be great, however. The most widespread experience of this lifestyle is the loss of control over one's time, space, finances, and the pursuit of one's career. Not all young dual earner families can afford a live-in nanny. Heightened stress, and its impact on health and relationships, is widely experienced, particularly when children are young. Concerns over the availability of quality childcare, guilt over not spending "enough" time with the children, pressures imposed when a child is sick, a babysitter is sick or quits, or children are at home during school holidays increase the stress and often displace the joy that new parents feel they should be experiencing in the life of their child. Pressures gradually ease as children enter school and become more independent. However, as the following professors relate, the long-term implications for one's career may be irreversible:

"Parenting has negatively affected my career, mainly because of the time requirements and physical fatigue associated with parenting young children … My inability to keep up an aggressive research/publication schedule has decreased my currency in my field. I will not be in a position to apply for full professor" (female, 43, married, school-aged children).

"Emotional involvement and physical/time requirements have frequently left me too tired to work on academic matters … It has somewhat derailed me as a researcher" (male, 48, married, adult children).

Most people wish they had more time for both family and career, and juggling work and family certainly can make one more efficient.

Many respondents found they had to adjust their priorities, scale down their ambitions, and find intrinsic rewards in the joy of their families.

"I achieved *almost* the peak of my career before my child came ... My child slowed down my career, but I enjoy him much more than promotions in my career" (female, 46, married, preschool child).

"Family provides a more lasting relationship more important in many ways than career" (male, 39, married, teenaged children).

"[The effect of parenting on my career has been] significant. Not as much time directed towards career. Priorities shifted towards family" (male, 35, married, preschool children).

"Being part of a family has been very important in my life, but the family has suffered from me devoting more time to my research and teaching than to family" (male, 79, married, adult children).

"One cannot work 100% and have children. Work needs to give, expectations need to be lowered" (male, 47, married, school-aged/teenaged children).

Some of the ways in which parenting limits those who are already established or seeking to get established include limiting the potential working hours per day, causing difficulty for scheduling meetings and classes; and limiting opportunities to travel to conferences, to travel to do research, or to enjoy sabbaticals abroad. When research is systematically curtailed over a number of years, one's marketability for other positions is reduced, as is one's likelihood of winning grants on the basis of a past research record. Time limitations also interface with teaching preparation, keeping abreast with the literature in one's field, and general effectiveness as a scholar. One colleague bluntly concludes: "I would be 'further along' had I delayed having children" (male, 32, married, school-aged children).

(4) For some, the fourth option, choosing career over children, is the only solution. The words of one "high merit" scholar about her publishing career reveal her rationale: "My publishing is above average because I have no kids, work every night I am home plus one day of every weekend. I chose career over children. I could see early on that I did not have energy for both career and kids and have never had a strong desire for kids" (female, 47, married, no children).

The idea of "life getting in the way of life" suggests that for individuals who seek to combine family and career two full "lives" are really being combined: an academic career can, and some argue must, really be a life-absorbing prospect, as can (or must) having a family. As one colleague puts it: "At present it seems that parenting is almost incompatible with an academic career. Unless the faculty member has a partner willing to take on more than a 50% share of parenting and family responsibilities, family life is difficult to the point of being impossible" (male, 48, married, preschool child).

Several respondents noted the relative absence of a "family friendly" attitude in the university, and suggested that this must be changed before those attempting to combine family and career will experience any real support. "All of us – we schedule classes, meetings, etc. as if families don't exist" (male, 47, married, teenaged children). "University tends to see 'professors' and 'students' rather than mothers and fathers" (male, 34, married, school-aged/teenaged children).

One female, however, defends the distinction between family and career: "In the 1970s I was a single parent with two elementary school children while working at [the university]. I did a master's degree part time as well as teaching two full courses, and coordinated another full course and published at least one paper a year. It was hard but I do not believe an employer is responsible for the personal lives of employees. We do make our own choices" (female, 62, married, adult children).

Do we? How much control do we really have? The various voices we have heard suggest that gender, age, and financial security are factors determining the answer one might have to that question, with younger women particularly feeling as if their choices and their ability to control, as understood by the academic clock, are limited. At the end of the day, for many women and men seeking to establish academic careers today, "life gets in the way of life."

NOTE

1 The questionnaire upon which this paper is based was originally distributed to the faculty of an Ontario university in the spring of 1993. Petra was Lesley's research assistant, and we worked together to devise a questionnaire that would access both qualitative and quantitative data on faculty's academic and family lives. We distributed 1672 surveys to both female and male faculty, and 317 completed responses were returned. Some of the data were analysed by Petra Remy for her MA thesis, "A Feminist Flip of the Coin: A Manifestation of Cultural Ideologies in Men's Family/Career Conflict," at the University of Guelph in 1996. The current article focuses primarily on the qualitative responses provided to questions regarding work/family conflicts.

On Being a Lady Professor

ALISON HAYFORD

I was born into an academic family, and while I made some feeble efforts to get into another sort of career, it was probably inevitable that I ended up in teaching. While plenty of my female forebears had fairly standard female roles, there were many notable exceptions. At least four of my maternal grandfather's seven sisters had college degrees, in an era when even most males didn't complete high school, and one of these sisters was a math professor at a college in Tennessee. My father's mother and her mother before her went to normal school and became teachers, and my grandmother continued in specialized training, including graduate courses, throughout her career. Indeed, my father was the child of an employed mother long before that condition became fashionable.

Note that I used the word "teaching" in my opening sentence. My father is recognized as a scholar in his field, but he has always been scornful of the research university culture that sees teaching as a kind of booby prize for people who can't hack the (self-) important work of creating ever-increasing levels of abstraction. As the son and grandson of teachers, he was proud to call himself a teacher, and he passed this attitude on to me (along with my great-grandmother's school bell). My mother was a college teacher too, and her father the president of a liberal arts college. Thus while I'm well aware of the importance of research as one form of scholarship, I was raised to see that the other elements of university life had equal intellectual importance.

Coming into the world as I did, equipped not only with this heritage but with two older brothers, I learned early (and learned often, older brothers being what they are) to be mouthy, even (especially in intellectual situations) assertive. I did spend three years (which I enjoyed) as a civil servant, but I was happy to take an academic job when one became available.

My background meant that I came into the university with a somewhat different perspective from many of my colleagues, male and female. The university campus is my natural habitat, and while I take it very seriously, I also don't take it very seriously at all. Unlike most of my colleagues, I am a born-to university person rather than a convert; and as we know, converts tend to be more serious about identities and institutions than those people who are born to them. The fact that I don't take a lot of standard academic values seriously, in particular the primacy of "Research," has been a disadvantage to me; I simply haven't been competitive enough. I'm guilty of other no-nos too: I switched fields, with my degrees in geography and my job in sociology, and I've failed to specialize in one topic that I write about over and over and over again, which is the traditional path to success for most academics, of any sex or none.

With all of this, I still have no doubt that the fact that I am female has been highly relevant to my career. A professor – a colleague – is male; a female professor is a woman-who-is-a-professor. When I was hired in 1977, it was as the department Woman, and not even my politically progressive sociologist colleagues saw anything weird in this. When I was made assistant dean, my sex surely was a factor; my university is ever so slightly embarrassed at the almost unrelieved white maleness of its administrators. Yet to be frank, while I have encountered sex discrimination – lots of it – it is sometimes hard for me to sort out which of my problems are the result of discrimination, and which result from other factors such as my family background, my personality, my having switched fields, and so on. This is not a situation unique to me. One of the worst effects of discrimination is that members of the subordinate group never know just where their personal actions end and the unfairness of the world begins, and it's hard not to spend a lot of time trying to figure this out.

After nearly twenty years in the university biz, I have come to the sad conclusion that many academic men, even those who support the principle of sex equality and are married to active and interesting non-academic women, have considerable difficulty when equality becomes practice rather than theory and interesting and active women intrude on academic turf instead of remaining safely in other occupations. A woman's academic career can come awfully close to being the death of a thousand cuts. The readiness of male colleagues to believe anything negative about you – the smallest criticism from

a disgruntled student can become proof that you have major problems in the classroom – is matched only by the difficulty they can
have in seeing anything positive – female students like you because
they want a role model, not because you're good at what you do;
you got your job because of feminist pressure, not because you were
approximately fifty times better qualified than any of the male candidates; and so on. The central problem we face as academic women
is surviving the petty but unending and ultimately corrosive slights
of academic life. I am trying hard not to let bitterness overtake me –
the first draft of this essay was angrier than anything I've written
here. Since I haven't figured out any real answers, I have only a few
recommendations for women starting out in academia, and since my
academic career has not been one of conventional success, women
who have ambitions may be well advised to disregard my advice.
But here goes – read it if you want:

1 Be a loud-mouthed pushy bitch. That's how a lot of the guys are
   going to react to you anyway, even if you're sitting quietly in a
   corner reading a book, so you might as well live up to your *a priori*
   unearned reputation (after all, you wouldn't even *be* here if you
   weren't an LMPB) and have some fun with it.
2 Actually, on second thought, be nice and sweet and follow all the
   rules and get tenure first and THEN be an LMPB.
3 Don't expect any of the informal "scratch my back, I'll scratch
   yours" support systems that are central to academic life. If these
   are extended to you, take full advantage of them (while never
   forgetting to watch your back), but don't expect them. From anyone. Women or men. Be prepared to be an individualist (which is
   where developing LMPB qualities is helpful) because the chances
   are that that's what you'll have to be if you want to get anywhere,
   or even just keep your head above water.
4 When you look at any male professor over about forty, never stop
   thinking for one minute that one of the main reasons he is where
   is, is that approximately 75 percent of the potential competition
   was knocked out of the running before they even got to the gate.
   Indeed, some (all people of African or Aboriginal descent, for
   example) didn't even make it to kindergarten before being marked
   as not worthy of much social effort in their education and professional formation. Keeping this in mind allows you to feel proper
   sympathy for these guys – after all, they really do like to think they
   got their academic positions because they were the best candidates
   (aka "best men for the job"), and it hurts them to be reminded that
   this isn't so (though one of your duties to your sex is to remind

them of just that). Keeping this in mind also allows you not to respect them overly, which will be necessary for your sanity, believe me! (Maybe younger males are less uptight about women than their seniors, but then they're uptight about the preference they think is being given to women in hiring, so to be on the safe side don't rely on them either.)

5 Avoid all orthodoxies relating to personal behaviour, academic interests, teaching styles (my own particular *bête noire* is something called "feminist pedagogy," but that's another story). There are many ways of being a feminist, of being a woman, of being a professor. Accept these in yourself and in other women and indeed in the men you work with (just to be nice). Avoid the temptation to think of other women as traitors to their sex because they've chosen a different road from yours. (OK, I realize this kind of contradicts the bit about "duties to your sex" in 4 above ... but I try not to judge.) Remember – the truest test of liberation is the freedom to be a jerk without staining the reputation of the whole social category to which you belong; allow that freedom to your female colleagues, and to yourself whenever it's necessary.

6 Have a sense of humour.

7 Try not to be long-winded (this is not gender-specific advice)!

A Wedding and Two Funerals

DIANE HUBERMAN-ARNOLD

I have taught, part time, in philosophy at the University of Ottawa since the mid-1970s. I have five degrees, and superb teaching evaluations. My service record is excellent, and my research is better than average in the department, and improving all the time. None of this matters. Because I am married to a full-time professor in the Department of Philosophy, I have been told over the years that I really do not need to work, since I have a husband to support me, and that when my children were young, I belonged at home with them.

I believe that learning philosophy is vital to a university education. I take great pride in teaching critical thinking, and I was rewarded several years ago, when an older woman who had reluctantly worked through a required term of logic with me, said that for the first time in more than twenty years of marriage, she was now winning arguments with her husband. I serve as a role model in a faculty where the majority of students are women and the vast majority of teachers are men. I believe I have an advantage, as a woman, in teaching controversial topics in ethics, such as abortion or homophobia.

The Philosophy Department at the University of Ottawa is a male bastion. Several years ago, the Canadian Philosophical Association (CPA) wrote to every Canadian Department suggesting that women were under-represented in the field and that each department should make an effort to find qualified women when there were job openings. Our Department sent a curt letter to the CPA, saying they had no right to set policy, and that the best man for the job was literally the best man for the job. A woman with a Harvard PhD did not have her contract renewed, because she specialized in feminism, and the general opinion in the department was that this was not "real" or serious philosophy.

I have sacrificed a lot to continue teaching, more painfully recently. In more than twenty years, I have had no say in elections, no input in departmental concerns or policies, no promotion, no status, no job security, and very little money. Last year, when I began to attend departmental assemblies as an observer for my union, I was insulted, and every attempt was made to evict me. The abuse stooped to the level of putting my name with that of the administrative secretary, in the attendance list in the minutes of the previous meeting. When I protested, the young man with two whole years of full-time teaching experience, who had written the minutes, asked me sarcastically where I expected to have my name listed.

Last year, I had the use of my husband's office. A colleague complained to my husband that the office was too nice and had too many windows for a part-time teacher. My husband reminded his colleague that it was his office, and that surely he could share it with whomever he wanted. The colleague said he understood, but couldn't my husband throw me out, as a conciliatory gesture to the department. When I went to the dean of arts to discuss the harassment difficulties, he said he had already received complaints from professors in the department, though they had granted that I was extremely good at what I did. I suggested that perhaps the motivation was professional jealousy, since I received better evaluations and more trust and respect from students than they did. The dean denied that motivation, and said that he was told that certain members of the department simply could not stand the sight of me working there. The dean's response to these problems was to rule that from now on, all part-time teaching in the Philosophy Department would be done by graduate students only. This would keep the peace, since I could no longer teach there. The only recent communication I have had from the dean was a brisk note telling me that if I insisted on applying to teach courses, I was not to use university stationery to do so.

At the instigation of a graduate student, and with her help, I organized a national conference on philosophy and feminism, called Women and Wisdom, with noted speakers from many other universities in Canada. I also delivered a paper at the conference. Influential members of the Philosophy Department disapproved; posters advertising the conference disappeared from walls, and the promised funding for the conference was withdrawn a week before the conference. We went ahead; the conference was a great success, with the best attendance of any philosophy event ever held at the University of Ottawa.

There were two deaths of colleagues in the last two years. Both had academic funerals, with an academic procession. For the first funeral, I naively thought that I too would have a place in the procession of robed colleagues. After much discussion of protocol, including the fact that my husband was giving the eulogy, I was placed at the end of the line, after all the men, including those with the enhanced status of a year or two of full-time teaching. The second funeral, last week, was for a colleague we had known for more than twenty years, who in fact had first hired me to teach in the Philosophy Department. Since I am no longer permitted to teach in the department, as the dean decreed, I could not show my respect by participating in the academic procession at all. So I can say that a wedding fixed my place in academia, and two funerals have spelled it out for me. Women are on the fringes of Canadian academia, hanging on by tooth and nail; some are pushed into the abyss, as I have been.

Managing Men-in-Skirts

MARTHA KENISTON LAURENCE

Why are some of my female colleagues better men than the men? Why do some of my female colleagues beat the meritocracy drum a little (and sometimes a lot) more loudly than their academic brothers?

I watch some of my female colleagues sinking other women at Senate Tenure and Promotion Committee, for example. I watch them bask in rays of approval from their male colleagues, most of whom have had to say little, while the woman champions the tenets of meritorious scholarship defined in traditional, scientific, objectified terms and heaps criticism on both substantive and methodological features of feminist scholarship, research, and politics. There is nothing quite so powerful as having one of the deviants cast aspersions on one of their own, on behalf of the dominant group. I used to wonder why they didn't see what was going on. I felt they were being used. In my own naïveté, I assumed that they didn't know what was going on even though I wondered why and how not. How could they be so closed to the possibilities offered by broader definitions of knowledge production and the validity of women's perceptions and perspectives?

Intellectually, I know the answer(s); so why do I ask the question(s) at all? Because, until I looked at the issues in an organized way I still found myself wasting energy in being angry when I watched it happen. And while being angry and frustrated by my inability to change the dynamics, I was derailed from focusing on those processes, as well as some people, over which I did have some "power-to-influence." When the opportune moment presented itself, I used the occasion to put together a little research project that allowed me to explore this issue within the context of my overall research foci on women and processes of change in universities and other organizations.

I am a mid-fifties White woman of privilege, a feminist and a professor in a graduate school of social work in a small rural, conservative and parochial university in Ontario, Canada. My substantive areas of academic pursuit, in teaching, research, and service/ practice, have to do with theories and practices of intra- and interpersonal change, organizational and community change – process as content. My focus has always been working for change. My organizing tenet for guiding decisions about how and where I will work is to work for change – for the improvement and expansion of opportunities and experiences for women and minorities.

The university is my client. In my earlier career I viewed the university as the vehicle through which I worked for change. I worked for change in care for and treatment of the elderly as a professor in a medical school and consultant/practitioner on a medical staff at a teaching hospital. My focus shifted when I came to my current university in the mid-1980s and encountered practices and events that were, in my experience, simply astonishing (panty raids, for example, and other sexist rituals of administratively orchestrated undergraduate socialization). I reacted and responded in anything but planned ways. I later made sense of it all by applying my professional, theoretical, and practice lenses to my experience. I recognized that the tumult arose from the yawning gap between me and the culture and the context in which I had landed (Laurence, 1999). Conceptual and practical shifts included reframing my university as my client. That may not be what they think they hired me for; but that is what they got. Viewing the university as my client redefines my relationship with it. I work *with* it rather than in it. Or under it. It helps me maintain the perspective whereby I can analyse situations and dynamics and decide how and where I shall spend my energy. It enables me to *choose.* It gives me a sense of control in a culture in which I often felt overwhelmed and out-of-control. It has all but dissipated that knot of urgency to act, react, and respond which has led me, and so many of my women colleagues, to burn-out, powerlessness, and depression (Laurence, 1998).

So what about the sisters who sink us? The opportune moment: fresh from a productive sabbatical in the early 90s, I sat as a member of the internal university research grants committee. I spent the year tapping my own drum on behalf of non-traditional research methodologies, questions for inquiry, and applicants. As the lone voice-for-difference, I decided early in the year that my agenda would simply be to confront the more blatant injustices, slow down the boy train as it chewed up proposals, and use rules of procedure (like tabling decisions to buy time) in aid of my cause. When I was unable to attend the last research committee meeting of the academic year, I submitted a proposal of my own so they would still have to deal with the issues of concern to me. It was a research study of intrapersonal identity construction in university women using qualitative methodology, and a conservative one at that. Astonishingly, funding was granted. The substantive analyses and findings were interesting (Laurence, 1996).

The process of doing the research was helpful to me as a practising feminist change agent in the university, because it enabled me to *let go* of some more of my own emotional debris, the presence of which reduced my effectiveness. This time it was about women who work against women (wittingly or unwittingly) and the equity agenda. Although the project served to reaffirm the focus of my work in general, it was in analysing the process that I identified some themes and pieces that I could use again, and which might be useful for someone else.

Listening. Hearing. I talked with women who had come into academia before we ever recognized the gendered and patriarchal fabric of the university enterprise, before we recognized or acknowledged that *truth* itself was politically, culturally, and contextually located and produced. As one woman said, "Mathematics may be objective, but mathematicians are not." I made a point of including women from the sciences, hypothesizing they might be less contaminated by some of the current valences of feminist consciousness and debate. I also wanted to learn more about their experience. Women described horrendous career passages marked by isolation, marginalization, servitude to (almost exclusively male) mentors, supervisors, colleagues, administrators. They portrayed self-effacement, self-blame for setbacks, and "failures." They assumed individual responsibility, even when it didn't make sense, for whatever hardships they had endured. They re-enacted, in professional life, their roles as women and wives, mothers and daughters, and for much of their experience they struggled for language to understand. Some were conscious and aware of their anger and hurt; few felt a great deal of hope for any significant change in the near future. Few had ever really talked about it like this before.

Pain. Hearing that pain, feeling that pain – from feminists and non-feminists alike – helped me by the very act of hearing and feeling.

Now, when I watch a woman being a better man than the men, being a man-in-a-skirt (some of whom would even describe themselves as feminists) and sinking or assaulting another woman, I am no longer distracted by my own outrage or anger.

Understanding. I think now that women who uphold the male-dominant cultural nuances of the meritocracy are the most vulnerable and have the most to lose. They can't afford to question – or *see.* The dynamics of power relations and rules of membership are universal; they transcend the particular context. The specific manifestations only reflect local politics and players; I have speculated about the inverse relationship between the relative status of the particular university and the virulence of the politics – the old saw, the politics are so vicious because the stakes are so low. But for the moment I have concluded that size or stature makes little difference. The power dynamics and the interpersonal jousting for position and sense of importance look the same. The intrapersonal needs and vulnerabilities of the players look the same. My greater clarity about the culture of the context and my understanding about what drives it have improved my facility at simply factoring all players, both male and female, when analysing power-to-influence forces. When I am analysing the composition of a particular committee, I don't get hung up on women members whose participation is likely to work against my agenda. I do allow for their possible increased influence "against" because they need the approval of the group in order to feel accepted. It is a lot easier to work with what *is.*

Expectations. I now connect my outrage with my own, often unrealistic, expectations. The process made me confront those expectations. Why do I expect other women to work for the same cause for which I work? Why do I expect anyone to work for equality and fight oppression? I have confronted some of my own arrogance in believing that when my cause is just and my heart is pure, others will embrace it too. Coming to terms with my unrealistic expectations of others has been one of my own stretches. I have struggled most with my disappointment when I hear the words but not the music – when I hear the verbiage of commitment to the sisterhood but see that the behaviour that follows is inconsistent. It reminds me of the complexity of intra-personal negotiations, witting or unwitting, of values and beliefs, training and socialization, wants and desires, skills and behaviours. When we place that complex personal organism into the collective expression of the parallel negotiations of the organism that is the university – it's little wonder we sometimes feel as if we are swimming in cold bouillabaisse. Struggling with my expectations of others has been another good exercise in *letting go* of what I can never control anyway.

I can kick myself every so often for not having reached this place of greater peace and focus (utility?) earlier in my life. But to keep that up for long is to give the lie to my greater belief that we are, all of us, products of our experiences, our observations, and the sense we make of them to this point in our lives. We can be nothing more. We need neither defend nor rationalize; we can only accept ourselves for who we are and move on from here. I often see women wasting themselves, their energy, their value, by berating themselves for not being something they aren't, not being as good as, as advanced as, as activist as, as whatever they think they see in someone next to them. Logically, how can we be anything other than what we *are?* This doesn't mean we want to stay there. It doesn't imply complacency or particular satisfaction. It simply means applying the phenomenological lens – observing without getting sidetracked into assessing before we have taken in the whole of what is going on within us, with us, around us. This is often hard to do in a culture devoted to valuation and competitiveness and in which dissatisfaction, especially of women for themselves, is akin to godliness.

My goals in life are simple: work for change for the improvement and increase in experiences and opportunities for women and minorities; and have a good life while doing so. The altar of self-sacrifice offers fleeting rewards at best and is ultimately destructive, to self and to others. I have transitioned through stages of being angry or outraged at women who are better men than the men, to hearing their pain and empathizing with them to the point of my own detriment on occasion, to my present point: a negotiated place somewhere between letting go and still protecting myself a little. My learning has also included not leaving myself open to avoidable assault or abuse, at least a second time round.

Disadvantaged? Not I!

ANNE M. LAVACK

I am always puzzled when I come across descriptions of women in academia as being "disadvantaged." For me, there have been nothing but positive experiences in my academic career. In fact, I feel that women in academia enjoy some tremendous advantages over their male colleagues.

Perhaps my positive experiences have something to do with the fact that I am relatively new to academia. Conditions in academia may have improved in recent years, so that women have become accepted as equals. However, I also worked for ten years as an executive in advertising and market research firms prior to my PhD studies and encountered virtually no discrimination in that career either.

In my business career, although there were a lot of women working in advertising and market research, when I attended meetings at clients' offices it was not uncommon for me to be the only woman in the room. I never perceived this to be a problem, but instead saw it as an opportunity. As an advertising and marketing consultant, it was my job to point out how the consumer thinks and what some alternate points of view might be. Since women do much of the household purchasing, it was easy for me to understand the typical consumer, and to present these points of view to clients and agency personnel. So being a woman was a definite advantage.

When I decided to leave the business world, it was mainly from a desire to expand my horizons, but also partly a desire to enjoy the more flexible academic lifestyle. The stability of an academic career was also attractive, especially given the fact that I had been laid off twice during my ten-year career because of business downturns. The initial academic salary that I expected was comparable to my business sector salary, although I would lose four years of income while completing my PhD. However, that seemed a reasonable cost for self-fulfillment and lifestyle change. Being a woman was undoubtedly an advantage in this decision. Not many men would want to go back and do a PhD after a ten-year successful business career, nor would they have the financial cushion of a working spouse which would allow them to do so. Women seem to have greater flexibility in this area.

So I started my PhD in 1990 at the age of thirty-one. In retrospect I can see that I really didn't have much insight into what professors do. At the time, I saw myself teaching and doing business consulting; I didn't understand the key role that research plays in the university setting. However, when I was introduced to the idea of academic research at University of British Columbia, I found that it intrigued me and that I enjoyed it.

As a PhD student, I received initial funding to cover living costs and tuition fees at the University of British Columbia in the form of an Outreach Doctoral Fellowship, a fellowship designated for women in Western Canada. While inwardly somewhat miffed at being awarded the "women's" fellowship, I accepted it graciously. After all, one can't turn one's nose up at fellowship funding, and there were no conditions attached to the fellowship other than remaining a student in good standing. Perhaps it was even advantageous being a woman, since I was able to qualify for "women's" fellowships as well as general fellowships. I later replaced my "women's" fellowship with a SSHRC doctoral fellowship, an award that I felt much more comfortable about. I wanted to be accepted on my own merits, not on the basis of my sex, and the SSHRC fellowship was all about merit.

During my time as a student, being a woman was never a disadvantage. I am a strong, assertive person who seldom hesitates to make my views known, and this willingness to speak out was a valuable trait. The fact that I was slightly older than some other doctoral students, and had experience in life and business affairs provided me with some distinct advantages. I was a mentor to new students, writing academic and thesis advice columns in our PhD newsletter. My relationship with my all-male thesis committee was warm yet businesslike. I was treated as an equal member of their team on research projects. And my ability to type nearly eighty words per minute, gained from my earliest business world experience as a pink-collar clerk-typist, was a tremendous asset in the computer age as I rapidly composed research papers at the keyboard.

When it was time to enter the job market, being a woman gave me tremendous advantages. During the summer of 1993 I was doing my initial job interviews, and virtually every business school in North America was keen to hire women for faculty positions. At the 1993 summer conference of the American Marketing Association where all of the initial interviewing went on in my field, the average female had fifteen to twenty interviews, while the average male had only about ten to fifteen. This discrepancy was tremendously encouraging to the women who were in the job market but rather discouraging to many males who realized that women were being given preferential treatment in hiring decisions. As additional anecdotal evidence, the only people that I heard of that year who didn't get academic positions were men. It appears that the female candidates were all able to obtain academic positions. So being a woman seemed very advantageous during this hiring process. I had twenty-three interviews at that summer conference, which ultimately resulted in five invitations for campus visits. Since most universities interview about twenty candidates and then invite three or four for campus visits, my five campus invitations were statistically somewhat greater than what I would have expected to get. My five campus visits translated into two job offers, one in Canada and one in the United States. I accepted the Canadian offer, which provided a more positive research environment and a lighter teaching load. Also, the American job offer was not financially attractive enough to offset the high cost of living in New York City. So I ended up at Concordia University in Montreal, where I was fortunate to be hired ABD, and was given up to three years in my first contract to complete my PhD. Because universities were keen to hire women, they seemed fairly lenient in hiring female candidates who hadn't completed their thesis. This definitely worked to my advantage.

On the job in my first academic position, being a woman again seemed to be a strong advantage. I was one of four women in a twenty-person marketing department. Every courtesy was shown to me, and male colleagues went out of their way to include me in lunch invitations and discussions. Male colleagues were generous in sharing information, as well as in invitations to join in as an equal partner on their research projects.

I enjoyed the teaching aspects of my new career, and this was perhaps the only area where being a woman was not an advantage. I often think that men are innately "funnier" than women, and are therefore better "liked" as professors. It means that I have to work harder at loosening up and having a sense of humour in the classroom, and I have to work at trying to make classes fun as well as educational and informative. This became easier over time, although I still feel that teaching is an area that I need to improve.

On the other hand, as a woman, I was sought after to teach in prestigious programs like Concordia's Executive MBA, where they have relatively few female professors. My ability to present a positive role model for female students, a large and growing contingent at business schools, was part of the reason I was recruited.

In terms of committee work, being a woman has been an advantage. Virtually every committee wants to have at least one woman as a member; however, there are often not enough women to fulfil this requirement. Therefore, women get virtually first choice of the committees they want to sit on, and are welcomed as valuable members on the committees they decide to join. Although some women complain about being overburdened with committee work because of the need for every committee to have a female member, I never personally found this to be a problem.

One of the interesting aspects of my new academic career was that I quickly became in demand as an "expert," giving radio and television interviews on advertising and marketing-related topics at least four or five times a year. It seems that it is often difficult for reporters to find female experts in this area, partly because of the absence of women in senior business positions, and partly because some women are reluctant to appear on radio or television because of insecurities about their personal appearance or fear that they may look foolish. When a willing female expert is available, producers and reporters will often choose the female expert over a male expert, if only to balance the scorecard for all the times when a female expert was unavailable. This imbalance partially accounted for my numerous media interviews, and meant that being a woman was an advantage in gaining media exposure. A female colleague at Concordia University and I both gave more media interviews than the rest of our male department members put together.

Because of my earlier business connections, my research publications, and my media exposure, I also became engaged in doing consulting work for the government. Governments have long been active in affirmative action programs, and as a result, government departments often employ senior women. Governments also seem to have a definite preference for choosing female consultants over male consultants whenever possible. So once again, as a woman I had an advantage in gaining consulting contracts.

Women often complain about having to make family sacrifices to pursue academic careers. I have been fortunate to have a spouse who has been supportive and willing to relocate with me to Vancouver for four years to pursue my doctoral studies, and then to Montreal for three years where I had accepted my first academic job offer. However, every relationship requires some give and take, and after seven years of living in the location of my choice, my husband finally expressed a strong desire to return to our home town of Winnipeg. Although my preferred choice of a position at the University of Manitoba didn't pan out, I was fortunate enough to obtain a position at the University of Winnipeg instead, where I was compensated with the higher rank of associate professor rather than assistant professor. While the level of research support is not as great as I enjoyed at Concordia University, the University of Winnipeg offers a very friendly and supportive atmosphere, as well as excellent undergraduate students.

Being a woman has been an advantage over and over again in my academic career. Advantages have included having my choice of committee assignments, having preferred access to plum teaching assignments such as the Executive MBA, having more media exposure than male colleagues, and having preferred access to consulting assignments for government. I could never view myself as being disadvantaged!

Teaching Doesn't Count

BLUMA LITNER

As I write this reflection on my experience, I have just submitted the required annual written report entitled "Evidence of productivity in research and scholarship" to the dean of my faculty, which will be used to determine my teaching load for the following year. This exercise always leaves me with a sense of malaise, bringing to the forefront, as it does, the contradictions I experience in my academic life at the university. In the past few years, I have managed to refrain from voicing the turbulence I feel each time I go through the productivity exercise, which is like the gun going off at the start of a race that I am made to enter each year and symbolically run the whole year through. I have refrained because I sit in the privileged position of being a full-time tenured faculty member while many other well qualified women are either on limited-term contracts or part-time ones, or, as is more and more the case with the hiring freeze in my own university, unemployed. Yet, as I make myself complete the "productivity" report, its very composition a testimony to what counts and what doesn't as academic currency, I find myself confronting the fact that much of what I care about in my life as an academic doesn't fit with the prevailing definition and dominant view of what is meant by and counts as productivity.

With this growing awareness, a chasm has developed between my sense of purpose and meaning and that of the university, so that I am increasingly living my present reality feeling disconnected from the university's goals or apparent direction. Simply put, being productive is measured on the basis of the number and quality of refereed articles one has published in a year and how much external funding one has managed to secure. Few, save for the all-but-forgotten students, seem to care whether a faculty member's teaching is effective. In fact, the only questions addressing teaching on the productivity report form in my university are those that ask for the number of courses taught, students registered, and graduate students supervised. Publishing articles in "quality" journals about the practice of teaching is considered proof of productivity, but the sustained effort of developing one's teaching practice is not. It just doesn't count. Beyond the public declarations and motherhood-and-apple-pie statements typically made by universities claiming that teaching excellence and attention to the learning experience of students are central priorities, there exists a parallel and contradictory reality. Teaching is the "loss leader" to get the students in the door, after which it is relegated to the margins.

In the absence of any explicit criteria with regard to the university's view on teaching capability, I can only conclude that good teaching is assumed when one is hired. In my experience, there is a major gap between that assumption and what often actually transpires in the classroom. Unless one's course evaluations are so dismal that they cannot be ignored or enough students, braving the risk of negative repercussions, file complaints, one's teaching is all but overlooked. "Good enough" teaching will get your contract renewed and will get you tenure and promotion as long as the more "worthy and productive" activities of publication and research are evident. In fact, if you don't publish enough or participate in funded research, your teaching load is increased. Since teaching is seen as a "second class" activity, having a greater number of courses to teach is seen as a punishment. This serves to uphold the prevailing view that anyone can teach, but only productive academics – the real academics – publish and carry on funded research. Teaching is something of lesser value that you do more of if you haven't done something else of greater value.

The turning point for me in the midst of my doctoral studies was precisely my fortunate encounter with several professors who really strove to engage students as authors of their own learning. This marked a critical shift in my education from which, without even knowing it, I had been disengaged. Until then, an education was something that had to be acquired – it was "outside in" rather than what it needed to be, "inside out." The unceasing efforts of these professors fostered a climate in which students, feeling visible and validated, could be fully present, ready, and able to learn.

My commitment to creating an enabling teaching environment for students, a place where they can retrieve their lived experience and use it as a context for learning and critical inquiry, is rooted in my own history. Much of my formal schooling from the time I was a child to midway through my graduate education can be characterized as one of marginalization, invisibility, and exclusion. It started in kindergarten at a private French *lycée* where I remained until I graduated at the age of sixteen. At the time, I was the only anglophone and Jewish child in the whole school and neither my parents nor I spoke any French. To borrow a metaphor, "I was an o in a series of x's." Though I managed to homogenize myself through my years at university, it was not until I was well into my doctoral studies that I began to understand my otherness not only with respect to my sixteen years of education but also with respect to my sex. Until then, masculine privilege and male dominance were as natural and as taken for granted as "father knows best" in my home and school life, as well as in that of my classmates and friends. When I started teaching at university, I wanted at the very least to work at developing a different educational setting for students. In reaction to the traditional male view of social sciences in which I was schooled and progressively disenfranchised, I have endeavoured to promote a classroom climate where students' experiences are welcomed, encouraged, and validated as a legitimate basis from which learning can take place.

Teaching, in my view, is a dynamic process that I am continually rethinking, adapting, and revising. The memory of my own voicelessness and the feeling of being a detached stranger throughout the years when "I was being educated" has fuelled my ongoing efforts to teach inclusively. From an initial preoccupation with the silences of women in traditional classrooms, I have become increasingly sensitized and attentive to other minority groups who have consistently been marginalized in university classrooms. I am, of course, referring to students who, by virtue of their race, ethnicity, age, disability, class position, or sexual orientation have been overlooked, discriminated against, or silenced. The changing complexion of the students on my university campus presents challenges to the teaching and learning dynamics in the classroom. If I am to take seriously every student's right to an equitable education, I must create enabling conditions for them in which to learn, not constraining ones. I value research and scholarship, but I also value teaching. Quality in my teaching is not an afterthought, nor is teaching an activity that is less central or worthy than my other academic endeavours. In fact, it is the raison d'être of my being in a university in the first place. I am accountable to my students first and foremost.

Now, sadly, I once again feel distanced and somewhat alienated from the academic milieu in which I work. I live my daily reality at odds with a definition of productivity that either weighs one's contribution to effective teaching inequitably, discounts it, or excludes it altogether. In a strange way, I feel that I have come full circle. I am back in school this time as an educator who cares a great deal about what she does in the classroom. I struggle hard to keep focused on what matters and not to allow my sense of purpose to be eroded or my sense of self to be diminished because what is central to my labour is devalued. If teaching is dismissed as an unworthy preoccupation, am I also dismissed as unworthy? Some days, as I sit in academic meetings where debates go on for several hours without the word "student" being uttered even once, the otherness of my *self* as a student slides back over my *self* as an educator – the recognition of that discomfort in that place of otherness all too familiar – otherness, namelessness, invisibility. It strikes me that the harder it is fiscally for the university, the more reactive it becomes. As a cost-saving measure, the university where I teach has all but dismantled its Centre for Teaching and Learning Services, pared it to the bone, a "luxury" that the university can no longer afford even though its services are widely used. The commitment to support the development of teaching has been all but erased in spite of the university's lofty mission statement. Since 1996, not one senior academic administrator has held a title where the word "teaching" appears.

I deplore an academic reality in which I am regularly pushed to favour activities that bring me brownie points on the university's scale of values over those that don't. Spending more time on course preparation or helping a student in difficulty, for instance, means having less time to write and do research, which in turn means that I will have, as one of my colleagues put it, fewer badges to show for my efforts, fewer badges as signs of productivity to display across my chest. As in a game of monopoly, fewer badges mean that I don't pass GO, that I don't collect $200, and that I won't be in a position to increase my power and influence to buy more hotels/tenure/promotion.

In the tundra of my academic institution, with its perplexing indifference to the significant work that good teaching necessarily entails, it is crucial for me to persist in asking what forms of academic endeavour are endorsed by those who are in positions of power to decide what qualifies as productivity. Holding on doggedly to my sense of what is important for the students we teach, I must now begin to challenge the prevailing definition of productivity that fails to recognize the commitment and effort that excellence in teaching constantly demands.

Downsize This ...
and This and This:
Women and Academic Hiring

JEANETTE LYNES

In her 1994 survival guide for academic women, Paula Caplan made the dismal observation that "women are less likely than men to be hired by academic institutions" and that "in Canada and the United States, 27% of all faculty positions are held by women" (Caplan, 1994). To this, Caplan adds the even more depressing fact that "in both countries far smaller and sometimes negligible percentages are held by women from non-dominant groups [such as] Black, Hispanic, and aboriginal women" (Caplan, 1994). More recent statistical work by Janice Drakich and Penny Stewart shows that in Canada, some slow gains have been made in terms of numbers of women hired (Drakich and Stewart, 1998). As encouraging as these findings are, it is also well known that the majority of part-time or sessional positions are held by women. This latter group forms part of an optical illusion that characterizes today's university campuses: an illusion that there are many more women on faculty presumably partaking fully of the resources and intellectual life of the university. A closer look at the conditions under which these women were hired and the number of resources to which they actually have access quickly dispels this optical illusion.

My concern is less with how many women get hired than with how hiring actually takes place. The former, quantitative issue continues to be tracked carefully by statisticians like Drakich and Stewart. Information on the latter – the physical and political conditions around women's hiring (i.e., interviews or the lack thereof, job offers) – must draw more on anecdotal evidence. The discussion that follows is based largely on my own hiring history, but is supplemented by the experiences of other female academics described in Paula Caplan's *Lifting a Ton of Feathers* (Caplan, 1994) as well as women occupying various part-time and full-time academic positions who responded to a questionnaire I circulated over electronic mail in December 1997.

Since 1985 I have been hired for seven full-time appointments, two part-time appointments, and several summer sessions. I probably had what is, for someone in the humanities, an impressive number of interviews; not all of these led to job offers, of course. These interviews took me as far afield as Kansas, Prince Edward Island, and the Kootenays of British Columbia.

Four dominant features emerge from my hiring history: 1) only one of the aforementioned "full-time" appointments was tenure-track; 2) the fact that my spouse was also an academic proved to be a complicating factor in significant ways; 3) in a depressing number of instances, the job offer was a downsized version of the original job I applied for; 4) never, in any of these hiring situations, did I feel confident enough to negotiate my salary or any other terms of my employment.

Looking back almost fifteen years later, I still find these four aspects of my hiring history enormously distressing. During the same period, Canadian university administrations often used recessionary rhetoric to lower faculty expectations. This recessionary tone set by administrations has likely gone some distance to sanction downsized offers and hiring on limited-term appointments. The one tenure-track job I was hired for was, interestingly enough, in the United States (but there is a story behind that, too). Three of the full-time jobs were sabbatical replacements for one year. One full-time position ran for two years but came with the proviso that there was absolutely no chance for conversion to tenure-track: very much a case of "don't even think about it." Two of the full-time positions came with the "possibility" of conversion to tenure-track. One panned out, one didn't. In the case of the latter, the selection process was highly suspect; four women were interviewed, myself included, and the one male candidate ("internal" in the sense that he had previously worked at that university) was not flown in for an interview because "they knew him." Although I was an internal candidate, too, I was put through a gruelling interview in which one senior department member attacked my presentation and humiliated me. In the months leading up to my interview, the department head harassed me by insinuating that I might not be able to perform competently even if I got the job because my husband taught far away at another university.

This is not the only instance where my personal life has come into play politically during the hiring process. In one of the sabbatical replacement positions I was in, I ended up being interviewed for a tenure-stream job. That institution had in the mid-1980s a policy that married couples could not both be on faculty. During my interview, I was asked "what my husband would do" in that small prairie town if I were hired (I was not). Ironically enough, three years later, my husband was interviewed at the same school, and never once was he asked "what his wife (i.e., *me*) would do" if he were hired. The American university where I was hired for a tenure-track position already had my husband on faculty. He was well-liked, and this went a long way in laying the groundwork for my own appointment. I was grateful to the university for hiring me, but I suspected that I did not get the job on my own merits. I was hired at a salary $4,000 lower than my husband's, even though I had received my PhD three years earlier and had more teaching experience. Once again, much to my chagrin now, I did not negotiate my salary; the situation seemed too delicate. Every situation seemed like eggshells, in those days.

Women who are hired on a part-time basis but whose partners have full-time jobs in the same university are often particularly vulnerable to having their personal lives used to manipulate them into substandard working conditions and salaries (Caplan, 1994:134–5). I could cite numerous examples, from various institutions, of part-time female faculty being forced into silence because of their connection with a full-time male faculty member. These hierarchies with women typically on the disadvantaged side, are entrenched in every realm of the university community, including the social-professional one. One questionnaire respondent who has taught sessionally for many years at a Canadian university where her husband is a full-time faculty member articulates this well: "In the department, I am just the wife of a professor. When I am with him and being introduced to someone from outside, he is introduced as faculty and I am not introduced at all. This has happened three times in the last year ... How could I not even be introduced as part of the department? I have taught at *** for twenty-five years. I feel totally invisible."

On at least four occasions, I applied for a position advertised at a certain level but was offered a lesser job. In one case, I applied for a tenure-track appointment, but was offered a two-year, non-renewable term with a salary of $17,000, no benefits or moving expenses. I took the lesser position; nothing else came up that year. In another case, I applied for a full-time position, believed I had gotten it (the whole situation was alarmingly ambiguous), and ended up being offered one off-campus course in a remote corner of the province. Another time, I interviewed for a full-time job and was subsequently offered two courses. Finally, I applied for a three-year position and was eventually offered a one-year appointment. In short, the conditions of my employment had often been downsized at or even after the hiring point. Three of the thirteen women I surveyed had also been demoted in some way; crude mathematics places this at almost one-quarter. One woman was hired on a two-year contract, but was subsequently switched back to sessional lecturer. When asked if she had ever been "demoted," another respondent told me: "Something similar happened. Oppressed at one time with a young child and things not going well, I had the bright idea of asking to go onto part-time work. Very quickly I learned that this would be the usual 3/4 of a job and 1/4 of the pay and benefits or worse. Once I realized that this was not what I planned for, I recanted. But nevertheless, I was put on what I regarded as punitive part-time for a year. Also, the probation years I had served were taken away and I had to do them again."

Paula Caplan advises, "When you are offered a particular salary, job category, and resources ... be sure to negotiate for more and better" (132). Sage advice, but how many women academics receiving a job offer actually do this? Caplan is right in suggesting, I think, that feelings of gratitude "to be hired at all" (Caplan, 1994:37) frequently prevent women from negotiating on their own behalf. She also cites feelings of unworthiness among "women in particular" as obstacles to negotiation, and also the fact that negotiation is an acquired skill that women have not necessarily been encouraged to cultivate (Caplan, 1994:132).

Of the women I surveyed, six did not negotiate their salary at the point of hiring, four did negotiate salary, one negotiated job category, asking "for assistant professor rather than lecturer, assuming there was a pay differential." Two did not respond to that particular question. Those who negotiated salary were more likely to negotiate other aspects of the terms of their appointment such as computer equipment and moving expenses. Women who did negotiate did so because, to cite several examples:

"The initial salary I was offered was at the same salary I was receiving in the position I was holding in government at the time. I indicated I would not give it up unless the offer was higher."

"The American Society for Cell Biology puts out a publication on how to find an academic position and this was one of their recommendations. Several of my postdoctoral friends have been through the process and we were constantly comparing notes on our experiences."

"I heard that you should try to negotiate. I tried to, but was unsuccessful."
"Colleagues told me to negotiate."

Women who did not negotiate salary or other aspects of their appointment cited the following reasons:

"I just accepted what they offered. Any full-time appointment sounded good after being a sessional for about fifteen to eighteen years."
"I believed the offer to be fair. I regretted that later. Others were offered more and better conditions."
"It seemed that the contract was non-negotiable."
"I was told that the administration was aware of the fact that the salaries were among the lowest in the country, and there was nothing that they could do about that. In retrospect, I probably could have negotiated, at least to include additional moving expenses, or a computer. But I think that I was happy to have been offered a position, and didn't feel that I should do too much to jeopardize the position, even if I was somewhat unsure as to whether or not I wanted this position."
"Ignorance and lack of advice at the early stages of my career."
"I thought it would be rude."

In my own case, failure to negotiate came from fear and naïveté. Moving from year-to-year contracts, I felt that negotiating salary or other aspects of my appointment was a luxury I could not afford. Like one of the above respondents, I was told, in one instance, that nothing could be done about salary levels. Being offered downsized jobs, as I sometimes was, made negotiating difficult since the subtext of these offers seemed to be: "Take this consolation prize or nothing." I was sometimes competing with at least thirty applicants for even a term position, which, I wrongly believed, undermined my bargaining power. During that period, I knew little about the role of faculty associations.

In the above responses, the women who negotiated the conditions of their employment at the hiring point were empowered to do so by information networks, through colleagues or written literature, or by virtue of already having employment.

The women who did not negotiate acted as they did because of current substandard employment that lowered their expectations, lack of mentoring or information networks, a sense of trust (which they later regretted), institutional cues that discouraged them to do so, or behavioural conditioning that has always urged women to act in a conciliatory, non-confrontational manner.

When asked what they see as the most valuable resources for women going through the hiring process, the respondents of my questionnaire emphasized networked support, sharing experiences with other women, and familiarization with literature on women and hiring. The respondents also believe that faculty associations should take a more active role in providing women with information during hiring. One respondent pointed out, quite rightly, that more work needs to be done on the hiring experiences of minority women. During the most active period of my own hiring history, Caplan's book did not yet exist; neither did electronic mail nor books like this one, committed to documenting women's professional experiences. These resources continue to validate my own experience in important ways. Let us hope that increased information resources empower future generations of academic women so they no longer respond as I did, when receiving a job offer, with, "That sounds just fine."

Don't Let Them Know You Care

HARRIET D. LYONS

My mother took early retirement at fifty-five, the age I am now. She was a mid-level civil servant who thought she deserved better. Never having heard of systemic discrimination, she believed (a) that most of the people in her office were personal enemies, and (b) that if only she had been satisfied with being a wife and mother, she wouldn't have laid herself open to such suffering. My mother wanted me to do better than she had but thought that "doing better" meant being more satisfied with the conditions of a woman's life, not changing them.

At fifty-five, I am a tenured associate professor, have been a department chair and a program director, and have served on my share of significant committees. A fairly successful career for a woman, nothing exceptional for a man. How did I get to this point?

One fact that perhaps ought to be made clear at the outset is that I knew from childhood that my options for the future were limited, though to many the situation might have appeared otherwise. I have always been unusually good at reading texts, and writing and talking about them afterward, and I probably possess better than average analytical and numerical skills. These are abilities that generally earn good marks in school, and they certainly did in my case. Because so much of a child's presumed potential is related to academic performance, my limitations were perhaps less obvious. To put it crudely, reading, writing, and arithmetic were the only things I was good at. My efforts at anything requiring manual dexterity were laughable. I made my gym teachers as miserable as they made me, and I was not particularly good at submitting to authority. What skills in interpersonal relations and diplomacy I now possess I learned at a much later date, and they did not come easily. In a world less mediated by the written word than the one I was born into, I would have been a likely candidate for starvation or fatal accident.

Many aspects of "women's roles" in North American culture – organizing domestic space, maintaining one's personal appearance, transforming recalcitrant matter into nourishing and attractive meals and well-cared for clothing – demand precisely the aptitudes I most lacked. My mother's hope that I would be a "better woman" than she was, was probably doomed from the beginning. Since one unspoken benefit of the private nature of women's work is that it is rarely formally evaluated, I have been able to muddle through whatever amount of it I have not been able to avoid. But I certainly was miserable at any time in my life when a conventional woman's role comprised any sizable part of my identity. It should be stressed, however, that I would have been equally unsuited for the sort of work most men do, and that my failure at it would undoubtedly have been more visible. On the other hand, I came of age at a moment when the previously elite status of a paid intellectual was opening up to the middle and lower middle classes. My parents were willing to pay for as much education as I wanted, even if they had to borrow to do it. They did pay – for a "Seven-Sisters" BA and an Oxford doctorate. Here my story deviates conspicuously from the likely history of a young man in my position.

Anthropology appeared to my parents to be as acceptable a subject to invest their money in as law or medicine or engineering. In my mother's case, it was decidedly more so. For her, sending me to college was akin to Mrs. Bennett's efforts, in Jane Austen's *Pride and Prejudice*, to keep her five daughters continually under the eyes of neighbouring bachelors. One of the biggest fights we had was over my decision to transfer from a co-educational to a women's college.

For years, I was torn between contradictory demands. Scholarship was something I could be good at, by means potentially under my control. Acquiring a husband seemed as frustrating a task as jumping over a wooden horse had been when I was in fifth grade. College was a long series of humiliations – awful dates with law students who never called again, Saturday nights working for the college baby-sitting service, one-sided relationships with men who weren't "ready for commitment" as they said in those days. The more the indignities mounted, the more marriage began to seem like my goal, not just my mother's, if only to prove I wasn't totally undesirable. All this took up an awful lot of my brain capacity at the same time as it shaped my future.

At some point in my life, as I said, I had been able to count, as well as read and write, and rather enjoyed formality and abstraction. A science career was very much a possibility. By the time I reached my second year in university, I was desperate to find a subject that offered some answers to the dilemmas I was facing. This narrowed my choices to literature and the social sciences – those were the only fields in which sex and women's emotions were ever mentioned. I tried literature first, but in those days, before feminist criticism, attempts to relate depictions of women in literature to the things my friends and I were experiencing were met with comments that it was "naïve" to "read for content." The latter comment was made by a female professor, when I questioned whether a class at a women's college might want to read Andrew Marvell's "To His Coy Mistress" in a way that at least acknowledged the dilemma of the woman being pressured into bed with all those clever conceits. In the psychology department, where I hoped I might find out whether I was as crazy as I felt, the direct study of human emotion was suspect – real scientists worked with rat models. Anthropology, then, came as something of a surprise. My college had produced a whole line of women scholars, most famously Margaret Mead, who actually asked questions about sex and women's lives and used data from other cultures to suggest that these matters didn't *have* to be organized the way they were in twentieth-century America. I was hooked.

In graduate school, in England, two things became clear to me: the things that had drawn me into the discipline were regarded as "mushy," and that if I was to be taken seriously as a scholar, not least by myself, I had to learn to view men, women, the things they did and even the food they ate, as categories in systems of classification. For a while this provided a welcome escape. My thesis dealt with the logical problems posed by socially conventional ways of criticizing social structures. It didn't mention directly any real people who might have been assigned to real suffering by those structures. Somewhere in it, I said that humour didn't really exist as a distinct analytical category, people's capacity for laughter notwithstanding. My English professor would have been proud of me – I certainly wasn't reading for content! Although I couldn't stop reading the new feminist scholarship that was beginning to appear, I regarded it as a secret vice, not part of my efforts as a "serious" intellectual. It took a long time, and the relative safety of collaboration with my husband (yes, I did find one) to start writing about the things that had brought me to anthropology.

My split perspective, English detachment warring with American, feminist *angst*, turned out to be a hot commodity. I could teach women's studies, while fairly dripping with Oxford irony. Irony, the art of dry understatement, in fact, may have been the most useful acquisition of my expensive education. It's what my mother lacked and what probably could have saved her. Irony is what stops you from "taking it personally" when a senior administrator early in one's career suggests that a department might save money by dropping "fringe" courses like The Sociology of Women. With any luck you'll even have a caustic reply on the tip of your tongue and know how to deliver it with just the right amount of *de haut en bas* asperity. Irony is what makes you able to make a witty story out of the time when forty men crowded round to congratulate the man who'd just taken credit for your idea. Irony is what keeps a safe distance between you and your feelings and reassures everyone you're not one of those women who are always feeling sorry for yourself. Irony makes it possible to discuss bodies and sex and love and exclusion without being accused of indulging in "personal" rather than "scholarly" discourse. Irony is something not traditionally taught to women, and even among men has tended to be associated with relative privilege. It is important enough to academic survival that its lack can almost be said to constitute a kind of systemic discrimination. I had to cross an ocean to learn it. Do I dare to imagine a university where I wouldn't need it?

An Alternative Vision: Creating a Life Vitae

GERALDINE (JODY) MACDONALD

My struggle began with my entry into academic life with the hope that in an academic career I would be able to balance my work and family life. Along the way I found myself resisting the university's predominant valuation of the curriculum vitae. I began constructing an alternative structure for personal validation, the creation of what I call a "life vitae." I share my story in the hope that it will give other academic mothers (and fathers) the courage to create their own life vitae. This is the perfect moment in time, the university is the ideal space, and together we can influence the academic environment as it unfolds into the future.

I didn't grow up wanting to be an academic; I grew up wanting to be a nurse and a mother. Neither my mother nor my father provided any role model for how I was going to manage this. Although I was very close to my mother and appreciated what a good parent she was, I didn't see myself following in her stay-at-home footsteps. Even in high school, I was aware of my interest in participating in the public arena as well as the private world. My father did not provide a role model that I could relate to either. He worked hard and was treated with deference and warmth at home, but we tended to communicate with each other through my mother. For my own family life, I wasn't willing to give up the emotional closeness my mother enjoyed with her children for the financial and status rewards my father enjoyed in the working world.

Fortunately, I was not intimidated by the need to create a new lifestyle. My eldest daughter, Liane, adjusted well to my working full time as a public health nurse and, although my busy life was tiring, I thrived on it. It wasn't until I had returned to work after my second daughter was born that I was challenged to reflect upon how my family was managing. Kristen was very clear that she was not happy with a mom who worked full time. In my research on mothers who are nurses I note that their children either adjusted well or "resisted their mothers working" (Macdonald, 1996, 182). Resisters invite their mothers to reconsider their choices and to pursue alternative life directions. It took many months, but one day I came home and told my husband that I was going to resign my full-time employment and investigate part-time opportunities. I trusted that the decision was the right one.

By September 1984 I had accepted an offer to teach part-time, on a sessional contract, at the University of Toronto, Faculty of Nursing, where I continue to teach today. The rewards of academic life are numerous. I have been able to contribute essential financial support to my growing family, while encouraging students as they undertake the complex challenge of becoming excellent nurses. Both continue to be very meaningful activities in my life. Working in a stimulating environment, with many of the brightest academics in my profession, within the wider university community, has been both exhilarating and exhausting. I have never had to worry about becoming stagnant or being bored, two cruel realities of all too many jobs in our contemporary life. My dean provides financial support so that I can report my research at conferences, and I have thoroughly enjoyed the opportunity to meet academics from across Canada. The years of learning and personal growth that followed as I completed my doctoral studies will have a lasting impact on my life. They have immeasurably enriched the contribution that I have been able to make, in both teaching and research, at the university. This enrichment has also had a positive effect on my home community and my mothering.

In my own home community, I devoted time to initiating and guiding an addition to my children's primary school and also to the creation of a new high school. My contribution was enhanced by my community health nursing and my university experiences. Throughout both of these projects, I felt totally engaged, committed, and thankful that my work life allowed time for me to make these contributions.

Although I have worked very hard, and often long hours, at the university, I have also had large blocks of time to be with my husband and four children, time that was available because of my sessional appointments. The many moments, weeks, and months that

I have shared with my children have created memories that we will always treasure. I feel like the mother in my research study who stated, when reflecting on the choices she had made in order to balance work and family life: "I don't regret any choices I've made" (Macdonald, 1996, 140). At the same time, I will argue that the price I have had to pay for my substituting an extensive life vitae for an extensive curriculum vitae has been extreme and the system that has exacted this price needs to be challenged.

The most obvious symbol of the response to my life vitae is the letter that I receive almost every December from my dean telling me, with regret: "I must inform you that I cannot guarantee that we will be able to renew your contract for the [next] academic year." It is important to understand the context of these letters. After being unemployed for four months of the year, I return in September, only to be advised three months later that my appointment will soon be over and that the university is not willing to make any further commitment to me. While I do understand the legal issues that prompt these letters, they symbolize the dominance of the curriculum vitae over the life vitae.

The absence of the possibility of a flexible career path remains a strong motivation for academics who choose to balance work and family life to give the curriculum vitae top priority. To be considered seriously within the university community, one must choose the curriculum vitae. At my university, there is not even a tiny crack in the glass ceiling that separates the full-time, tenured academic from the part-time, sessional teaching academic, regardless of gender. As an academic pursuing a life vitae, I have been warned, when sharing that I was pregnant, "I hope you are not going to do this again." I was also told that my graduate degrees were not appreciated; that it was understood that I would be looking for a tenure-stream position elsewhere; and that it was expected that I would be available to come in for meetings during the summer if I were needed. Meanwhile many new faculty members have been added to our tenure-stream faculty, all of them with full-time appointments.

As more and more faculty members commit to a life vitae, one that promotes both excellence and humanistic values and will contribute to building a culture of peace in our private and public lives, the university will be called upon to respond with flexibility and determination. Flexibility will be essential because, in the course of any one career, the need for balancing work and family will be continuously shifting. Within the university there will be a wide variation in the ways faculty members wish to balance their work and family life.

Academic institutions will also need determination to make a long-term commitment to part-time and sessional faculty. They will be required to create a variety of opportunities to meet the diverse needs of a generation of faculty members who wish to combine career and family responsibilities. Such a complex package of options would include part-time tenure-stream appointments, mentoring to all faculty members with yearly sessional appointments, programs targeted to move sessional faculty members into tenure-stream appointments when they are ready, and recognition that faculty members who wish to devote time and attention to their parenting and home communities are making a contribution to society. They should be appreciated rather than penalized for this within the university environment.

We each are called to a unique journey, one that we must live authentically. While those who commit themselves to the curriculum vitae journey continue to be favoured within the university, it needs to be acknowledged that faculty members who are on the life vitae journey also offer a qualitative contribution that is invaluable to both the university and to society at large.

A Different Balance

JENNIFER MATHER

Unlike many women who work within the professoriate, I "have it made." I have a full-time tenured position within a well-established university and will not likely be out of a job unless the system collapses. I have a chance to do the whole range of activities that the professorial system allows, and that range of activities is immense. Formally, professors are requested to spend their work time on Teaching, Research, and Service. There is a lot of leeway for individual preferences, and my colleagues and I vary widely in how we interpret that set of assignments.

Theoretically, recognition of our excellence in the profession comes from how well we fit the complex definition of what matters in all these areas, how well we do our teaching, our research and our service. I have it here with me, Article 21 of our Faculty Handbook, filling a whole page. To do all of it well would be impossible, but to do much of it passably and some very well indeed is quite likely. The trouble with the definition of our performance, however, is that only part of this performance *really* matters. Faced with a complex set of functions, academics mostly retreat to the view that basic research comes first and the conveyance of the information gained in that research to waiting passive students is only the necessary second step. All else is nice, useful, but not esteemed.

This discrepancy matters to me because I do a lot of the "other," and in the process have trouble convincing my peers that I am attaining excellence and should get promotion. Some of this variety of function comes almost inevitably from my sex. Women are expected to do more of the "support services." Women should care more about teaching and spend more time with and be more supportive of students. Women are expected to fulfill the role of student advisor because students feel comfortable with this. If over 50 percent of the students are female and there is only one female professor in the department, lots of students will simply gravitate to her. Women spend more effort on more committees because "we have to have a woman here." Some of my diversity has to do with my educational background. Yes, I changed research areas because a jealous professor threw me out of his lab (as he had several others, male and female, I discovered later). Yes, I teach in several unrelated areas because the small university at which I work needs diversity – but none of my male departmental colleagues do so. And so, when I ask for promotion, my record looks like a mishmash to focused scientists with a keen view for the swift advancement of knowledge in a narrow specialization.

It was with a sigh of relief, therefore, that I read Boyer's *Scholarship Reconsidered: Priorities of the Professoriate* (Boyer, 1990). Here was a person who understood what I meant in my career. Here was someone who saw scholarship as intricate and interdependent, who talked of knowledge as developing in a multidirectional rather than a linear manner. He felt that the categories of teaching, research and service were narrowly defined and rigidly held, that we needed a new view of the scholar. He talked of "Scholarship of Discovery," "Scholarship of Integration," "Scholarship of Application" and "Scholarship of Teaching" (Boyer, 1990). Following these categories I found my work, and probably the work of many women in the professoriate, better understood and more logically linked together.

First, Boyer's Scholarship of Discovery fits a part, not the largest, of what I do with my days, weeks, and months. Like many women in science, I chose to sidestep the hotly competitive and trendy newest areas and decided on a specialized part of knowledge to develop as my own. It's very "pure," totally without present practical application, and not acknowledged by many others. From time to time we joke about it; there may be two dozen people in the world who care about the behaviour of octopuses! But its obscurity allows me to think, to compare and to range widely in my reading and speculation, to be what a scholar should. In the last little while, public attention has caught on that these are fascinating animals and I'm in demand for film interviews and popular accounts, getting a reputation as an expert in the obscure. I can't say that I mind.

The second area, Scholarship of Integration, involves making connections across disciplines, putting specialties into larger context, and seeing data in a wider way. I never though about doing this, but conducting research on octopuses and teaching in psychology makes it almost inevitable. And here the two-way street of knowledge transfer comes in. So when I was doing a paper on personalities in my octopuses, the information of the development of human temperament that came from the context of my child development class proved to be the best theoretical base. Teaching a couple of seminars to the Introductory Psychology course, I reached into my research and tried to understand why both the molluscan octopuses and the vertebrate humans would have developed lives that depended on learning. Attending meetings of ethics comittees, I came to work for ethical consideration of my sensitive, intelligent, and often poorly treated "dumb invertebrates." And watching my octopuses manipulate things with their flexible arms and listening to my colleague specializing in play, I put the two together and extended the phylogenetic scope of that behaviour to them as well. I'm in funny diverse places with the same brain; I notice and connect things.

Maybe my commitment to the third area, the Scholarship of Application, comes from my gendered role to help and make the world a bit better. Certainly my activity in the Alzheimer Society arose out of my teaching the Psychology of Aging and their request that, as such, I join the local board. After over ten years, as the Person Who Knows Research I have found myself enriching the society, myself, and my students in several different ways. Yes, I report research in the newsletter. Yes, I have twice conducted a research study for the society when they needed someone to do so. In return I have a new depth and balance for my class (and me; we'll all grow old), and a priceless opportunity for the many students who have worked on the research for me or followed me to do applied study projects. Two of them are with me now on the board. I'll always remember the comment of one, as she learned about Alzheimer's, "It was just a paragraph in the text, but out here it's a whole world." I gave a presentation to the university senate one year about combining research, teaching, and service in this way, weaving together a diverse but unified whole. I understand it better as the Scholarship of Application, far from the mindless minutae of meetings that service is reputed to be.

My commitment to the fourth area, the Scholarship of Teaching, may stem from the expected feminine focus on teaching, but also definitely from the diversity of areas in which I teach. I always expected to be a researcher and never had any explicit teaching training. But there are all those students out there ... I began to look at and think about teaching. I did a teaching dossier, decided that I believed in active learning, and designed non-traditional classrooms (which make some of my colleagues suspicious). I attended a teaching discussion group and organized a local seminar on teaching issues. I can be seen arguing about whether a particular teaching technique might work in a specific setting, not just about whether a particular scientific method might produce a specific result. I discovered the annual STLHE (Society for Teaching and Learning in Higher Education) teaching conferences, and am now an enthusiastic presenter. Teaching goes far beyond the classroom; even a simple research study on something you're trying to do with teaching opens up huge new areas. Several undergraduate students have done applied study courses while being teaching assistants in my course, opening a new world view as they move to the other side of the table.

Of course there isn't enough time, and sometimes my Scholarship of Discovery suffers as it gets postponed for the other more immediate areas. But I do a lot of interesting and useful things in this job. I know a lot of fascinating people from many different worlds. I don't think of myself as a second-class citizen of the world of academia, but as a professional doing a complicated profession as well as I can with my particular talents. Boyer's four types of scholarship help me see how the different strands all knit together, and I'm proud to call myself a SCHOLAR, especially using his definitions.

Now, if I could just persuade my colleagues.

Why I Didn't Have Time
to Write This Article

DENISE S. McCONNEY

Carter Revard "is working on a new and selected gathering of poems, *Unzipping Angels*, while tracking down a fourteenth-century scribe and his patrons, and may considerably improve the world if given half a chance and fewer distractions" (sage, poet, literature professor, scholar and dancer).

I think Carter Revard wrote at least this last sentence of his biographical sketch himself. I find both encouragement and despair in these brief words. The portion about being "given half a chance and fewer distractions" certainly rings true for me. I wish I had time to write and get my words published. But I don't.

I didn't even have time to write this article. I didn't have time to write it because:

· I am a single parent;
· I am a sessional lecturer;
· I teach in the Native Studies Department;
· I am a non-Native member of the Department;
· I teach at the University of Saskatchewan;
· I am currently teaching two consecutive Intersession three-credit courses;
· I am currently teaching for the Indian Teacher Education Program (ITEP).

I feel really badly that I don't have time to write this article. I think I have some interesting insights and concerns that I would like to share with a wider audience. I am a person who likes to think about the how and the why of university teaching and not just the what. I wish I could have found the time to do this. I also know that while the "publish or perish" rule is not strictly one that sessional lecturers stand or fall by, it is one of the critical markers that will help us eventually get out of the "sessional box."[1] I wish I could have done it.

If I had had time to write this article I would have written about each item on the above list and how they come together to use my time in important ways that mean I rarely ever get to writing, even when I want to. I would have talked about the joys and pain involved in each of them. I would have shared some of the strategies that have worked, and pleaded for feedback with the ones that I do not have solutions for. I would have also concluded by talking about how important it is to be at a university at this juncture; how important my teaching, my department, my colleagues and, most of all, my students have become to me. I would have talked about why I will continue to do what I do and continue with the way I do it. I could have written a powerful and moral message and maybe even an intellectually stimulating one. But I didn't have the time.

A small but important part of why I didn't have the time is because I am a single parent. Parenting my four-year-old daughter, Wynonah, is the most important thing I do in my life. Of course I love her dearly but I also love our time together. During the spring and summer we plant a large vegetable garden. Much of the produce will get us through the winter. Wynonah helps by being the row marker during planting and this year she has started helping with the watering and weeding. This may not sound like much but it is an important part of what I am trying to teach her about the world. We do the work of growing our own vegetables because I want her to know and appreciate that the food she eats comes from effort on someone's part. I hope she will also be able to garden and contribute to what she and her future family eats so that she understands what it means to be able to take care of herself. This takes a significant amount of the relatively little time we have together but I hope it is time well spent.

She will be starting school in the fall and that marks the beginning of her move away from me into the wider world. To this point I have been able to choose what she gets exposed to and what she does not experience.[2] One of the important experiences that I have chosen for her is that she has powwow danced every season since she could first walk.[3] She is Blood of the Blackfoot Confederacy and although we live in what is now Cree territory, it is important that she understand who she is and who Indian people are. The powwow is just one of the ways I do this with her. This too takes a lot of time for a single parent, not only the time travelling to attend powwows but the time to make and care for her outfit and regalia, prepare and pack for the trips, drive and clean up afterwards. I in no way begrudge this time. I like powwows too and when we can attend them with our family I sometimes get the opportunity to dance too. I am simply stating my priorities. I feel time as finite and I make choices that I think will best serve her in the long run. Before she starts her public education experience, I want her to have as firm a grounding in her "Indian" identity as I can possibly manage. I have visited her school (reputed to be one of the best in the city) and spoken with the principal there about who my daughter is and who I am. Soon I will be adding meetings with school staff to discuss issues of cultural awareness and sensitivity to my list of things to do. There may be even less time for writing in the future.

I am a sessional lecturer. As many of the people reading this will know, that means if I am not teaching I have no income. As a single parent who receives no child support, what I earn is all we have to live on. So, as long as I can get course assignments, I teach straight through the year. While the teaching is in itself time-consuming, I do not think I need to go into the details of what a conscientious instructor does to prepare for classes. I will add to this point that this is the first full term that I have not had at least one new course[4] to prepare. I have frequently had more than one. That is part of the crunch in the "sessional box." Those of us who are attempting to make a career of this, teach whatever we can get. While these courses may not be "out of our field of expertise" (although they sometimes are), any new course means substantial amounts of preparation time before the course and during it. I also "pick up" courses at the eleventh hour. And why are these typically new ones? I have been hired to teach new courses two weeks before they are scheduled to start. This may not be typical for many departments. It is an on-going structural reality and source of stress for sessionals in my department.[5] Time?

I teach in the Native Studies Department. This adds a number of layers to the time problems. I sometimes feel that if I miss a single newscast I will be behind in my field. It is certainly part of the dynamism of the field, but I do wish I could hear a news report about a court decision and not think, "Drat, I will have to revise that lecture now."[7] In our department we deal with Indian and Métis material. Not only can our course content change on a daily or weekly basis, but our entire approach to Native Studies is undergoing a long overdue change. We can no longer treat Native peoples as objects of study. Some of us are engaged in promoting a systemic and therefore seismic shift. We are not satisfied with changes in our own teaching.

As academics and intellectuals, we are missing vast amounts of history, science, politics, literature, and sociology when Aboriginal knowledge is excluded. All of our disciplines will benefit from the inclusion of Aboriginal knowledge. As with all systemic changes, however, there is great resistance. Dealing with that has taken enormous amounts of time and energy. This may seem obvious, and even morally and practically right,[7] but none of that means it is either simple or easy.

I am a non-Native person in Native Studies. I came into Native studies at the express invitation of an internationally renowned Indian scholar. She is well respected both amongst the First Nations and other more recent geo-political entities.[8] I wonder if it is like being a man in Women and Gender Studies? I recognize that this example is not likely to happen, yet it happens all the time in Native studies with no particular questions being raised about its appropriateness.[9] I also feel a tremendous responsibility towards my Aboriginal colleagues and students. I carry a primary responsibility to them to be supportive in myriad visible and invisible ways. I am aware both theoretically and personally of the horrible experiences they have had and continue to have in their lives both inside and outside of the university.[10] They live with "in-your-face" racism almost every day of their lives. They are also bound up in the systemic discrimination that structures and limits their opportunities. I feel it is another part of my responsibility to identify and raise challenges to these barriers, especially with my non-Native colleagues (and students).

It seems to me that if all the identifying and challenging is left to the survivors of racism, then this process will take far too long and have too little effect on the structures that maintain it. I have come to believe, therefore, that non-Native peoples must also be held accountable by their non-Native peers. Sadly, albeit ironically, this is as necessary inside my department as it is outside my department. Being a vulnerable sessional is no excuse for letting these situations slide, although, realistically, I have little power to exert.[11] Assisting students, supporting Aboriginal colleagues, looking for ways to address systemic barriers, speaking out and then protecting myself from the backlash all take enormous amounts of time and energy. All too often I leave campus in the depths of despair. Given that my overall goal is to make the university experience a safe one for Aboriginal peoples (including my daughter, nieces, and nephews), I wonder – frequently with tears streaming down my face – if I, a fairly privileged White woman, cannot make a safe place for myself on this campus, how can I ever hope to make a safe place for the Aboriginal children to come?

I teach at the University of Saskatchewan. It is my understanding that the University of Saskatchewan sessionals are still the lowest paid in the country. I was startled to hear a couple of years ago that sessionals at York University earned about 50 percent more per course than we did. We are also limited in the number of courses we can teach. Again this did not seem to be the case at York. Add to this the recent cutbacks in UIC and it becomes financially impossible to have a break from teaching in order to do research and writing. This means writing articles like this gets squeezed in around the edges of an already overloaded schedule.

This article was requested early in May 1998. At that time I was about to begin teaching back-to-back Intersession courses. Although neither of these courses were new for me, Intersession and Summer session courses move at a breakneck pace. Even with most of the initial course preparation already completed, the daily preparation and continuous marking take a great deal of time. The first course also had its own special glitches. I had scheduled a number of guest lectures.[12] To my on-going frustration, most of the guest lecturers cancelled, often at the last minute, so I spent many nights and early mornings writing up lectures on the topics they had chosen to address. I also want to note here that I understand the realities of these women's lives. I in no way blame them for the turbulent circumstances which more than occasionally overtake them. I would structure the course in the same way again, although I would have fallback plans prepared. The second course was one of my favourites. As I had taught it six times, preparation was a real non-issue. This course, however, had a strong energy component. Most of the students in the class had had at least one class with me before and many of them were in their third class. So we knew each other quite well. The class was so engaged that we often took an hour and a half to go through three points out of the eight that I usually cover in the same time period. It was a wonderful experience but it took a lot more energy than I ever thought it would. My miscalculation here was in not allowing for recovery time! It takes considerably more energy to "teach" a class in which the majority of the students are eager and more than willing to discuss each and every point in the lecture[13] than I had counted on expending.

It is important to note that for the courses I was just describing as well as for many of my regular courses, I am teaching in the Indian Teacher Education Program.[14] While I consider this a distinct advantage in terms of class content and activity, it does bring with it a responsibility to work with students who are coping with stressful lives. I spend about three hours a day in addition to the class time with students. Phone calls at home and responses to e-mail messages took even more time. Again I am not complaining about this. I am pointing out that Aboriginal students are more likely have needs that go beyond the academic ones, and it is vital that their teachers meet these needs. Their communities entrust these students to our institutions (despite the overwhelming historical, and contemporary evidence that this is a risky thing to do). We therefore have a responsibility to safeguard that trust. This time it is a matter of honour.

In conclusion, I empathize with Carter Revard. In the past two years, I have come to love writing. When I find the time to get started, the words just pour out of me. Writing has helped the morass, chaos, and subliminal pain of my experiences feel more manageable. I thank the editors of *Tundra* for their request and wish that I had time to write the article for them.[15]

NOTES

1 Thanks to Patricia Monture-Angus, not only for this phrase, but for her help and encouragement in doing the things that it will take to get me, in particular, out of the "sessional box."

2 Perhaps as an incest survivor this is a more important measure of control for me than it is for people who had less turbulent childhoods.

3 She attended her first powwow when she was five days old. By the time she was three months old, she had been to six powwows. She first danced at one year old.

4 By "new course," I do not by any stretch of the imagination mean that sessionals are granted the opportunity to develop special topics courses. I only mean being assigned (or "requested") to teach courses that we have not taught before.

5 With respect to stress, think about being worried four times a year about whether you will get enough work to pay the bills, and then at the last minute being overloaded with new material.

6 I completely messed this up this winter term, much to the delight of my Indian legal colleagues, Patricia Monture-Angus and Sheldon Cardinal. I was teaching a history course and scheduled a discussion of the Delgamuukw case for the first week of January. The appeal decision was announced in late December. The rest of the world has still not caught up to me. I heard on the radio today (7 July 1998) that neither the BC nor the federal government had decided what this new decision means. I knew politicians needed to go back to school.

7 The University of Saskatchewan is approaching numerical equity in student admissions for Aboriginal peoples. We have a long way to go before their experiences in the university become equitable.

8 For more on this story, see "Dear Wynonah," *Native Studies Review*, vol. 11 (2).

9 Monture-Angus is one of the few other people to raise this question. As she says, "I have often wondered how women professors would respond to the suggestion that men can, could, and should teach courses about law and feminism. It is so apparent that this would create quite a contoversy." *Thunder in My Soul.* Halifax: Fernwood, (1995).

10 I have recently completed reading a class set of essays in which Native students contextualized their life experiences. Many of them chose to write about their extensive experiences with racism in primary and high school. I remain in awe of the determination that has carried them through their education in what are clearly hostile mainstream educational institutions.

11 And the ironies can get quite overwhelming when senior non-Aboriginal male colleagues earning more than $90,000 a year tell a lowly sessional struggling to earn $24,000 that she is the one standing in the way of equity initiatives.

12 I was teaching a course called Native Women in Canada. The main reason for the many guest lectures was to ensure there was ample space in the course content for the voices of Native women in Canada.

13 I would like to pay tribute to the members of the ITEP 203 1998 Intersession class for showing me what a truly wonderful experience this can be.

14 I have also had the great good fortune to teach in the Northern Teacher Education Program (NORTEP). The bonus of these classes, for me, is that they are largely, if not entirely, composed of mature Native students. This increases the level of comprehension and discussion to an advanced level that is pure bliss for someone who is largely limited to teaching first and second year courses.

15 Now I only have to: finish teaching a six-credit course; write another article; complete two book reviews and edit an LLM thesis – this summer. And that is good, because I will start my PhD this fall and be ABD as of May 2001.

An Academic Life as I Have Experienced It

SUSAN McCORQUODALE

Some would describe me as a member of a double minority. Before I retired I worked in the virtually all-male world of political science and am a disabled female in a university setting. The polio I had as a twelve-year-old left me with a virtually useless left leg. All my life I have used crutches to go "long distances" as I defined them. However until I developed rheumatoid arthritis nine years ago, I could walk around a classroom unaided, even if I did limp a bit. I should add that I took early retirement in 1996, but I am keeping my contact with academia, teaching one course in the fall terms of both 1997 and 1998.

When I first came to Newfoundland from Ontario I remember being introduced to a St. John's man who asked me point blank, "What is a nice girl like you doing in politics?" It is a good question, and the smart answer I gave him is mostly true: "I fell in love with J.A. Corry." For those of you not familiar with the field, Alex Corry was head of the Political Science Department at Queen's University. A distinguished scholar and a lovely man, he completed his career as principal of Queen's. In 1955 he taught first year political science. I could never tell where the balance lay between the man and his discipline. When I graduated with a bright, shiny BA (Honours) in political science in 1959, I went to see him with a problem. I had to make a choice between a job with the Government of Saskatchewan and two scholarships (not the choices that today's graduates face). My father, a Scot, thought any government job, especially one that paid $5,000 a year was *the* answer for his disabled daughter. I have no remembrance of what Corry said to me on that visit, but I came out of his office sure that going to Manchester, England, for an MA was the right thing to do. That decision affected my whole life.

I had a great experience in England, learned to travel solo, did research inside the Lord Chancellor's offices in the Parliament Buildings and had a summer job that paid seven guineas a week in law offices in the Inner Temple. This job left me with two guineas a week, after I had paid rent in Mecklenberg Square, to explore an exciting city in an exciting time.

On returning to Canada by ship in the spring of 1961, another great opportunity, my first real job, was obtained through the Queen's old boys' network. The Royal Commission on Government Organization had another of my Queen's professors, J.E. Hodgetts, as one of its commissioners. I mention this because it was yet another connection that landed me at Memorial University in 1962. A friend of Hodgetts, Moses Morgan, at that time dean of arts and science, came to Ontario on a head-hunting expedition, and Hodgetts sent him to interview me. In 1962 I was thirty years old and I assumed I was destined to go into the Public Service of Canada (as many of the Royal Commissions staff did). I did not realize the discussion with Morgan was a job interview. When Morgan asked if I would like to come to Memorial for a two-year probationary appointment, I was totally surprised. I accepted because I thought two years in a university would look good on my curriculum vitae when, at last, I did join the public service.

As I remember it, that first year of teaching was hell. I used up what I thought was three lectures in one 50-minute period, I had deep doubts when it came to marking, and half the time I did not know where I was going. Somehow my equally green office-mate, a young woman teaching German, and I got through it. I think wearing gowns helped. Yes, that first year I followed a dying custom at Memorial and wore a short black gown. It helped my self-assurance and it helped keep chalk dust off my clothes.

At the end of the two years, I had decided that I quite liked this academic game, and I also had the wit to know that if I was going to be in the male world of Canadian political science in the 1960s, I should get a PhD. As a result I returned to Queen's and in two years did the required course work for my degree. With various scholarships, I got through three degrees and ended up with zero debt; another difference from students' situations today! It took until 1973 to finish my PhD thesis, travelling back and forth to Kingston each summer. During these early days there was money enough to send me to conferences around the country, whether I was delivering a paper or not. I was elected to the national offices of my professional organizations, and during the heady days of constitution-making in

Canada, the 1970s and 1980s, I attended, participated in, organized, and made media appearances, locally and nationally.

As I look back on my career now, I recognize that I have taught in one institution for thirty-five years, but I know I never taught the same course twice. The students were different, course outlines were different, the issues were different. I was lucky to be living in interesting times – not exactly a curse for someone interested in politics. I published enough to be respectable but I was not any kind of a breakthrough scholar.

How was it being a female political scientist all these years? Well, to tell the truth Memorial was, for me, a good employer. I was promoted to full professor in the normal way; I was paid on a par with my male colleagues, I was encouraged toward professional development and I was given leave to work for royal commissions, both provincial and federal. I was encouraged to experiment in the early days of distance education and, above all, I was never interfered with or directed as to what I was to teach or how I was to teach it. The only thing I wanted that I never had was to be chosen head of department. My colleagues had a policy of rotating the headship around the department, but somehow it never got to me, in spite of my making it clear that I wanted the job. But this was the assessment of the colleagues, not of university administrators, and I just had to live with it.

Nothing of what I am saying should lead readers to think Memorial was an equally positive experience for all women working there. When we finally unionized, it was partly because of the unequal salaries. Women working in the ghettos like nursing or English, were terribly underpaid. My period of service on a union committee after our first contract showed me that racial minorities, too often to be coincidence, were kept on one-year contracts, for as many as sixteen years, by a department unwilling to regularize their appointments. I was lucky enough to work with colleagues who were reasonable and fair (most of the time!) and got along well with each other. As a department we avoided the internal disputes that have ravaged other departments in this same university, disputes that inevitably work hardship on the vulnerable.

Now I turn to the second minority status, being a disabled female academic. Again my experience at Memorial has been positive; however, this is obviously not the universal experience of women in other places. About a year ago I was sent a publication from OISE by a woman who had had awful experiences with her university, such as difficult parking arrangements, uncooperative staff, and departmental hostility. Wanting to write of my contrasting experiences, I checked around Memorial with four other faculty women who are disabled. None of us had had bad experiences. Memorial has always been positive and cooperative for disabled faculty and students. One of those I interviewed was the first disabled student in the residences. The building was made accessible just for her. She now teaches in the Psychology Department. My physical situation changed when in 1989 I developed a galloping case of rheumatoid arthritis. I was put on long-term disability with no questions asked for as long as my physicians thought it necessary. From the 1960s on I have had nothing but help from those Very Important People, the parking commissionaires. When I returned to work in 1991, nobody questioned my right to teach from a newly acquired scooter, sitting down and writing on transparencies instead of a blackboard. A colleague in earth sciences permitted me to leave my scooter locked in one of his labs, which I now share with two disabled students using scooters. The parking commissionaires painted a new blue parking space just for me in the attached underground garage, thus making it dead easy to get to work in winter.

I think the positive experiences of each of us at Memorial have two sources. First, many of the administrative staff are dedicated to the idea that the university should be accessible, and money has been spent as necessary to achieve this goal. Second, much that happens depends on the individual attitudes of each employee, faculty, and staff member. If a person, a lecturer, for instance, refuses to wear a microphone to aid a deaf student because it is against personal and religious beliefs, we are all diminished. The world is not a perfect place.

I hope this brief biography does not come across as too "syrupy." I am fully aware that not all females and not all disabled persons have had as positive experiences. Much, I think, has depended on the attitude which I have brought to the table, but I am equally sure that I was lucky, lucky with my timing as to when I started an academic career and lucky with the people with whom I have worked. I feel compelled to report that so far retirement has also been a good experience. Let us hope it stays that way!

Equity Coordinator: Change Agent in an Unyielding Power Structure

SHAHRZAD MOJAB

In 1990 I was hired as a full-time employment equity coordinator to initiate the employment equity program at a medium-sized university in Ontario. Introducing equity into any inequitable institution is a formidable task. This is also true in the case of universities, despite the fact that they boast long histories as major centres of enlightenment. Since universities are formed out of autonomous units such as departments and faculties with external professional and disciplinary links, they are often viewed as organizations with decentralized structures. And this type of organization, with an elaborate distribution of power, is expected to be more hospitable than others to equity reform. However, I soon found out that at both the administrative and academic levels power was centralized and hierarchical. This structure eventually worked as an obstacle to equity, which aims at representation and power-sharing.

Resistance to equity reform began as soon as our efforts were initiated. To begin with, the senior management of the university decided to assign the equity office a rather low status. Instead of positioning the new office at the level of senior management, the office was linked to the Department of Human Resources, which was a low-profile unit. This decision is significant in a system that values status, authority, and power. My perception is that faculty often do not value the staff or even the part-time, temporary teaching staff. Thus, the majority of faculty did not perceive the office as a credible source to intervene in equity related issues. The equity office was not allowed, for example, to provide training for "Equity Assessors" who were members of the faculty and played a major role in ensuring that equity was practised in faculty hiring.[1]

In my job interview, I raised the question of profile with the president of the university. The main problem was that the administration did not view equity as an intervention aimed at redistributing power. Senior management seemed to view equity as no more than a set of discrete measures to be taken in order to satisfy the requirements of the Federal Contractors Program.[2] Although I was interviewed for the employment equity position, for example, the contract letter specified "Status of Women Officer" as one of my responsibilities. While this decision was apparently a result of financial considerations, it indicated the administration's view that equity was a hodgepodge of problems related to women only. The management's perception was that the employment and educational equity coordinator was a technocrat hired to ensure that the university complied with government requirements. My own view was quite different, however. I considered equity reform to be a cause, one that I had been advocating for years. I considered myself an agent of change. My approach to equity was inspired by feminist and anti-racist perspectives. These two contesting views of equity were a continual source of conflict.

Applying participatory methods, I believed that I could reverse the administration's top-down approach to a more democratic and bottom-up intervention. I was sure that I could mobilize the campus community and especially the four "designated groups" (women, visible minorities, people with disabilities, and Aboriginal People) in support of a full-scale intervention. Although I was under pressure to take the first steps as soon as possible in order to ensure compliance with government requirements, I devoted considerable time and resources to educating and training the campus community. Soon, however, I realized that in spite of my participatory approach, I was still working within the top-down system that is integral to traditional organizational culture. Let me elaborate by providing a few examples.

I started my work by familiarizing myself with the community and introducing my mandate to as many people as possible. I included student organizations, unions, faculty members, advocacy groups, activists, the local media, and various other employee groups. The first major step was to conduct an employment equity census to determine the representation of designated groups in the workforce. Based on my previous experience at another university in Ontario, I was aware that it would be difficult to get the required participation from all employees. I devoted about a year to informing the employees about the significance of the equity program and the census. In order to democratize the decision-making process, I formed several advisory groups with members representing students, staff, and faculty.

I made extensive use of the weekly student newspaper and the administration's newsletter, in order to keep the campus community informed of the equity program, and I distributed posters and flyers. The information package sent to every employee included a letter from the president reaffirming the institution's commitment to equity, the coordinator's letter of introduction, the university's employment and educational equity policy, the mandate of my office, the composition of advisory committees and their terms of reference, and a brief history of employment equity at the university. The culmination of this educational process was what I called "information sessions."

The invitation to the employees to participate in the sessions was done entirely on a top-down basis. The letters went from the president to deans and heads, and from them to directors and supervisors and finally to the employees. The philosophy behind this approach was that the employees would better respond if the invitations were issued or endorsed by senior management. Although the sessions were intended to be informal so as to encourage full participation, employees most often did not participate. Several factors contributed to this lack of participation. Too much material was covered in a short period of time. Employees were reluctant to speak out because employee groups were colleagues and often had their supervisors present. Generally speaking, the participants in the session were indifferent and passive. There were few questions and most of them were negative; the dominant topic was their concern about employment equity as a "reverse discrimination" practice.

In some of the sessions, I experienced negative reactions from one or two outspoken participants whose comments were supported either by the silence of the others or by their encouragement to make similar points. One such session was with the campus police. The White male members did not hesitate to show their outright hostility to equity and to create an atmosphere of harassment for women and members of minority groups present in the session.

Hostile opposition to equity was also expressed by a number of individuals through other means. For example, one faculty member tore the promotional material into pieces and sent it back with a simple message: "Stuff it!" Another package was sent back with the following note: "I find this type of thing inordinately offensive in an academic community. I do not need a) your office or anybody's office to tell me about equity; and, b) if equity and quality come into conflict, I shall opt for quality." One faculty member sent a signed letter which in part reads: "I find your politically correct presence on campus offensive and objectionable in terms of intellectual inquiry and free thought. I deem your office – like several others – to be unnecessary and, frankly, an inordinate waste of limited financial resources. For the amount devoted to assuring that this university is 'politically attuned to current correctness' we are squandering public money which otherwise could be devoted to the primary purpose of the university, teaching and research."

These are examples of active opposition by individual employees. More passive forms of opposition were practised by the administration. For example, my office was excluded from some public functions such as equity workshops for department heads, or consultation on issues related to equity that were held on campus by government officials or the administration. Also, senior management often avoided direct contact with me preferring to go through the organizational hierarchy by communicating through my supervisor. Even when I directly contacted the senior management, they responded through the supervisor. Another form of administrative resistance was playing down the significance of the equity program; for example, its annual reports were not given prominence at the senate and board of governors, the two highest decision-making bodies in the university.

I must also mention that some participants conveyed their support for the program and for my work privately through personal contacts. The greatest support, however, came from women faculty who were also organized and had a visible pressure group. Feminist faculty members, both as individuals and as a loosely organized group, pressed the administration for decisive and active equity reform. As individuals, women faculty effectively used the local media, professional meetings, and other occasions to criticize the administration's equity policy. Being sensitive to public relations, the administration reacted, both positively and negatively, to these interventions. On the positive side, the administration speeded up certain processes while, on the negative side, they demonized some women activists. Earlier, these faculty members had formed the Non-affiliated Action Group for Equity (NAG for Equity); they played the role of an "equity watch" that monitored the progress of the equity program.

From the beginning, I got in touch with the feminists on the campus and sought their advice and support. I did this not only because I am a feminist, but also because the feminists had been the most vocal force behind the whole intervention process long before I arrived on the campus. They were familiar with the potential and the obstacles, and were ready to assist me. I kept in close touch with this group and participated in some of their meetings. The administration indirectly reacted to my close alliance with the feminists. For example, when a top administrator found out that the Interim Advisory Committee that I had established included feminists, he did not hesitate to warn me. He exclaimed, "Red flag! Red flag! There is a tradition on this campus whereby interim committees become permanent committees!" He immediately called my supervisor and warned him about the feminist presence. To give another example, when I submitted the first annual report to the senate and board of governors, my supervisor had been asked by the president to accompany me for the presentation. When I inquired about this, I was told by the public relations officer: "The president wants to protect you because you have built an image of allying with minority women [feminists] on the campus."

Support also came from minority students both as individuals and organizations such as the Black Student Alliance and the Womyn's Centre. Members of the staff were supportive, too. Another source of support was the off-campus community-based organizations, especially those that represented members of the designated groups.

I cite these experiences in order to emphasize that factors such as ideology and politics play a fundamental role in the process of reform. I have described the role of employment equity coordinator as that of an agent of change. However, the administration appears not to view the coordinators as such. They see us as technocrats hired to ensure the institution's compliance with government requirements. Many universities expect equity coordinators to play the role of public relations officers. They expect us not to criticize the institution in public statements, in the media, or even in academic conferences. My own experience, as well as the experience of other practitioners, indicates that both the government and the universities, as major employers, have a limited view of employment equity. Thus, these two *agencies*, the state and the university, are themselves inhibiting factors; they exercise the power to limit the scope of change. When we add structural barriers to these limitations of policy, it is easier to understand the frustrations of equity coordinators in Canadian universities.

It is not surprising, therefore, that the pace of change has been slow; women are still under-represented, and members of other designated groups continue to be excluded. Equity reform was imposed on the state and the institutions engaged with the state by the social movements of the 1960s. The reform process, however, began only after a considerable lag, in the 1980s when the movements had slowed down. Under such conditions, individual advocates of change are in a much disadvantaged position to resist the age-old structures of power.

NOTES

1 An "equity assessor" is a member of faculty assigned to serve as an observer in a faculty hiring committee; the assessor is a non-voting member who is expected to ensure that the hiring process complies with the university's equity policy.
2 This program requires that organizations with more than 100 employees bid on government contracts of more than $200,000, to comply with the Employment Equity Act.

On Being Homeless: Aboriginal Experiences of Academic Spaces

PATRICIA D. MONTURE-ANGUS[1]

I use the notion of "homelessness" with hesitation. I acknowledge that I exercise much privilege in my life (income, education, profession, and so on). I have a physical home. My quest, since I started teaching nine years ago[2] at Dalhousie Law School, is for an intellectual home. After my first two years of teaching on term contract, I secured a tenure-track position at the law school at the University of Ottawa. Restlessness, a feeling I now understand as "homelessness," set in before that first move from Halifax to Ottawa. This comment is both my story of the last decade of my university teaching and a reflection on my "conquest" of the university. I still seek a space in the university where my Mohawk self is safe.

After a few years as a law professor, I felt[3] I existed in a cavern. At first it felt like a tiny, deep crack in the wall or floor of legal knowledge. Now and again I could peek over the side of that crack and peer at the institution that surrounded me. Eventually, I began to hear an echo in this crack (probably my own spirit cries, trapped). I recognized that the shape of my experience and perhaps the shape of my oppression had changed now that I was no longer a student.

As a law teacher, I was forced to teach ideas that I found both unconscionable and often ridiculous to my Aboriginal way of knowing. The clearest example is teaching property law. I must digress for a moment and note that I did choose to teach property law because it allowed me to displace some of the standard curriculum in first-year law with a full semester on what might be inappropriately labelled "Aboriginal Title."[4] I thought that displacing mainstream curriculum in a required first-year course was an important strategy for transforming the perimeters of legal education (that is, I taught some students who would not otherwise have signed up for an upper year "Aboriginal" course with "someone like me"). The unconscionable edge in teaching property law was presenting the idea that "the crown owns all the land." This concept will always be difficult for me to present in a convincing fashion with due regard to the "knowledge" that the idea was, and still is, the philosophical underpinning of the entire property ownership system in Canada.

I had been interested in law, perhaps dragged to it because of my life experiences (orphaned, adopted out, sexually abused, as well as abused in several other ways, including the ones I self-inflicted).[5] As I recovered my life, these experiences developed into an interest in social justice and the rights of Aboriginal people. Sadly, the list of course options at Canadian law schools did not provide me much opportunity to develop these interests in the classroom. What I wrote about, thought about, and read about was separated from what I taught about. After the time required to prepare classes and teach them, there was little time for the intellectual pursuits that I was most interested in.

It is important to understand the way in which I did not fit within the established law school curriculum. My interests might look deceptively as if they would fit into "criminal law" courses. These courses, however, do not consider the systemic impact of the appli-cation of criminal law to "peoples," which results in the extreme over-representation of Aboriginal Peoples as "clients" in institutions of criminal justice. Less recognized is the extreme under-representation of Aboriginal people in positions of power and authority in the crim-inal justice system (as judges, lawyers, police officers, prison guards, parole officers, and so on) (Hamilton and Sinclair, 1991). More impor-tant, "standard" criminal law courses do not offer any opportunity to address solutions to the systemic problems that Aboriginal people face in the existing system of Canadian criminal justice. Although I, as a professor, do hold the power to shape my courses as I see fit, if I deviate from the "standard" curriculum taught in other criminal law courses then at least a few of my students will suggest that we are not doing "real law." Because I am a Mohawk woman, the aca-demic freedom I possess is diminished against this idea of a "stan-dard" course if I do not conform.

An obvious solution to the problem of mainstream curriculum would be to develop some of my own courses. Unfortunately, by the time I began teaching law, fiscal restraint was already the reality in Canadian law schools. Seminar offerings were being actively limited if not reduced. Just before I left the University of Ottawa, the dean had advised me I would only be able to teach criminology every second year. New courses, especially courses in "alternatives" were not being encouraged. As a result of both fiscal restraint and the very structure (and presumptions) of legal education, it became very difficult to hope that my future experience of law school as a law teacher would be anything other than alienating.[6] I did not agree that my "perspectives" were in fact "alternatives" and saw clearly that the structure of law school curriculum was a central problem in the marginalization I was experiencing.

Reflection has made me realize that the precondition to my participation in an institution of mainstream society is my ability to maintain hope that the institution is in a process of transformation. Generically, my frustration with law school resulted from the recognition that systemic and structural change was not forthcoming. Although Aboriginal professors were welcomed into the law school, our participation was silently conditional on our acceptance of the already entrenched pedagogical structure. Law school curricular visions are rigid, especially in first year when students take some combination of contracts, criminal, constitutional, torts, and property law courses. This structure is not generally or specifically critiqued (for example, why is an "Aboriginal and Treaty Rights" course not a required first year course?) The failure to contemplate structural change and the tendency to be pacified by cosmetic change alone (that is replacing a few white faces with brown ones) led to my final dissatisfaction with law teaching and law schools.

I do not remember when I first started thinking about Native Studies as an "alternative" (alternative meaning only as a discipline different from the one I had been educated and trained in). It is an alternative that is parallel to wanting to be back home in the First Nations community where my "cultural" safety is not threatened and assaulted daily. I suspect it was when I was still a law student. It was probably on one of those all-too-frequent days when the only conscious thoughts I had were of quitting law school and going home. After all, for Indian people, committing to post-secondary education either as a student or as a teacher most often means living out of the community. This commitment means yearning for your people and your place. It means accepting that the constant spirit screams will be the steady and constant backdrop to your education experiences.

I joined the Faculty of Arts and Science, the Department of Native Studies, on 1 July 1994.[45] After much consideration, I had decided that I would not be satisfied with my place in a law school until I had some experience elsewhere in the university to compare that experience against. One of the attractions of a Department of Native Studies was the opportunity to assess from the "inside" the development of a "new" discipline – a space that was envisioned for the very same reasons I had thus far felt "homeless" in my academic career. Native studies was unheard of in Canada prior to the 1970s. For me, Native studies provided an opportunity to consider whether an Aboriginal law school was a realistic dream. It is still a dream, but, I believe, a necessary solution to the issue of indigenizing legal education that floats through my mind from time to time.

There is no doubt that my classroom experience has significantly improved. Law fragments knowledge in general but also moves Aboriginal understandings to the margins by sequestering "Aboriginal rights" courses as upper-year electives. Native studies does not marginalize Aboriginal people in this manner but instead has Aboriginal people at its centre. This is not to suggest that the problem of fragmentation of knowledge does not exist in Native studies; it does. This is the general problem of bringing Aboriginal knowledge into an institution that does not belong to us.

It is clear that I am a much more satisfied teacher as a result of shifting my university "home." It is also clear that my classroom is a safer place for me. My teaching evaluations have been consistently above the department requirements (presuming that these evaluations measure to some degree what is going on in the classroom). I no longer face the indignant assault of students who just cannot accept a Mohawk woman teaching them Canadian law (as it is "their" law not mine). I no longer have to read comments on evaluations such as "she wears too many beads and feathers to class." This is one fewer assault I have to carry. But it was not so much the evaluations themselves that I found so disturbing in law school. It was knowing that some of my students thought racist things about me as I stood at the front of the classroom on a daily basis. It saddened me deeply that even one of my students was compromised in their learning potential solely because their teacher was a Mohawk woman and they could not accept that I knew more about the Canadian system of law than they did.

The other advantage that my move to Native studies facilitated was that I now teach solely in my area of interest, Aboriginal justice (which includes, but is broader than, mere criminal justice) including a class on "First Nations Women and the Law." Now what I read, write, and teach fits together in such a way that I do not feel as if my mind and my energy are divided between what I teach and what I research. It has alleviated one component of the workload burden I have carried as "outsider."

Although, my move to Native studies has generally improved my classroom experiences, it has not had a significant impact on my relationship with the university. In some ways, I am more marginalized in Native studies than I was in the law school. Native studies is a very young discipline, and its position within the university is in some ways still tentative. There is a dynamic tension in the department, between mimicking other disciplines and their rules of legitimacy, and embracing Aboriginal ways of knowing as legitimate. As this tension is not being significantly addressed by the Native studies community (both at my university and elsewhere), there is little room to address questions such as gender equality. This unfortunately compromises my position, in the department, at least.

One of the most important lessons I have learned because of my move from law to Native studies, is that the degree to which I am marginalized is really a condition of the university. This was a very difficult lesson, because in many ways it means that I am powerless to do much to change my marginalization, since that marginalization is based on systemic factors. I doubt very much whether, if I had stayed in the law school, I would have come to understand that the problems are much larger than the structure of the law school. This knowledge of my own powerlessness within the university does not leave me feeling hopeless. Questioning the contours of my university homelessness brings me back to the recognition that I have the power of voice. This is the power of naming, and it is frequently the only power I have. This recognition means that I understand just how important it is not to be silenced. As more and more Aboriginal people come to the university, both as students and as faculty, the power of our individual and collective voices cannot be underestimated. I am part of the first wave of a movement that will see a critical mass of Aboriginal voices converging in Canadian universities. This view gives me great hope that structural change is within our grasp.

NOTES

1 Patricia Monture-Angus is a Mohawk woman from Grand River Territory who currently resides at the Thunderchild First Nation. She is an associate professor (tenured) in the Department of Native Studies at the University of Saskatchewan.

   A longer version of this paper was published in Frances Valdes, Jerome McCristal Culp, and Angela P. Harris, eds., *Crossroads, Directions, and a New Critical Race Theory* (Chicago: Temple University Press, 2001).
2 It was not until 1 July 1989 that any Aboriginal person was hired on a full-time basis in a Canadian law school (all three were women). Sadly

and of note, none of us continue to teach law. I am the only one left in university teaching, although I no longer teach in a law school.

3 I have chosen to use this "emotional" concept (feeling). It is not that I do not know. It is not that I have no knowledge or theory to ground this analysis. I do, and it is the knowledge and knowing that took me to the conclusion. And the conclusion is a feeling. In my way of under-standing (which includes being a survivor of sexual abuse) feeling is a harder place to reach than thinking.

4 I must also acknowledge that I did not participate in this "mission" alone. Two talented and courageous law teachers had already begun this initiative when I arrived at the University of Ottawa. My regards to Darlene Johnston and Cynthia Peterson.

5 I have discussed this at length in "Self-Portrait: Flint Woman" in *Thunder in My Soul: A Mohawk Woman Speaks* (Halifax: Fernwood Publishing, 1995), 44–52.

6 At this point, I would not like to fully close the door to the possibility that I may one day return to law teaching within a law school. How-ever, my participation could never be that of the "usual" law professor. It would have to be negotiated based on my difference.

   I have discussed my experience as a law student in "Ka-nin-geh-heh-gah-e-sa-nonh-yah-gah" in *Thunder*, 11–25: my concerns about legal edu-cation in "Now that the Door is Open: Aboriginal Peoples and the Law School Experience," 90–118; and my experience of the academy in "Flint Woman: Surviving the Contradictions in Academia," 53–73.

7 There were also personal and family reasons behind our move to Saskatchewan that space limitations do not permit me to discuss here.

Biologist from Birth:
Mother by Instinct

ANNE MORGAN

I grew up in Kent, the county known in Britain as the "Garden of England." I have always loved "nature" and some of my fondest childhood memories are associated with the world of wildlife. It is hard to know where the strongest influences came from – perhaps helping my parents in our large garden, perhaps from time spent on family farms, or perhaps from excellent teachers who encouraged an appreciation of the outdoors. One of my favourite activities in elementary school was "First Finds," a competition to be the first person in the class to bring in a particular flower that season. I spent hours roaming the countryside on weekends looking for new flowers and inadvertently learning the local flora.

Throughout grammar school, my love of biology continued and ultimately led to botany, zoology, and geology in my first year at university. The problem came the following year when I had to choose a specialty; was it going to be plants or animals? My father was a beekeeper and so entomology seemed a logical choice. Searching for an appropriate graduate program, I was attracted to work being done in Saskatchewan on leaf-cutter bees. On arrival in Saskatoon I found that the main research was on blister beetles, and so I switched topics to be part of the team effort. Beetles, then, became an important focus for my future research.

By this time I was engaged. Alan had graduated from the same university in England and, coincidentally, had applied for research at the University of Calgary. We had travelled to Canada together and we eventually got married in Saskatoon. Upon completion of our

MSc degrees, we returned to Britain where Alan started his PhD at the University of Birmingham, while I began earning. Already I was taking second place career-wise! However, I was very fortunate in that my job involved full-time research on fossil insects, and the university allowed me to write a thesis on this work. I truly *earned* my PhD!

We returned to Canada and were awarded joint postdoctoral fellowships with the Universities of Western Ontario and Waterloo. Thus began our intertwined history! However, two jobs were not as easy to obtain. After a year, Alan joined the faculty at the University of Waterloo and I continued as a post-doctoral fellow for another year. The Department of Biology then hired me as a research assistant professor to continue with my research and do some teaching. This led to a temporary appointment, replacing a faculty member on sabbatical leave. By then I was thirty years old and I felt that delaying motherhood was going to be increasingly risky. Knowing that I had a guaranteed job for one year only, I planned my pregnancy to begin near the end of that academic year (1974), so that I could complete my obligations without looking too large! (A quirky idea when I think about it in retrospect, but I was in a predominantly male environment!)

Following the birth of my daughter, the Department of Biology continued my position as a Research Assistant Professor; this post enabled me to hold NSERC research grants, but I had no office and no remuneration. For the next six years I juggled motherhood with research, all without maternity benefits, salary, or even tax deductions for the many hours of babysitting that were needed to allow me to work. Fortunately (or unfortunately in retrospect) I was able to share research facilities with my husband, who was in the Department of Earth Sciences, and with whom I did collaborative work. In 1977 I had a second child, and then concentrated periods of research became almost impossible. Babysitting had always been a very difficult choice for me because I could not find anybody who met my high expectations, and so I was trying to do more and more work at home to allow me to care for the children myself.

However, by this time my husband had left his original field of stratigraphy and completely moved over into my field of fossil insects as they related to climatic change. This meant that he was doing the bulk of the paper writing, but I was able to make small contributions and keep my name on publications. This, I felt, was very important if I had any hope of ever getting back into academia. Even in 1978, when my husband took his first sabbatical in the United States, we gave joint seminars at our host institutions and I continued my research interests.

In 1980 two events changed everything for me. I was offered one of the new University Research Fellowships (URF), and my in-laws moved to Waterloo. This gave me a full-time paid academic position, and provided caring, full-time babysitting. The URF ran for five years and provided the opportunity to teach and continue research that I found very stimulating and exciting. Once again I was going to conferences and feeling that I was part of the scientific community. However, I still found it difficult to combine full-time employment with responsibilities at home and often felt the frustration of failing all around.

In 1985 my fellowship came to an end and there were no permanent positions available in the department. I was told that the Science Faculty at the University of Waterloo was not keen to have two faculty members in the same research field, even though our teaching covered different areas and was, in fact, complementary. I felt that we made a very successful research team, an observation that had also been recognized by NSERC with the award of several Team Grants. Perhaps part of the problem was that I was in a field of research that was far better understood and appreciated by the geological community, so it was difficult to gain acceptance in a biology department, especially one that had an emphasis on microbiology and biotechnology. In addition, the decision-makers were not in a position to appreciate the international reputation that I had acquired by this point. However, my husband was planning another sabbatical, and we were both very glad to get away for a year. We took the children out of school completely, did a lot of travelling between extended visits to universities that welcomed us in different parts of the southern hemisphere. It was the best family experience we have ever had, giving us quality time with our young children and allowing both of us to meet and work with many academics in the rest of the world.

On our return to Canada, I re-evaluated my life and decided I did not want to continue the struggle of unpaid research and child-rearing, but would rather opt out of academia for a while. For me, academia has always been more than a nine to five job, and I was not willing to do a job poorly with all the concomitant stress. The lack of available positions in Waterloo, coupled with my unwillingness to drive any distance under the prevailing winter conditions for jobs elsewhere, dampened my hopes for an academic position. As the years went by, I felt more distanced from my research field, and it became obvious that I was unlikely to return to academia. I became more involved in community activities. Earning a salary became subsidiary to being a good mother and making a difference in the world around me. I took several horticultural courses, qualified as a master gardener and started giving talks to community groups on a variety of topics related to growing native plants, saving habitat for native species, and eliminating the use of chemicals. I often wonder if a career in horticulture might have been more suited to my inherent interests and encouraged me to continue in academia despite the difficulties. Nevertheless, my training in biology has provided an excellent background for my current activities.

Now, after a few years of an empty nest and over ten years of community volunteering, I look back with mixed feelings. I regret that my children were not old enough to see me as a role model when I was working as a full-time academic (I think this would have been especially important for my daughter who is now in science herself and struggling with career choices). They only remember me as "the stay-at-home Mum" who went out to give occasional lectures or appear on TV. They, on the other hand, assure me that this does not matter to them, and that I have had other important influences on them by always being there. Another concern is that I do not have my own pension fund for retirement. The final regret is that I can no longer claim to have a real career. I often feel undervalued in society and find it difficult to respond satisfactorily to questions such as, "And what are you doing now?" Somehow volunteering does not gain the respect that it should.

Women are often considered fortunate in having a choice to work inside or outside the home. I bought into this particular philosophy at one time, but now realize that I did *not* have a choice. My children were my priority and, in order to give them adequate time and attention, I *had* to stay at home. My husband held the traditional belief that he was not responsible for work in the home and that it was important for the wife to be there. I did not have enough time or energy to look after children, house, and career and do each to my high standards.

Hearing about similar problems from other women academics has helped to validate my own situation, but not to reconcile it completely. Was I forced out by the system or should I have changed my attitude to child-rearing? I try to tell myself I did the right thing for my children because they have grown up into wonderful human beings. But would they have "turned out" just as well if I had been more "brutal" and put them in full-time child-care? We will never know, and I suppose it comes down to the fact that one usually follows one's heart in these situations. The head is secondary even for some women in academia!

Women on Campus: Mosaic Myth or Melting Pot Reality?

MAXINE C. MOTT

In recent years increased attention has been given to the issues and concerns of women faculty and students in Canadian universities.[1] Similar attention has not been given to women in leadership positions in these same institutions. There is a small but growing body of literature that relates to women in educational administration at the primary and secondary school levels (Reynolds 1994). However, most of the published literature that examines gender issues related to higher education leadership is from the United States. There are several possible explanations for the lack of Canadian scholarship on women in higher education administration. One reason may be the relative lack of women in administrative positions. Caplan (1994: 180) notes that "Rarely are women made department heads, deans, or other top administrators, and despite being placed on many working committees, infrequently do they hold positions on the powerful ones or on funding bodies or editorial boards." Or, it may be that the majority of scholars have accepted the notion that leadership is *genderless* and that male versions of administrative issues are representative of women's perceptions. One step toward correcting the *genderless* dilemma is to identify women participating in leadership roles and listen to their experiences. This collection of women's stories is one such step in the process.

In Canada, the image of a *mosaic* has been used to describe our diverse population. A mosaic implies a work of art composed of a collection of brightly coloured pieces that fit together to create a unique wholeness. The use of the term implies that all individuals (including women) are valued for their unique contributions to our culture. The term used to describe population diversity in the United States is the *melting pot*. A melting pot suggests that the ingredients are put together with a blending of the various differences and the final outcome a oneness. However, if one element in the melting pot is particularly strong, it tends to dominate the flavour and appearance of the final product. In the past, the United States' melting pot has been dominated by a White male bias. The resulting expectation has been that all components of the melting pot will look like and assume the ideologies of the White male. Individuals, women, and minorities who do not, will not, or cannot "melt down" are often subjected to a life of *less than*. Canada's equal opportunity efforts and the United States' affirmative action programs were introduced to prevent and reduce the *less than* outcomes that have affected women and minorities in the past. The success of these programs in higher educational institutions, however, is questionable.

As is likely the case with many others, my interest in issues of women in academe stemmed from my own experiences, which I felt at times during my career were *less than* equitable. These experiences triggered my curiosity to learn more about the obstacles other women face while in leadership positions. In the fall of 1996, I undertook a self-funded research project in an attempt to satisfy some of my curiosity. The main objective of this project was to develop a better understanding of what women leaders in academe consider to be issues or concerns for women in the post-secondary milieu. A questionnaire[2] was sent to eighty-nine women in leadership roles at universities, community colleges, and technical institutes throughout the ten provinces and two territories, asking them to identify areas they saw as problematic for women in higher educational institutions. Fifty-six (63%) of the questionnaires were returned. The majority of the respondents held formal administrative positions, while sixteen were faculty members. The average age of the women was 50.5 years, and their average length of service in higher education was 17.5 years.

The study's findings indicate that institutions are *not there yet* with regard to equitable practices toward women. The responses suggest that higher education has assumed a melting pot mentality, rather than acknowledging and valuing women as unique pieces in a mosaic. Most of the women surveyed (forty-three of the fifty-six) felt that discrimination in academic institutions currently exists for women students, faculty, support staff, and administrators. There was strong agreement that greater discrimination or differential treatment of women took place the higher up the administrative ladder a woman was positioned.

What follows are written comments from the respondents. Their comments fell into two broad categories: concerns related to women in formal leadership roles, and concerns related to all women in higher education. The expressed concerns that related to women in formal leadership roles focused on the "maleness" of the higher education administration culture and conveyed a tone of frustration that efforts toward improving campus experiences for women have resulted in minimal change.

· Upper management still operates on the old boys' network principles and tends to hire only women who will play that game (because they want to or because they cannot do anything else).
· At the administrative level, we have almost no women. Therefore, the "atmosphere" is very male. I would have no interest in promotion because at the higher administrative level there are only men and I would find working with that group very difficult. I am interested in developing a non-traditional management style. The men in administration at my institution are not at all interested in this. I find this issue very interesting and important – even if the college is interested in hiring women for these jobs, women may not want to participate in the existing management culture.
· At senior level positions, vice-presidents and presidents, individuals and organizations are quick to attribute behaviours to "being a woman" rather than to individual differences. This is especially true of behaviours or interactions that differ from the norm.
· Too many women suffer from "triple-A syndrome" (acting, assistant, associate) versus "the real thing." As part of the "triple-A League," I could do less for women than when I was in charge of an academic unit as director.
· The very male culture [with its] emphasis on "team solidarity" and constant overt sexism to other women was an issue of concern for me. All other women in the "senior suite" were secretaries. Frankly, I lasted eighteen months and am now free again to be an advocate.

· Many comments reinforce the struggles encountered by the respondents in their attempts to improve the academic environment for women. Comments included: "Women who are openly advocates [for women] have a much harder time getting into administration"; and: "Although women in positions of leadership should (and do) support gender issues, it is not *what they do but how they do it* that is often criticized by peers/co-workers."
Some women wrote of how discrimination toward women has become more subtle, and made observations such as: "Much of the

discrimination now is more polite, better disguised than ten years ago, hidden in workloads or the scheduling practices (late classes, for example)"; and: "I think all universities are trying to recruit women at the top levels in visible positions. At the department level, where recruitment is more likely to be internal, discrimination still exists." I think the gender battle has reached a new stage. By and large institutional policies are in place. Curriculum transformation is happening, albeit more slowly than we might like. It's true that the financial crisis has stalled change in some quarters, but some of the delay is certainly due to resistance, some of it at times quite nasty and vicious.

Other comments made by these academic women reflected the realities of their postsecondary environment. It was noted that: "Even those who advocate inclusive curriculum and positive classroom climate don't always put theory into practice"; and: "With respect to recruiting, we are currently involved in two searches for new faculty members. It is hard enough finding suitable candidates; if additional requirements for gender and/or minority status are added on, we would never succeed."

Still others identified concerns related to family life and women's multiple roles within the family unit: "Child care services on campus are still an issue and have been for my over twenty years in Canadian universities." Time commitment was also an issue of concern.

· Not all universities and granting agencies acknowledge women's different educational and career paths, e.g., time out for childbearing and child-raising, care of elderly relatives, work requirements. Some universities and rating agencies, [magazine surveys, for example] still see a four-year degree as the norm and anyone taking longer is being tardy.
· I have not noticed discrimination toward women in general. However, women who wish to devote more than a minimum of time to their children have a *very* difficult time in academia. It is hard to get any research position that does not require 40–60 hours/week for satisfactory performance. I would like to see far more part-time positions (20–30 hours/week) and I would encourage *fathers* as well as mothers to avail themselves of the opportunity.

The final words of this paper are from a woman administrator who reinforces the observation that the Canadian higher education culture has assumed a "melting pot" mentality toward women and women leaders on campus. "Although I am embarrassed to admit this, now is not the time, given current leadership styles, to openly and successfully be seen to be a blatant women's advocate. My heart is sickened by this, but one knows after thirty years in this business when a battle or a war can be won. Neither is possible now using the overt approach. So I continue to do what I feel committed to do, regardless of the fact that it is not blatant, overt, and as aggressive as I would like. Thank you for doing this research."

The myth of a mosaic that celebrates differences is just that – a myth. There is much work to be done if we hope to put to rest the melting pot situation in which women are considered "less than," and make the myth a reality, so that women become acknowledged as unique pieces of the Canadian higher education mosaic.

NOTES

1 Resources are: Caplan, P. (1994). *Lifting a Ton of Feathers*, Toronto: University of Toronto Press; CAUT Bulletin, *Status of Women Supplement*. (1995,1996). Canadian Association of University Teachers; and, Dean, J. and Clifton, R. (1994). An evaluation of pay equity reports at five Canadian universities. *The Canadian Journal of Higher Education*, 24–2, 199487–114; Epp, J. (1994). Women's perceptions of Master's level educational administration programs. *Canadian Journal of Higher Education*, 24–2, 1995, 43–67; The Chilly Collective. (Ed.) (1995). *Breaking Anonymity: The Chilly Climate for Women Faculty* Waterloo: Wilfrid Laurier University Press.

2 A copy of the questionnaire is available, upon request, from the author. The questionnaire was adapted (with permission) from Touchton, J., D. Shavlik, & I. Davis (1993). *Women in Presidencies: A Descriptive Study of Women College and University Presidents*. Washington, DC: Office of Women in Higher Education, American Council on Education.

What's a Girl like You Doing in a Nice Place like This? Mothering in the Academy

ANDREA O'REILLY

My history as an academic began close to seventeen years ago when I, at the tender age of nineteen, left home to attend university in the big and bad Toronto. My career plans were anything but concrete, though I envisioned myself in a smart and sexy career like law. Given that I had done well in law and economics in high school, such a future seemed possible. However, I made the fatal mistake of enrolling in a course on women and literature; since then, women's writing has been the undying passion of my life. There went the high-powered, and, I may add, high-paying, job. However, I excelled in English and Women's Studies and decided to pursue my studies at the graduate level. Twenty-two, with an A average and a decent boyfriend (a first for me), I felt as if I was finally in control of my life, awaiting a future full of promise and hope ... And then I learned that I wasn't just late ... I was pregnant.

Motherhood was something I had planned to do at thirty something, only after both the career and the guy were firmly established. I was not supposed to be pregnant now and certainly not this way: young, poor, and in a dating relationship. Well, we decided to have the baby, and three weeks later I found myself setting up house (if such is applicable to student residence) with this man; obscenely happy, eagerly awaiting the birth of this child. (Fourteen years later we are still together.) I believed my life would go ahead as planned; I reassured my mother that with my child in daycare at six weeks, my studies would resume as scheduled. I did not know then, could not have known, how completely pregnancy and later motherhood would change my life. In the early months of pregnancy I was horribly ill with unrelenting nausea; in the later months I developed a quite serious case of pre-eclampsia, which necessitated the daily monitoring of my blood pressure. I wrote a brilliant paper on the plight of fallen women in Victorian literature as my feet swelled and my back ached; I went into labour having just completed a major paper on sexuality and the empowerment of women; the ironies, in retrospect, are splendid. Labour destroyed any remnant of complacency left over from my pre-pregnant self. I hemorrhaged during labour. I had never experienced such pain, terror, or aloneness.

Nothing, as any new mother will tell you, can prepare you for the numbing exhaustion and psychic dislocation of new motherhood. Nor can anyone warn you about how deeply you will fall in love with your child. "Motherhood," as Marni Jackson so aptly puts it (Jackson, 1992:5), "is like Albania – you can't trust the descriptions in the books, you have to go there." Motherhood radicalized and politicized me; it brought me to feminism. Though I had identified as a feminist for a number of years, motherhood made feminism real for me and radically redefined it. At twenty-three, I knew in my gut, though I could not yet fully articulate it, that my feminism was to be about motherhood and that any social or political gains made by women through the repudiation of motherhood were to be seen not as achievements but as compromises and sellouts. If I had to deny or downplay my maternal self (as if such were possible) to be successful, I was not interested in playing the game. As Audrey Lorde reminds us, "the master's tools will never dismantle the master's house." I now realize that, had I been willing to cleave off my maternal self and "pass" as a nonmother, my stay in academia would have been less difficult, though less rewarding. A well-meaning friend advised me, when my son was two, that if I kept my son in daycare longer hours (he attended six hours a day) and if my spouse were to mind him on weekends, I would find mothering less of an interference. That I might want my son in daycare six, as opposed to ten, hours a day and that I might enjoy my weekends with him, had simply not occurred to her. Another friend who had a ten-year-old and a two-year-old confided to me, with much conspiratorial glee, that she had been a student for more than five years and no one in her department had figured out she was a mother. When I became a mother, I realized that feminism was to be about changing the system, not about securing a niche in it. Getting some of us in, I understood, would not set us free.

The months after my son's birth were spent finishing my honours thesis, due in July. The university agreed, after laborious petitioning, to extend the date to December. With a new baby, poor health, (due to complications of birth) and no childcare, I was nonetheless told, in no subtle way, that I should be grateful for their generosity in allowing me the four months to write my hundred-page thesis. My son never slept; as an infant, his naps seldom lasted more than forty minutes. I remember phoning La Leche League hysterical about my son's lack of sleep. They reassured me that it was normal ... but then again they didn't have an honours thesis to write. We had planned to enrol our son in daycare when he turned one; but in November we learned that we had a daycare subsidy and that if we turned it down our name would go back to the bottom of the waiting list; motherhood also awakened me to the insensitivities of state bureaucracy. Though our son attended only part time the first year, he was constantly sick and ended up being hospitalized at six months for bronchitis and at thirteen months underwent an ear operation. The night he was hospitalized, I had a seminar to present in my graduate course. When I explained to my professor that I would be missing class due to my son's stay in hospital and that I would have to reschedule, she suggested that, since my seminar was already prepared, it might be best that I do it as planned. This was one of many moments in which I felt I had to assert my identity as a mother. I spent the night with my son.

In my master's year, I worked nine to three while my son was in daycare. I would cram into six hours what my classmates would do in a full day: no dawdling over the paper and morning coffee, no phone calls, no lunch or TV breaks. My son cried, screamed, and clung to me each and every morning I dropped him off at daycare. I often would see him – my bedroom window overlooked the daycare playground – still standing at the gate where I left him with tears and snot running down his face. These mornings I did not work; I sat and cried, paralysed by grief and guilt. The day I was to teach my first class as a tutorial assistant, I ran into my son's daycare group out for a walk; of course he wanted to leave with me, and when I left he threw himself into a fury I have seldom seen since. I entered my first classroom as a teacher with his cries still ringing in my ears.

I worked exceptionally hard that year and I was rewarded with A grades and an Ontario Scholarship which I held for four years. My professors were overwhelmingly supportive of my work. But, looking back, I realize that, despite my insistent affirmations of my maternal self, my motherhood had not in any substantial way challenged the way the university worked: I seldom missed class, I was never late, I always had my readings done, and my course papers, though handed in late, were of the highest calibre. I was behaving, for the most part, as the good graduate student I was expected to be. And then I found myself pregnant *again*.

I began my PhD six months pregnant, with a son just turned two. Looking back now, I am amazed at both my defiance and naïveté. I firmly believed that if I just continued to work hard, all would be fine. My daughter was born on December 30; I was back in class on January 4, hospital bracelet still on. There was no maternity leave for graduate students then, though I did have a six-week maternity leave from teaching. My students today are amazed when I tell them this story; they cannot believe that as recently as 1987 a major university lacked maternity provisions for graduate students. The month our daughter was born we lost our daycare subsidy; we had to remove our son from daycare. Child Services reasoned that my spouse's teaching contract did not constitute full-time employment, as they counted only in-class teaching hours. We fought, and our eventual victory resulted in a change in municipal policy. However, for nine months I was a full-time graduate student and a teaching assistant, with two young children and no childcare. To make matters worse, my daughter refused to take a bottle until she was nine months old; this meant that I could not leave her for more than three hours at a time. That term my spouse finished teaching a class at one; my graduate course started at one on the other side of campus. I would nurse my daughter at twelve-twenty, bundle her and her brother up in their winter apparel, dash to my spouse's classroom (as much as this is possible with a stroller and a toddler in tow), hand them off to him, and then I would quite literally run to class. During this time I managed to attend classes, do my readings, present my seminars, and begin the research for my course papers; lack of childcare prevented me from completing the papers on time. Due to the December birth of my daughter, I had enrolled in one full course and a half, which ended in December, putting me half a course behind schedule. I had hoped to complete my outstanding course work in the summer. The department, however, argued that since I was a half course behind I should take a course in the summer to get back on schedule. So here I was, taking a full graduate course in four months, again with no childcare and, of course, not completing the outstanding papers. In September, though ahead of schedule by a half course, I was put under informal probation because of my incomplete course work. That year I finished my courses and got caught up on some of the earlier incomplete work. Most of the time, I felt as if my life was spiralling out of control; as one assignment was finished, another came due, and the whole time my progress was under constant surveillance. Such stress triggered what we euphemistically term a writer's block; weeks would go by and I could not write a sentence. I was undergoing a crisis of confidence, faith, and, no doubt, exhaustion. In the fall of 1988, my status was assessed again, and it was determined that I was to sit my minor field comprehensive exams (an eight-hour exam) in May; by that time all course work would be completed. Failing to honour these commitments would result in my status being changed to part-time. Part-time study is frequently championed as the option of choice for mother students (though, of course, never asked of father students). For me it would mean the end of my academic career; as a part-time student I would lose my scholarship and no longer be entitled to a Teaching Assistantship. As well, I would be ineligible for daycare subsidy, student loans, and even student housing.

Though my children were still quite young (1½ and 4), I was determined to honour my commitments. And then I found myself pregnant *again* (all three pregnancies were the result of birth control failures). I hid my pregnancy all winter, knowing that if my pregnancy were discovered, my full-time status would be jeopardized. Reflecting back on this, I feel shame, guilt, fear and, I may add, disbelief. It was 1989 and a straight A student who is an Ontario Graduate Scholarship recipient, majoring in women's studies in literature, was compelled to hide her pregnancy. I felt like one of those Victorian fallen women I had been studying. The day of my minor field exam, my pregnancy was discovered; I could hardly hide my protruding belly on a hot day in the middle of May. The chair, as I had feared, applied to have my status changed to part-time that same day after learning that two of my three course papers were still incomplete. I believed he thought that such a gesture was well-meaning and well-intentioned. In reality, it meant the end of my academic career. Fortunately, when my professors learned of this they lobbied on my behalf, struck a committee to investigate the experiences of mother graduate students, which resulted in the first-ever maternity provisions for graduate students, and I was awarded a retroactive maternity leave which, appropriately enough, put me ahead of schedule.

I *finally* completed my PhD in June 1996. In 1993 I withdrew and wrote my dissertation as I worked full time as a part-timer, another one of the ironies of university life. I have been quite successful in presenting and publishing my work and I hold what is considered to be an impressive cv. I am hopeful that I will secure a tenure-stream appointment; though, like many women with partners, I am unable to move to obtain such a position. As I look back at my graduate career, I am less bitter than I was a few years ago; though I still mourn for that young woman whose stress, guilt, and anxiety I can still taste today. The requests which that young woman made were quite modest: a recognition she was a mother and that this affected the progress of her studies, and also an extra six months to complete course assignments. Last year I received a call from a graduate student seeking advice on how she should implement her maternity leave. During our conversation, she expressed her incredulity at the difficulties I had experienced as a mother *back then*. I did not have the heart to remind her that *back then* was a mere five years ago, and that, no ... I didn't think that we were out of the dark ages quite yet.

McTeaching

MARIANNE D. PARSONS

Between 1993 and 1997 I moved six times. Four of these moves were for teaching jobs; all of them were motivated by economic necessity. In 1996 (for the first time in nine years) I could no longer afford to live independently and had to share accommodations with my younger sister who is a single parent and full-time student. From September 1997 to August 1998 I taught seven courses, at three universities, for the handsome sum of $27,100.[1] My work experience of teaching university students part time for the past sixteen years[2] has a historical and social context that is shared by a number of part-time faculty, particularly women part-time faculty. Prevalent views and practices in the academic world regarding the treatment and "place" of part-time faculty serve to marginalize and devalue the highly skilled, necessary work that we do. As a result, part-time faculty have become the "McTeachers"[3] of the university system.

Several social and economic factors have contributed to the current dependence of postsecondary institutions on part-time faculty. In the period following World War II, a dramatic increase in student enrollments necessitated the establishment of numerous colleges and universities in Canada. New faculty were hired and many students pursued graduate studies. However, in the 1970s, while student enrollment continued to increase, government funding to universities declined. To fill the labour gap in the most economically feasible manner, universities hired faculty on a contractually limited, part-time basis (Rajagopal and Farr, 1989). Today "more than a third of all Canadian faculty are part-timers" (Rajagopal and Farr, 1992: 317).

I have worked in university departments where part-time faculty outnumber full-time faculty. Unless a radical decrease in student enrollments occurs or government funding to universities dramatically increases, the maintenance of a part-time labour pool will continue to be necessary in order for universities to be able to offer degrees. "As a cost-efficient highly skilled workforce, part-timers have become an integral part of academe not in spite of their low cost, but because of it" (Rajagopal and Farr, 1992).

Part-time teaching offers dead-end jobs with virtually no opportunity for advancement and no job security. Part-timers have little to no political voice in university and departmental governance (Gappa, 1987) and generally receive the less attractive teaching assignments, typically teaching the lower level, larger courses (Rosenblum and Rosenblum, 1994). We are the "last hired" (after teaching assignments have been allocated to full-time faculty), and the "first fired" when courses are cut. Sharff and Lessinger compare the low pay and unsatisfactory working conditions experienced by part-time faculty to sweatshop work: "the majority experience working conditions that to some extent resemble the conditions of low-skilled labor ... akin to industrial 'homework' in terms of isolation, low pay for long hours of effort ... the characteristics generally identified with sweatshop work" (Sharff and Lessinger, 1994).

These working conditions include overcrowded office space, last-minute course offerings, cancelled courses with little or no compensation, and fewer resources than those available to full-time faculty (Rosenblum and Rosenblum, 1994). I once taught in a department that "housed" part-timers in a huge room where there was no computer, no telephone and no place to hang your coat. There were rows of desks separated by partitions and a sign-up sheet where you could book a desk for a couple of hours a week. If a student had to speak with me in private, we would have to go for a walk on campus and converse in an empty classroom, the hallway, the parking lot or, as one occasion, the washroom!

Underlying the treatment of part-time university faculty are some basic assumptions about the place of part-time teaching in the university. Members of administrations and full-time faculty have told me that the best candidates for part-time teaching are "moonlighters," who have full-time jobs outside of academe, retired academics, and graduate students who need some teaching experience in order to apply for tenure-track jobs. In other words, the best worker for the job is someone who, in the long run, will not remain in the part-time pool and will not be dependent on part-time teaching for the mainstay of his or her economic existence. The implicit underlying assumptions of "opportunity" and "choice" serve to reinforce the marginalization of part-time faculty.

Colleagues who espouse these liberal analyses fail to recognize the real structural barriers to full-time employment (including non-academic employment) which now exist, and the fact that universities require a steady, reliable pool of part-timers. How should I perceive myself as a worker if I don't fall into one of the above categories? It is not surprising that part-time faculty are often referred to as "the underclass" (Committee G, 1992), "second-class educators" (Thompson, 1992), and "gypsy scholars" (Rajagopal and Farr, 1989).

Women are more often employed as part-time faculty than men and are particularly vulnerable to remaining as part-time faculty for the duration of their academic careers (Rosenblum and Rosenblum, 1994; Warme and Lundy, 1986). Married women with children represent a significant proportion of those employed as part-time faculty.

In the words of a woman part-timer (mother of three children) who has taught at three universities for the past decade: "I would like full-time quality employment that I could feel some sort of empowerment through. In order to use what we've been trained for we need to be hired as full-time academics. I feel like an underpaid, under-valued robot who processes students. I am scrambling in an economy which is anti-worker. Part-time teaching is a sad reality for many of us."

A Quebec study found women part-time faculty to be more "dependent upon the university for a major share of their income" than their male counterparts, for whom the majority (76%) enjoyed "regular full-time non-university employment" (Rajagopal and Farr, 1992). For many of us, part-time university teaching has become just another one of the "Mcjobs" available in the 1990s, which force us to piece together our economic lives. In keeping with the "Mc" analogy, the propaganda presented in the media regarding the work environments of workers in fast food-chains closely resembles the false impressions generated by universities regarding the work environments of faculty.

In a recent television interview, the 1997 media image representative for McDonald's fast-food chain talked about her experience of being discovered by public relations moguls interested in capturing the "essence" of what it means to be a happy, dedicated worker at McDonald's. With the exuberance that only a high school student can muster, she attributed her success in landing the media spot to her "sunny" disposition. Her main concern was maintaining her excellent customer relations skills now that she had become a media image representative for the fast-food chain. Advertisements for McDonald's also exploit retirees, who appear to be finding fulfillment flipping hamburgers in their twilight years.

This euphemistic display of worker satisfaction and opportunity masks the hard-core reality that for many of these workers their labour force participation will consist of an endless string of "Mcjobs." Universities attempt to project the same kinds of positive images to the public at large; for example, calendar pictorials that depict university faculty as a monolithic group of secure, happy, dedicated workers, and mission statements that emphasize excellence in teaching and student centred learning environments. Without adequate pay or satisfactory working conditions, a significant and growing number of part-time university faculty are unable and unwilling to pretend that this reality exists or is remotely attainable, given the conservative political and economic climates within which we work. Those of us who struggle to meet the teaching standards we have set for ourselves, despite overcrowded classrooms and shrinking resources, frequently suffer from teaching "burnout" and mental exhaustion.

"McTeaching" is the inevitable result of economic exploitation and a lack of critical understanding of the work environments of part-time faculty. This dependence on part-time faculty within the university system has far-reaching effects on staffing, collegiality, and the quality of education. Departments that depend heavily on part-timers to teach the core of their program may be unable to deliver their programs during labour shortages, as the number of part-timers available to teach fluctuates: with a high proportion of part-timers it becomes difficult to build up strong departments with a clear sense of future goals. And, because of last-minute course offerings, inadequate resources, and part-timers' being forced to teach the "leftovers," quality teaching and quality curriculum are severely jeopardized. The dependence on part-timers affects the entire academic and university community. The effort of all concerned needs to be mobilized in order to effect change.

In January 1997, as I contemplated my sixth move in four years, I painted a self-portrait that I have entitled "Employee of the Month." A realistic "poster girl" for part-time university faculty.

NOTES

1 The seven courses included three full courses and four half courses.
2 My teaching experience includes eight years as a teaching assistant, seven years as a lecturer, and one year as an assistant professor. My work experience as a teaching assistant included many of the duties assigned to course instructors.
3 For a full discussion of the concept of "McDonaldization" see George Ritzer, *The McDonaldization of Society.* London: Pine Forge Press, 1993.

Some Stones and
Some Mountains

LINDA JOAN PAUL

I was auditing a women's studies course. The subject was global abuse of women, and we watched a documentary[1] of the June 1993 United Nations World Conference on Human Rights held in Vienna. One hundred and seventy governments met and deliberated. It was the largest human rights gathering ever. While the heads of states and officials met in one area, women held a smaller tribunal of their own – to "tear down the walls of silence" that surrounded the abuse and debasement of women.

One stark scene showed drawings of three sizes of rocks which might be used in one country to stone women who had supposedly committed adultery: one size was too small to kill; another was too large – it would kill women too quickly. The medium-sized stones were the best. They would kill women slowly and painfully. A horrifying picture. An analogy occurred to me: in Canada we do not stone women to death, but we do kill them – in society and in the Canadian academic tundra – psychologically, painfully, slowly. I thought of my own career(s) with its bruises and broken bones.

I do not mean to paint a totally negative picture. There have been happy days too, just like the moment when Julie Andrews welcomes the hills in the first scenes of *The Sound of Music*. It is naïve to expect a career path filled with such moments. But it would be a welcome relief to dodge some of the stones and sing on the Canadian hilltops occasionally.

Feminist theory affirms that we live in a patriarchal, male-dominated society. Male decision-making tends to ignore or downplay gender, race, ethnicity, and class. The experiences and aspirations of women are largely absent from such a world. Universities are generally part of this patriarchy and have been so since their inception in medieval times, following the monastic tradition. Over a millennium before that, Plato and Aristotle articulated the patriarchal line to their informal gatherings of students. This academic tradition continues in our day. Many women sessional instructors like myself seem invisible to most levels of the male-dominated administration. The systemic discrimination encountered by women academics often feels like hurled stones; the psychological bruises cut deep.

A similar effect from these invisibly thrown stones relates to the lack of female academic role models. I grew up in an era of few women professors. At the University of Alberta, I had precisely one female professor, for one course, in my three undergraduate years. During my MA studies in geography, there were no full-time female professors. One woman professor taught as a "visiting professor." Consequently, when I graduated, I had virtually no female role models. That I might become a university professor never crossed my mind.

I married, worked for the provincial government in the Water Resources Department, had my first child. We then moved to Regina where my husband obtained his first university teaching position, straight out of graduate school. Job offers were proffered, unsolicited. He had a choice.

Universities were growing rapidly. I soared like Julie Andrews when the geography chair asked me to teach as a sessional. I would never have considered doing so on my own. However, the chair also pointed out I could never become a full-fledged department member because my husband was already a geography professor.

At that time spouses were not allowed to teach in the same department. Because we shared the same discipline, discriminatory rules disallowed my permanent appointment. In similar situations, men are still usually hired first, their wives or partners often following them to their places of employment. Thus men tend to obtain the tenured position, their wives remaining in less secure sessional jobs. What was the effect of this stone? It erased from my mind completely the idea of obtaining my PhD. Since the nearest university was three hours away, and we were not prepared to have a long-distance marriage – and it appeared I would never be hired by this university even with a doctorate – there seemed no incentive to obtain it, even though I loved teaching. The stone hurled by a blind patriarchy destroyed my vision.

Biological blockades also tend to affect women more than men. Our family expanded, although not entirely as anticipated. We had not planned on five lost pregnancies – two miscarriages and three stillbirths. These losses were debilitating physically and psychologically. I was in and out of hospital many times. I was twice in hospital for a terror-filled month, flat on my back, only to lose the babies anyway. We adopted twice, and finally another child was born to us, twelve weeks prematurely. He was extremely ill and required much help in his first few years. As a result, a ten-year segment of my career never materialized. But how often do academic hiring committees consider women's applications if they contain few publications, less research, and no PhD? None that I've been involved with. And what is the impact from this projectile? A sad ring of truth appears in a comment by a women's studies professor in Regina: as long as women's roles are related to biology and they produce babies, females will be in inferior positions.

There were benefits, however, other mountain views to enjoy. While the children were young, I taught when requested by the university. I grew in confidence. That I could work inside and outside the home was an advantage at the time. I was also an ardent volunteer – with UNICEF, Amnesty International, the church, refugees. Life was interesting, but after a decade in this situation, I wanted more. Society seldom values its non- or low-earning members. For many years now, I have taught virtually full time, as a sessional, not as a tenured professor. I once taught full time at one of the federated colleges on a two-year contract that I had been assured verbally would continue indefinitely. When my two-year contract came to an end, my job was cut, the result of being part of a non-unionized staff. (This stone was big, almost killing.)

Over time, I have come to realize how poorly most sessional teachers are treated across Canada. They are generally invisible at the administrative and department level. They mysteriously arrive, teach their classes, conduct their research and leave. This stone cuts deep.

For years, I had no office. How does one focus on a class, meet students, take part in department life without one? Eventually, frustration loomed so large that I became politicized. I joined a pre-negotiating committee of our faculty association, trying to get sessionals onto the bargaining agenda. I was elected to the faculty association council as a sessional representative. I eventually joined its Status of Women Committee, later becoming its chair. (More hills climbed for me as my confidence increased.) I instigated a survey on sessional conditions through the SWC. Consciousness-raising is extremely important.

Gradually, the University of Regina Faculty Association (URFA) has become proactive and initiated gains, especially for long-term sessionals. A new category was created for us "sessional instructors." We now receive some benefits: dental care, as well as prorated pension plans. After twenty-six years in the academy, if I were to retire now, my pension would be a mere $1,500 per *year*! We also receive an accountable allowance and, very important, the right of first refusal for teaching four classes in our area of expertise, per year. The administration, too, is becoming more aware of our working conditions.

However, my work still goes mainly unnoticed. In another college where I have taught, I applied for two term positions but came out empty-handed. A PhD is the only passport that exists. While I was treated well, and the college gave receptions for all staff, including sessionals (a welcoming hillside for sessionals to wander), I found myself back in the Geography Department. Geography is a discipline in which few women hold tenured positions. A quick straw count of prairie universities indicates that approximately 6 percent of geography positions are held by females. How do women geographers obtain jobs if little or no consideration is given to systemic discrimination or women-centered problems such as family concerns?

It appears I will have to take the advice of one sympathetic (female) department chair who commented, "I think they have come to see you only as a sessional. They can't see beyond that. You are going to have to find satisfaction outside the university." Unfortunately, I think she is probably right. (This stone has caused constant, throbbing pain.)

Where, then, does satisfaction lie? I love teaching. This must show. Time and again, my students comment on this in my class evaluations. They like me. They think I know my work. They think I am fair, kind, and fun. This means a lot. (I embrace this mountain.)

I have found tremendous fulfillment in being elected to the Canadian Association of University Teachers (CAUT) Status of Women Committee (SWC). I have grown in confidence, knowledge and, I hope, in usefulness as a result. I have come to know even more of the stones thrown at academic women across Canada and, for that matter, across the world. But I have also learned the camaraderie of becoming friends with, and co-workers of, women with a cause. Though I am mindful of all women's and minority issues, I have pushed especially strongly the plight of part-timers. CAUT, too, is becoming more aware of this constituency. This spring for the first time a part-timer won the Sarah Shorten Award for outstanding achievement in promoting women's issues in academe. CAUT has also created the Working Group on Contract Academic Staff to try to identify who part-timers are, describe their working conditions, and report on the solutions that universities are implementing to alleviate problems for them. (The new pathway CAUT has chosen has led to many joyous alpine walks for me!)

At the CAUT-SWC Conference in Halifax in the fall of 1996, I organized a session on part-timers. The fact that women in these lower-ranked positions have a forum is very important. When I edited the CAUT Status of Women Supplement for the *Bulletin*, it was again possible to publicize women's issues. I recently specifically highlighted part-timers' concerns in an article I wrote entitled "Dilemmas and Solutions for Part-timers" (Paul, 1998:3–10). I have discovered that while part-timers are numerous, they have little opportunity to meet with others. Therefore many do not realize how similar their problems are across the country. I have been surprised by how many sessionals have written to me as a result of this article, wanting to discuss the problem further.

Networking. So often, we hear of the old boys' club in relation to positions of power within the university. My involvement with the Status of Women Committee has introduced me to a wide network of university academic women. I have come to know that I am not alone. Empowerment and encouragement from this caucus have given me strength and hope.

While editing this book, we three co-editors have developed a deep friendship in our fascinating quest for the roots of women's survival. Finding the writers and participating in their narratives have sent us singing to the hilltops.

This summer, I reviewed a 1,000-page geography manuscript for a publishing company. This fall, I was invited to present a keynote address to a conference on part-timers at the University of Ottawa. My professional work beyond the campus seems to be expanding. What is so annoying is that the number of courses I am projected to teach appears to be declining as a result of budget cuts. I enjoy teaching! I am also worried about the impact of this reduction on my meagre pension as well as its immediate effect on my salary.

Does one end a story by describing the impact of hurled stones or the ascent to mountain peaks? Perhaps a bit of both. Consider experiences related to me by part-timers and contract teaching staff. One institution periodically circulates a list of all former employees from bottle-washers and maintenance staff to librarians and past-presidents. The assumption is that present and past staff like to keep in touch. The only people NOT listed are sessionals. How do sessionals feel when student representatives can vote on important issues in department meetings but sessionals cannot? How does it feel when a husband faculty member is introduced as such within a social situation, but his sessional wife standing next to him is not introduced at all?

Where do priorities lie when a secretary is told not to type the exam of a sessional, which was submitted ten days early, if he or she is too busy? What about a chair who never speaks to workers in contract positions between department meetings? What about universities or departments who hold retirement parties or ten- or twenty-year receptions for their staff but exclude sessionals from celebrating their benchmarks? Part-timers have many more stories to tell.

And for me, has it been easy? Not always. This fall, as I frantically made final preparations for the CAUT Status of Women Conference to be held in Regina and worked on the final editing process for this book, I asked rhetorically of my CAUT-SWC co-workers, "Why Am I So Tired"? This summer alone, I had to move my office three times, a frustrating exercise after teaching for twenty-six years. Conference-arranging was frantic. The articles for the book, while fascinating, were often depressing, especially for sessionals. And I thought of my salary. I was teaching a full load – five classes – but my husband, who had started teaching only a year before I did, was being paid four times what I brought home in pay.

It is often suggested that sessionals don't do research or work on committees. Since I had been putting in fourteen-hour days for weeks, often when I was neither teaching nor getting paid, I found this particularly ironic. My work was all university-related, involving the CAUT-SWC conference and the editing of this book. But to many academics, sessionals don't do research or work on committees. Therefore to them, I was apparently doing nothing!

To end on an upbeat note, however, I have found both projects fascinating and invigorating experiences. It has been uplifting to encounter interest and support from administration and the faculty association.

Some women have climbed to the highest peaks, scaling the Mount Everests of academe. Others, like me, have found the pathway more rocky, have felt the impact of the small stones and the larger stones hurled in our direction. These have inflicted the bruises, and perhaps even broken bones, that impede our embrace of the mountain. Hopefully, though, most of us can point to a career that has some verdant hills to wander, with *The Sound of Music* echoing through our minds.

NOTE

1 "The Vienna Tribunal: Women's Rights are Human Rights," 1994,
Augusta Films and National Film Board of Canada.

Princesses and Physicists: How Women in the Lab Shattered My Stereotypes

AMY ROWAT

"What's a young lady like you going to do with a big book like this?" This is my favourite reaction to my identity as a female physics student, uttered by the cashier at the university bookstore as I was purchasing my copy of *Quantum Waves*.

I am rather humoured by the sheer outrageousness of this comment and others like it. But I have been fortunate not to have had to deal with any sort of outright discouragement during my three years as an undergraduate physics student at Mount Allison University. In fact, I have found much support and encouragement to pursue my interests in physics. An excellent physics professor (one of many men instructors) provided a great source of motivation. And through my experiences in research, made available to me through gender-specific awards and scholarships, I was able to discover the satisfying creative aspects of physics at a critical time when I was contemplating the study of science. My undergraduate experience at university has thus generally been a very positive one.

There have been moments, however, when I have become very frustrated and discouraged. Dealing with my male classmates can be exhausting at times, particularly when my ideas are dismissed in a brash manner and I am left feeling incompetent and stupid. When the same ideas are suggested from the mouth of a male colleague, they suddenly take on a new sense of importance. I have never encountered a female physicist – professor or peer – who talks instead of listening and doesn't acknowledge my ideas. It wasn't until this past summer, when I worked in the research group of a female academic physicist, that I came to realize these subtle differences in communication.

Seeing and interacting with a real, live woman physicist was truly an empowering experience. I was able to witness, for the very first time, a woman who was not only an intelligent physics and biology professor but also had a family: a life outside of the lab. I realized that I was not the only one who had been discouraged with the intellectual dynamics of the physics community. She, along with other women in physics, had learned to adapt to such different styles of communication and had come to accept that respect can be a challenge to gain. This woman added an entirely new dimension to physics, banishing all of my preconceived images of physicists and expanding my perceptions of science. I have always felt that women can achieve in the same way as men, but still, the concept of a woman as a physicist was no more tangible than the possibility of my becoming a princess. Working with a female researcher, however, made me realize that it was truly possible. Never before had I had a role model with whom I could completely identify.

I was intrigued to learn more about women and physics and embarked on a project to interview Canadian academic women physicists. In the process of meeting and talking with these scientists, I discovered a group of inspiring people. I was strangely surprised to discover that each one is entirely unique – was I expecting all women physicists to fit into one mould? I discussed with them their experiences as women in physics: how they first became interested in science, their role models (or lack thereof), their preferred teaching style, the perceived "cut-throat" attitude of science, their treatment compared to that of male scientists, the objectivity of obtaining funding, the problems with physics education, and the future of physics as well as their personal dreams and ambitions. From this series of interviews, I gained many insights that are applicable not only to my understanding of the structure of science but also to my own life and potential career as a physicist.

To begin with, the very structure of a career in the sciences provides a major challenge for a woman. The vision of myself researching obsessively for the next ten years of my life so that I can publish as many papers as possible is not an attractive one. But this sort of effort is required at this stage of life if I hope to gain success – and an academic position – in my field. Having children during this process would be a huge burden, inhibiting the required "maximum performance." Some of the women I met had children and confessed that there is no easy way to fit motherhood into a career as an academic physicist. Taking time off at any point while trying to establish myself in science would be a challenge, whether I was searching for a job or finishing a graduate degree. Either way I would be at a disadvantage, losing valuable time during the important process of proving myself in the physics community.

Is there any alternative to this traditional structure? Some universities seem to be gradually becoming more flexible in the employment opportunities they offer. I have realized that this is essential if women are to increase their representation in the academic world.

Personally, I have not experienced the "partnering-of-physicists" phenomenon, but all of the women physicists I met are either married to or involved with men physicists. This trend makes it difficult for them to find employment in academic physics, especially since they tend to be younger than their male companions, who are generally more established in the field. Universities will have to acknowledge this need in the design of more flexible hiring procedures. The fact that job-sharing is still discouraged at most institutions creates an obstacle for partners who both want to pursue a career in physics. I have observed that it is often the woman who makes the sacrifice, either forfeiting her career in science or seeking a position elsewhere and committing more time to commute.

Part-time appointments represent another alternative, but unfortunately seem to be accompanied by a certain stigma – and lower pay. Yet it is certainly possible, and even more productive for some, to conduct research and teaching on a part-time basis. To disallow such positions denies the flexibility that is necessary for men and women who wish to spend more time raising a family. In a field that is already competitive and saturated with over-qualified people, the options of spending more family time or pursuing non-academic interests seem more attractive to me.

I am aware of the many challenges I face, should I choose to pursue an academic career in physics. Yet at the same time I am hopeful that some of these attitudes will have changed by the time I reach this stage in my career. I want to have children and I want to be able to spend time raising and enjoying them. Is it too much to ask to do physics as well?

While I am aware of these challenges ahead of me, I imagine that the rewards of an academic career could be very satisfying. To unearth new knowledge, to provide new insights, to affect the lives of others: these are all alluring objectives. Furthermore, I find the possibility of advancing the frontier of women in the field of physics to be a worthwhile goal. Women physics professors have made an indelible impression upon me, and I hope that someday I could provide the same sort of inspiration for other young women. Perhaps at some point in the future, students – and bookstore clerks – won't think twice about meeting a woman physicist.

Women have much to offer the physics community, not only in an intellectual way, but on a more profound level. We have the potential to change the entire style of physics, to broaden the field with new dimensions. The women physicists I know all strive to incorporate some sort of human element into their profession, whether branching into biological research, encouraging interdisciplinary collaborations, or valuing the social interactions within the international scientific community itself. These women professors also try to bring this "life" connection into the classroom. Their lessons provide a format for integrating different concepts and ideas, and they usually try to establish a personal rapport with their students. Within the lab, I sense how a woman's presence can alter the dynamics of the traditionally masculine environment, and provide a balance in social interactions. Physics shouldn't and doesn't have to reside in the domain of men.

I am left questioning the future of science. Can the traditional structure of academia ever change? I envision a more human and personable atmosphere: where universities are more liberal in granting freedom and flexibility to professors; where scientists are not judged solely on the basis of the first ten years of their research and the number of papers they have published; where people are not evaluated for a tenure-track position exclusively on the basis of their academic performance during one of the most maternally and paternally demanding periods of life. Granted, a healthier and more accepting attitude is already being achieved at some universities. Research is a major focus, but family life is also acknowledged. Some administrators accommodate women's needs, allowing part-time maternity leaves and joint husband-wife appointments. Science does not die in such an environment, nor is its reputation jeopardized. Rather, academics continue to prosper, as does the well-being of scientists themselves. We need to broaden the scrutinizing filter of physics if we are to incorporate more diversity into such a narrow field. Yet in such a self-perpetuating academic community, any sort of transition can evolve only with a conscious effort.

Different Parts of the Margin

JOAN SCOTT

Two disclaimers. After years spent on different parts of the margin of academic science, I don't claim the identity of academic woman. Also readers might expect to find a male-type career structure – a set of stages, with increasing access to institutional resources. There are only fragments of such structures in my story.

As is the case for many women in science of my age and older in Canada, I grew up and was educated elsewhere – in my case the United Kingdom. In the circles our family moved in, women stayed home if they had children, or, if without children, they might be office or retail workers. But my family had more ambitious plans for my sister and me. My mother and father were skilled eldest children from large families that had never sent a child to university. They married late and controlled their family size. Having no sons, my family fiercely prepared their two daughters to "get on," and propelled us towards the professions.

In World War II, there were food shortages and bombing raids. There were also newly flexible gender boundaries that were probably relevant for our future lives. We were evacuated from our coastal Suffolk home and lived for eighteen months in a series of friendly households in a Leicestershire village, with only occasional parental visits. From this we gained confidence and independence. Later, when we ran into some brick walls that thwarted our aspirations, a good head of steam from earlier days helped us to persist.

Once we were home again, our mother, who was always thrilled to receive bouquets of wildflowers, taught us their names. She used economic motivation to get us to sew and knit for ourselves. These activities all involve spatial and counting skills, as well as the use of templates, all of which are important in science. We raised rabbits to eat. We collected wild greenery for them – another route to learning about plants. We saw where little rabbits came from. When they were large enough for the table, we watched our grandfather, an old poacher, silently and elegantly kill them. We could recognize the internal organs. With all our experience in nature and cycles of life and death, it was easy for us to excel in biology.

The 1944 Education Act of a socialist government opened a pathway to university and the professions for children like us. We both passed the "Eleven Plus" exam, and attended the local grammar school.

This was an all-girls' school with a very stable history. The teachers, virtually all unmarried women, had worked there many years. All the informal and formal positions in this student society were filled by girls. The jock, the swot, the loud, the quiet, the bad, the beautiful, the form leaders, the prefects, the Head Girl … all were young women. In that atmosphere it is easier for girls to become achievers, especially in subjects like the sciences, and I did decently in mathematics and chemistry, and really well in physics and biology.

At sixteen years of age, each sex took different courses. The boys in the school next door took physics and chemistry separately, while the girls did the combined physics-with-chemistry, which was easier. This inequity was a product of sexist assumptions, which were then consequential, as they were fulfilled in our lives. It was assumed that girls would fail the more difficult separate courses. That was the first time I remember hearing explicitly that girls couldn't do science.

We then had two years to prepare for another public exam at age eighteen. I wanted to do botany, zoology, and English, but this combination was not permitted because it was seen as useless for "getting on," so I did botany and zoology, with a choice between chemistry and physics. As it was "well known" that girls couldn't do physics, I did chemistry and did it very poorly. It was harder for girls because we had done easier prerequisites.

As we entered these two years, there was another gender-related stunt to deal with. At this level numbers and economics dictated that the science classes would be co-ed. Girls would go to the next-door boys' school for chemistry, and boys would join the girls for biology.

While our parents were fiercely ambitious for us, no one at school encouraged either my sister or me to take challenging paths. It still amazes me that there was so little institutional encouragement and so much sexism from an all-female staff. Their class position was generally above ours, and perhaps they found it impossible to imagine that we could "get on" intellectually in the 1950s in the UK, because of our class origins.

For me, access to postsecondary education depended on getting a grant. University grants went only to people with three subjects or more at the Higher Level, and so there was a further consequence of the assumptions of the educators. With good grades in only two subjects, I would not be funded for university.

I think these details are worth exploring because they show the construction of success and failure for some young women as they go through the different stages of schooling. I have used the word choice, but as individual women we have only limited choices and no power to shape what those choices will be.

From about age seventeen, I was, "going out with," one of the chemistry teacher's prize students. Did I imagine at some level that marrying chemistry would make up for failing exams in chemistry? When I was finishing school in 1953, he was working on his PhD in London. Following a path now well-known to be disastrous for women, I moved for my boyfriend's career rather than for my own. Without a grant to go to university I took a two-year teacher-training course in London. I remember rejoicing in the recent gain by the National Union of Teachers of equal pay for women and men.

After the teacher-training, we married and, in the next seven years, moved for my husband's career five times, through three countries on two continents, and I had three different and interesting teaching jobs. Such moving, which has been required for the standard male-type science career, requires domestic support. No wonder that professional men usually have wives and that professional women often are NOT wives. It was not until we finished moving and I was pregnant with my second child, at the age of twenty-eight, that I started on the road to becoming a scientist myself.

We conceptualize the "juggling" of career and family. This suggests that individual women are in control of the juggling, an assumption that is flattering but not realistic. "Juggling" suggests that the items juggled are equivalent, but they are not. In fact, institutions such as universities have all the power. Only they can offer or withhold the educational and job opportunities that can make up a career. With their power they also shape families, through their time-demands. While institutions have much power to control family decisions, families have virtually no power over institutions. For instance, families can successfully help prepare young women for science careers with experience and skills that cross the gender barriers. But, consider young women who are trying to build equal relationships with their partners, while at the same time attempting to have careers equivalent to those of their male partners. Until very recently, the institutions, guided as they usually were by older men, made sexist decisions about what opportunities would be extended to women. Thus, institutions have successfully deprived young women of the real opportunities needed to realize their plans of equivalent careers.

After all of the moving, we settled in Newfoundland. I was diverted from school-teaching there by the low rate of pay and the religious domination of schools. However mental health and planning for my own income in the future decreed that I do something. I took a university course in math that would, my husband declared, be used as an indicator of whether or not I should register for a science degree. By 1968 I had an honours degree in biology, with which I moved into teaching in a Catholic high school.

I continued to be a good little wife, putting my husband's career first but finding it harder all the time. In 1969 I moved with the two children to Calgary with my husband for his sabbatical, and I spent my time gaining experience teaching grade XII biology. When I returned to Newfoundland, pregnant for the last time, this experience helped me obtain a university position teaching first year biology at Memorial University. This was then equivalent to Grade XII, which was not then taught in Newfoundland schools. It was 1970 and I was thirty-five years old.

It was a time when people holding PhDs were beginning to look for teaching jobs like mine. It was time to become qualified for the untenured job I held. I registered for a master's degree in biology, notwithstanding that I had a full-time job and three young children.

At that time tenure arrived effortlessly by today's standards. It was a time of insights, probably facilitated by the financial security that tenure brought me. The master's work became unrewarding, as my research organisms died out in a pond where they had been accessible from the shore, and I could not get help to work on other populations from a boat. Instead, I began to inch along a new library shelf – the one that carried books such as Mary Daly's *Beyond God the Father*. The renewed feminism of the times felt good to me and I began to conceptualize it as a foundation for an intellectual future that might be useful to others as well as myself. Simultaneously I re-evaluated my relationship with my scientist husband and brought the marriage to a close.

Before long, I was giving papers at conferences instead of listening to them. I began a study of science subject choice and achievement in high school girls in Newfoundland and was commissioned by the Science Council of Canada to produce a national equivalent. I moved to Toronto with my youngest daughter, then nine years old. Within a year I had completed a master of education degree and was registered for a doctorate, at the Ontario Institute for Studies in Education (OISE). At home, Grade XII was added to the educational system, and for that year no students entered first year. As a result, any professor who had a project away from Newfoundland was encouraged to stay away, which suited me very well.

I had started my time in Toronto on a sabbatical salary and spent the next three years on study leave with a one-third salary. It sounds impossible, but I sold my car and my RRSPs and also had a secret weapon. I had a special housing arrangement. Instead of living in a cheap and awful high-rise apartment, this single mom and her child lived in a splendid shared household with a total of six professional adults and three kids. When a rent increase was unavoidable, my increase was shared among the more affluent adults. I found the advertisement for that wonderful accommodation on the wall of the Toronto Women's Bookstore. Some of those people are still good friends of ours nearly two decades later.

For my thesis, I decided to study the careers of women university faculty in science who I thought might want to change the science workplace. Because of my inadequate sociological background I had to take numerous courses, mostly quite wonderful! It was a good time to be at OISE. While I was in Toronto, women's studies was created on our Memorial campus. Soon after I returned, I was teaching women's studies courses including one on women and science for half the year, and, in the other half, I taught biology. With the faithful involvement of my supervisor, I completed my thesis in the early 90s, within sight of mandatory retirement. The thesis offered an advance on discrimination theory as an explanation of the situation of women in science. It identified career practices that are experienced by both sexes, but which disadvantage women more than men. It showed that women predominate among those with no or low research grants, and that however hard those academic women work, their limited resources and consequent restricted options for organization of their time necessarily curtail their output. They can only spiral downwards in productivity.

In spite of extensive rewriting, so far I have not found a publisher for this work. One told me that all of his books that were critical of universities had bombed. He said that universities want to study everything but themselves.

I am still engaged in equity committees and teaching, but new challenges are upon us. This is the period of APEC, NAFTA, globalization, privatization, backlash, and the dominance of the corporate agenda. Our equity issues are being moved onto the back burner. The new "level playing field" issues are bringing a downward-levelling of Canada's labour standards and environmental regulation as well as, increasingly, our right to peaceful demonstrations. Universities are affected by these forces.

Some changes are positive, especially advances made by and for those who Sandra Harding has called the "other others." Racialized peoples, disabled people, lesbians, bisexuals and gays, and other marginalized people are organizing and increasingly making gains. They are being included under the equity rubric, in the intellectual activities of women's studies, and in new legislation. Lastly, in Newfoundland, a long battle against religious domination of schools appears to be coming to an end.

The New Roads Scholar or the Effect Of Hypergyny on Universities

STEVI (M.E.) STEPHENS

The term "roads scholar" is not my own. Dr. Rick Garvin, an archae-ologist and colleague, used it in conversation. At that time he was teaching courses in two universities and one college in southern Alberta. When I attended the CAUT Status of Women Conference in 1996, I was reminded of the term when I met women who were simultaneously teaching at several different colleges and universities.

Ironically, teaching five courses at three different colleges pays less and offers fewer benefits than teaching a three/two split as a term instructor at a single university. For example, contracts for single courses pay about $3,200 per course and give an instructor no benefits. A five-course contract for a nine-month period would probably pay about $30,000 and include benefits. Term contracts remunerate quali-fications and teaching experience but single-course contracts do not. Some community colleges pay as little as $1,700 per three-credit course.

Despite the origin of the term (the original Rhodes Scholars were men), it seems that the majority of "roads scholars" tend to be women. I personally traverse the Rocky Mountains twice a week. I do not live where I work, and this point should provide a graceful segue into an explanation of the hypergyny section of the title.

Why do I drive 300 kilometres twice a week? Why does my car bristle with so many deer whistles that it looks like a space ship? Why do I curse the elk that mob mountain highways in search of road salt? Why do I threaten to flatten the mountain goat that is wandering down the centre-line of the highway? Last year I consid-ered sacrificing a fatted calf to El Niño since it kept the highways clear of snow and blizzards. (Besides that calf would be one less specimen of fauna to avoid while driving!) Why do I do these things? I am the perfect example of someone who married hypergynously and is reaping the consequences. My POSSLQ (sociology jargon, pronounced possel-que, person of opposite sex sharing living quarters) has a better paying full-time job.

Hypergyny is a marriage system in which women tend to marry up in socioeconomic status. In North America women are expected to marry men who are older, wealthier, and better educated. This marriage system has resulted in a form of systemic discrimination for academic women. Systemic discrimination is a form of discrimination that is not necessarily intentional but is a side effect of the social system in which it occurs. In our society women are expected to marry, and when women who pursue academic careers marry older professional men, this pattern has some negative consequences. (On the positive side, one might note that senior communities are becoming matriarchies as a result of this marriage pattern. All of the men in them are either dead are too old to wield power.)

In the late 1970s I took part in a lively discussion in the faculty lounge at Simon Fraser University. One of the education faculty members mentioned reading a study of career success among academics in North America. It concluded that the major factor that negatively influenced career advancement was a professional spouse. The rationale was that when both spouses have professional careers, an academic does not have the freedom and mobility to negotiate a higher status. Since women in North America are expected to marry up, the negative consequences of having a professional spouse fall most heavily on women. In our discussion we considered the many married academic couples of our acquaintance and finally concluded that the study was probably accurate.

If spouses are in the same field, the husband may have a position in the only university in the area. At one time there were rules against nepotism which prevented spouses from working in the same department. There are still negative views about married couples in the same department. Colleagues fear that a married couple may exert undue influence on departmental decisions. There is often an unspoken but strongly felt idea that two salaries should support two families and not enrich a single nuclear unit. In addition there are fears that married women will demand pregnancy leaves and special schedules to allow them to care for children.

If a woman marries a professional in a different area, she will face some similar and some different problems. There is a prejudice against enriching the families of doctors, dentists, architects, for example, by giving a married woman a full academic salary. These professional husbands also have vested interests in remaining where they are. If his wife can't find a full-time or satisfying job in the area, it's a rare professional husband who can pull up stakes to follow a wife to a job. The usual compromise tends to be made on economic grounds. The wife takes a part-time job and tends to be exploited since "she doesn't need the money anyway."

This situation can exacerbate other problems. I once pointed out to my family that the southern tradition of educating daughters was to ensure that they would "marry well." My mother's response was, "and often." This was her less than subtle way of referring to my own poor marital record. Perhaps my focus on the societal strains for academic women in a hypergynous marriage situation is really just a rationalization for my own lousy track record. However, the combination of being exploited at work and bearing a double shift of work at home is tough on any marriage. How serious is a wife's job? When I was married to an architect, my husband's boss once introduced me to some clients by saying, "This is Peter's wife. She has a doctorate in anthropology. Isn't that cute?"

The results of combining professional and wifely status tend to be far-reaching. Married women tend to end up in the part-time and term positions at colleges and universities. This seems to lead to a mind set that part-time and term positions are the preserve of women. Now, many of the women in part-time and term positions are divorced parents or single women. The justification for exploitation – she doesn't really need the money – is no longer relevant. However, an unfortunate truth is that once a person proves that she can be exploited, she will be.

Obviously the economic systems and family systems of the world are changing. Are these changes influencing the world of higher education? From the personal perspective of someone who began university teaching in 1968, I would say, definitely. Very few of the enticements that lured me into an academic career still exist. I loved the opportunities to discuss ideas with professionals in varied fields. I loved my area of research and loved getting students excited about anthropology. Much of this has changed. Now I start my lectures by warning students that the economic rewards of anthropology and an academic life are very sparse. Enrol in anthropology in order to be interesting at cocktail parties but do not hope to make a career of it. Discussions with fellow academics are almost impossible. We are all overwhelmed by teaching and paper work.

The academic life has definitely changed. We have all made fun of the old professor who lugged out his notebook of cracked and yellowed pages and read the same lectures to bored students. The more he bored the students, the happier he became. He had tenure. Bored students meant smaller enrolments and more time for him to pursue personal interests. That world is gone. The old criteria of research, teaching, and community commitment are no longer the criteria by which faculty are judged. Tenure is becoming an anti-quated notion. The modern institution of higher learning takes pride in being flexible and responsive to the needs of employers. Such flexibility is only possible when faculty members are on contract. They may be easily replaced as needs or whims of administrators change. Last year I distributed an article by James Traub from the October 20 issue of *the New Yorker* about franchise universities and their "McDegrees" to students in one of my classes. When we dis-cussed the article the students were appalled and felt that degrees should confer more than earning power. However, a copy was sent by a university administrator to the college president with a little yellow sticky reading, "There are some very good ideas in this article."

On my bleaker teaching days I feel that I spend half of my life trying to outsmart the administration so that I can teach my students and the other half trying to outsmart the students so that I can teach them. There is a new emphasis in colleges and universities; my present college has people in charge of "marketing." How does this influence the allocation of resources? Here is an example. Last year around Christmas time most of the faculty were frantically tied to their computers in an attempt to get grades calculated before the holiday. The staff of our public relations office used the e-mail to send faculty and staff a Christmas card as an attachment. The graphics on the card were very sophisticated. In fact, they were so sophisticated that the computer of any faculty member who attempted to open the attachment did not have the capacity to handle the graphics. Those computers froze. This did not help in meeting grade deadlines but it says a great deal about university priorities. Which departments have the expensive computers?

Universities are now about business. In the summer I teach at a university that has an interesting summer-school policy. If a course enrolment does not reach seventeen students, the contract to the instructor is negated and the course is cancelled. It takes tuition from twelve students to pay the salary of the instructor. It takes the tuition of an additional five students to pay the administrative costs and overhead for the course. Tuition for any students beyond the mini-mum of seventeen is sheer profit for the university. I have considered writing to the university president and suggesting that the profits from additional students beyond the basic seventeen should be split equally between the university and the instructor of the course. The instructors do much of the work and take most of the risks. Why shouldn't they share in the benefits?

Our students are also changing. More than half are women and many are mature students. Most students have jobs and many have jobs and families. Women are now gaining the education needed to take over academic positions. This could be wonderful but academic positions are also changing. As tenured professors retire, newly tenured professors rarely replace them. Instead, academic jobs are becoming contract jobs. As women move into these positions the status and pay are dropping.

As institutions of higher learning become more market-oriented, the number of "roads scholars" can only increase. There are positive aspects of this phenomenon. For example, women in academic positions provide role models for women students. However, this kind of "feed-back loop," with more women academics meaning more women students, could eventually lead to the redefinition of universities as part of the "pink collar ghetto." And, what happens to men in this situation? Where will they fit in the new economic and educational world order?

I will end this article by noting that "times, they are a'changing." Education is changing. The economy is changing and gender relations are changing. At present it seems that the economy is directing change. It is clear that the old system of universities and gender roles is not viable but … is it not possible for wise people to examine the new economic order and devise a university system to deal with the new realities?

A final word of advice. Remember, a horse is only as good as his feet and a car is only as good as its tires. Check tread wear often and drive carefully.

Left Out in the Cold ... Who? Me?

CAROL STOS

When I first saw the call for contributions to this book on Canadian women in academia, my immediate gut reaction was one of personal denial. "That does not include me," I thought. "I have my PhD, I am doing what I love, teaching full time at university, and I have a tenure-track position." But I could not stop thinking about the topic, and I soon found myself jotting down notes for this article.

In many ways, I think, my experiences are those of other married women of my generation. When I was doctoral candidate, having just completed the written and oral comprehensive exams at the end of 1976, my husband and I had to choose between staying in the city where I was doing my degree (where neither of us had any immediate prospects of employment) and moving to a much smaller community in order for my husband to take advantage of an opportunity to establish himself in the career he truly wanted. We were aware of the potential problems that a move would present for fulfilling my aspirations, but my work at the time seemed portable, his job opportunity definitely was not, and so we moved. Five years later, after two extensions and one baby, I completed the dissertation and received my degree.

For the first couple of years, with an active toddler at home and a full-time retail business in which my husband and I were equal partners, just having the doctorate was enough. I did not actively seek a position in my field, knowing full well that there were no openings at the local university. Nor did I consider applying for any of the positions advertised at other Canadian universities: most were one- or two-year appointments, and having been on the fringe of academia while working on my dissertation (and running a business, having a child, and doing volunteer work in our community), I did not have the necessary teaching experience or publications for tenure-stream positions. Besides, we had returned to our home town, where both sets of parents lived, our business was well established and thriving, and we had bought a house. How could I ask my husband and partner (or myself, for that matter) to abandon the security of a profitable livelihood, our home, and our son's doting grandparents to leapfrog from one temporary position to another, hoping against hope that one of them would turn into something permanent?

Fortunately, although entirely coincidentally, I had made the acquaintance of the faculty in my discipline at the university, and when one of the professors fell ill and needed a six-month leave of absence, I was asked to substitute for him. That led to eight years of part-time teaching, until finally there was a retirement and I was able to apply for a full-time position. After three years of limited-term contracts, I was offered a tenure-stream position and also became chair of the department. This year I was awarded tenure and, as well, I am now vice-dean (anglophone) of social sciences and humanities. So, despite the difficulties and delays in my career that resulted from a mutual and pragmatic decision to follow my husband's opportunities since they presented themselves first, I am at last doing what I have always wanted to do. I think that I am extraordinarily fortunate. The granddaughter of Finnish immigrant farmers, the daughter of two people who never managed a high-school education because of the Depression, I am now a university professor. But ...

I remember, as an undergraduate, that the lone female professor in my department (a tenured PhD, an excellent instructor, and a scholar with a profound and incisive grasp of her subject) was invariably addressed as "Mrs" while not one of her male colleagues was ever "Mr" but always "Doctor" or, at the very least, "Professor." At the time, it did not occur to me to ask my professor if she would have preferred a more academic form of address, nor did she ever ask her students to use her professional title. Even after I received my own doctorate, this was not an issue for me, perhaps because as a sessional instructor working full time outside the university, I somehow felt that I was not really a part of the academic milieu. But ever since I have been teaching full time, I request that my students – those who are uncomfortable using my first name – call me either "Professor" or "Doctor" Stos. My son's friends, the serviceman who repairs the washing machine, and telemarketers call me "Mrs Stos."

I recall being told by a colleague, several years ago, how nice it was that my husband "let" me teach. Because he was a generation older than I, from a cultural background which encourages the assumption of male superiority and authority, and because I knew that there was no question of having had to seek my husband's permission to pursue my academic interests, I merely smiled in response. This same colleague remarked on another occasion, in discussing a textbook by a female author which we both preferred for a first-year course, that yes, it was a very good book and women, of course, were best suited for writing works at this introductory level. Because it truly was an excellent text and because – given the source – I was more amused than angered by his comment, I smiled (rather ironically, this time) and agreed, emphatically that *she* had, indeed, written a fine book.

Not long ago, as I was standing in the doorway of a colleague's office speaking to her, I greeted a professor from another department, whom I know very casually, as he strolled down the hallway. As he passed by, he returned my greeting and patted me on the head. It was a completely innocuous gesture, and totally inappropriate. I was speechless with shock, and surprised by the vehemence of my reaction.

And then there was the time that the chair of the committee for the teaching excellence award extolled the maternal qualities of a female candidate, implying that these attributes were an asset to teaching, but said not one word about the other (male) candidates' parenting skills. I suggested that if we were to consider all candidates equally, then we should not be so unfair as to not discuss the teaching skills of each person, male or female, in light of their parenting skills. The chair was very startled and quickly assured the committee that he had meant his comments to be construed in only the most favourable way, as an indication of how the candidate's professional and personal lives admirably complemented one another. Interestingly, we never did discuss the men's paternal qualities, but the image of "Mom" did squeeze in along side the female academic *persona*, and while I do not believe that this impression cost her the award, somehow there seemed to be an implication that this other dimension to her life diminished rather than strengthened her professional role. But, speaking up and drawing the committee's attention to this patronizing attitude counted as a small victory, for me, at least.

Is it a disadvantage to be a female in academia? Yes, insofar as it is also generally a disadvantage to be female in a society that is defined by patriarchal systems and values. Most of the twists and turns in the circuitous route that I have taken to reach this point in my life resulted from choices I had to make as a woman: to marry, to have a child, to live with rather than apart from my husband and son despite the limitations those personal decisions imposed on my career. I do not know how I could have made those choices any differently, given who I am. And I have no easy answers for all the other women who are grappling with these same choices in the years to come.

However, if there are not immediate and wide-ranging solutions to offer to help us all come in from the cold, I do see that we must continuously work to counteract the subtle – and not so subtle – discrimination and stereotyping that we all run up against as we go about living our lives, in and out of academia. As I acquire more experience, I appreciate more and more the determination and strength of my female friends; I value the wisdom and courage of those older women who have been and still are my mentors, and I admire the energy and fearlessness of younger women colleagues, all of whom continue to make significant contributions to their professions despite the obstacles they encounter. And I am encouraged by the number of men I meet who are more sensitive to the inequities we face and are willing to work towards a better balance for us all. I am still surprised when someone judges me first as a *woman* and not as a *person*, but they are even more surprised when I point that out. We must speak up for ourselves and for each other. It is the first of many steps that we must all take together to get out of the tundra.

A Few Things Learned

MARILYN TAYLOR

For twelve years (1986–98), I was actively involved in improving life and opportunities for women within my own university, through the Fédération des Professeurs des Universités du Quebéc, and through the Canadian Association of University Teachers.[1] At the university level, during the first third of this period, I participated, with others, in establishing university infrastructures and developing policy to foster change for women. During the last third of the period, most of this work has been dismantled. On one hand, this is a debilitating loss. On the other hand, it is provocation to reflect, to learn from our experiences and to develop stronger, more durable initiatives. Our efforts to change the university have created tremendous opportunities to learn how it works and how better to approach fostering change. It has been important for me to focus what I have learned. I offer six salient themes generated from my own story in the hope that they may be useful to others also.

Stay mindful of the big picture and the size of the project. I must remember that the last twelve years have been only a small portion of the period during which people, primarily women, have been struggling for fair treatment of women in society. It has taken 100 years for women to be present in significant numbers, as students and, as a significant minority, faculty. Further, not only is the pattern of progress very gradual but it seems to have an "ebb and flow" pattern. Each period of advancement is followed by outstanding retrenchment; hence the image, waves of feminism. The long view not only offers hope that progress toward fairness is not vanquished by any given downturn but also suggests that different activities will be productive. Tough times force us to reflect and re-evaluate. These are very helpful activities, since it seems that opportunity favours the prepared mind! Recently, I have worked with colleagues[2] to launch a new electronic journal, *Strategies*, in November 1998, for just this purpose.

The gradual and laborious pace of change for women reminds us that we are working on a vast project, far beyond our first imaginings. Gender inequities are deeply embedded in every corner of the work place and in our private lives. The expectations of both men and women, often tacit but always powerful, are still largely consistent with the millennia-old culture of gender inequality. Akin to what seems at first the simple task of removing a tree from the garden, the project ends in a massive upheaval due to the invisible root system that reaches everywhere. Change means chaos, rude awakenings, and pain. Strong resistance and powerful, often irrational, adversarial reactions are inevitable and unavoidable.

Until changes are embedded fundamentally in the life of the university, don't stop bouncing the ball or the ball will stop bouncing. A series of common initiatives across universities in Canada, such as status of women, sexual harassment, and employment equity offices, and status of women committees in faculties and unions) were and remained adjunct to the main theatres of university business. While these initiatives were important as spaces in which to develop more integral changes in the academy, they were also mistaken for real change. Many of us relaxed as we saw people with dedicated dossiers "on the case." Without the consistent presence of people, particularly the constituencies of women, these impulses lose their momentum. Political concerns and pressures, such as those that generated equity initiatives in the first place, drive the priorities of institutional leaders who wish to remain in their positions. When the pressures against equity exceed those for it, these people will turn predictably in the politically rewarding direction. We are too early in the journey to retire from consistent vigilance and efforts to exert and maintain influence.

Be ready to find allies everywhere and adversaries anywhere. I have learned that there is a vast range of responses to equity initiatives and that stereotypical expectations about support and opposition often do not materialize. It is facile and misleading to assume, for example, that men will resist changes and that women will affirm them or that women's organizations will support women and unions will not. I found that some male colleagues in unions are committed and effective advocates. Rather than being simply members of categories, allies are likely to have such qualities as: confidence in themselves and their positions in the university; respect for fairness; a strong commitment to inquiry; and a genuine love of the university with concern for its future and its contribution to the wider world. Women may have an edge on valuing fairness for women since empathy is not required. But we do not have a monopoly on it. Further, for us, it can be counteracted by fears, insecurities, hopelessness, and intense survival struggles that come with the prodigious task of establishing our own thematic sense of entitlement to be in the academy, not only as students, but as professors and leaders. Being simultaneously a member of one or more additional disadvantaged groups intensifies these challenges. It is important to approach everyone in the academy as a potential ally first and leave it to *them* to choose membership in the opposition.

Respect differences among us concerning our readiness to take risks in being active. For women in the university, the costs of, and margins for, action are different. Faculties and departments across the university differ enormously in their climate for women as faculty, as staff, or as students, and in their readiness to foster change and recognition for women as women. In general, this variety corresponds to the proportion of women and men within a given unit or organization, as Rosabeth Moss Kantor (1977) has observed. As a faculty member in a social science department identified with social change, as a visible actor in change, I risk much less within my own academic unit, where personnel decisions originate, than do my female colleagues who are appointed in units where there are few women.

Spend at least as much time and effort building understanding of changes as "pushing" for them. Policy changes won on the floors of faculty councils, senates, and union councils are very helpful achievements. However, changes will only endure if a critical mass of the members of the academy understand these policies and take ownership of them. This is a long-term investment involving the development of more refined cultural norms, expectations, and values within the academy as reflected in the university's everyday practices. These changes are likely to be achieved over a longer period of time but are also more likely to last for subsequent generations of women.

If we're in for the long haul, make it fun, restoring, and energizing! It is easy to succumb to a dismal outlook when we are struggling so hard for changes in things that hurt us so much. While we will experience discouragement, as a thematic outlook, it is devastating to the project.

Cynicism and hopelessness are de-energizing and unattractive to people who could bring new energy to the work. It is easy to rivet our attention on the people who are aggressive, even unscrupulous, opponents. Again, while we might need to obsess about the villains for a time, this focus distracts us from our ultimate purpose – productive revisions in our own ways of approaching the work, new opportunities for action, and appreciation and enjoyment of the intelligence, creativity, and humanity of other colleagues. I am grateful to have met exciting, talented, and delightful people in my own university and across the country in working for equity. It is possible and important that our project be highlighted with joy, humour, and friendship.

My experiences in working for change for women have been punctuated by astonishment, anguish, and anger, to mention only a few of the feelings associated with the work. However, I have also benefited as much as I have contributed. I am wiser about institutional change, having seen what works and what does not. I am less fearful about negative consequences, having lived through them and survived. I am more mature in my expectations and in my behaviour under duress. Finally, I am more confident in the importance of the project, that of fostering change toward equitable conditions for all in our universities.

NOTES

1 As an instructor in a course entitled Women in Organizations, my name was suggested to my faculty association as a possible representative to the Comité sur la condition des femmes at La Fédération des Associations des Professeurs du Québec. I accepted and served as a member of this committee and its chair for several years. Simultaneously, I chaired an ad hoc committee of my faculty association to develop proposals for negotiating procedures for employment equity into the collective agreement. I was then invited to join the Status of Women committee of the Canadian Association of University Teachers, where I served as a member and chair (1990–93). I served on advisory and appointment committees for offices of employment equity and as the status of women advisor at Concordia University, and I chaired an Advisory Committee to the Academic Vice-Rector on Gender Equity in Matters Academic.

2 Feminist Stratégies Féministes (www.unb.ca/par-l/NEW/strategies) is an interdisciplinary, bilingual, scholarly, electronic journal associated with the PAR-L network headed by Michèle Ollivier (Ottawa) and Wendy Robbins (UNB). It was generated collaboratively between PAR-L and a SSHRC-funded research network project involving Linda Christiansen-Ruffman (St. Mary's), Francine Descarries (UQAM), Keith Louise Fulton (Winnipeg), Carmen Lambert (McGill), and myself (Concordia).

Pioneering at the End
of the Twentieth Century

DOROTHY R. TOVELL

My grandparents were pioneers, leaving their established communities in Ontario, England, and the United States and coming to Alberta to build new lives and participate in building new communities. We no longer speak of Alberta in 1900 as unoccupied, having belatedly acknowledged the Aboriginal people who had lived here for centuries, but we know that the people like my grandparents, of European descent, did bring with them different cultures and ways of living in what was to them new territory. In this way, women may bring to our universities (relatively new territory for us in large numbers) aspects of women's culture and introduce new ways of living in the institution. The world of work is changing for all of us, and expectations of one secure job for a lifetime are disappearing for both men and women. What does this mean for women in academe? How might we pioneer new ways for women, especially, but also for men?

My last seven years have been an adventure in constructing work at the University of Alberta out of my own interests, skills, and abilities. In some ways, I feel like a pioneer, finding ways to be authentically myself in a setting suffused with patriarchal values and with well-established procedures and expectations of conformity. I believe that the choices I have made are good evidence of women's self-determination: we function within the limitations of "the system" as it presently exists and at the same time attempt to change it. I also suspect that I and other women developing similar unconventional career paths may turn out to be good role models for the next generation of women in the academy.

I entered graduate school in the mid 1960s, not because I had long-term career goals but because I thought the work would be interesting. I earned a PhD in biochemistry and spent three years in post-doctoral positions, a standard pattern for science graduates of that time. I then chose not to seek a faculty position because I did not want to commit the time and energy necessary for a successful career at that level. Later, after many years as a research associate, first at Queen's University and then at the University of Alberta, it became clear to me that I did not have the intense personal curiosity about biochemistry that I needed for fulfilling work within the boundaries of that discipline. I did, I think, contend with a fairly typical collection of experiences of gender stereotyping, but it was primarily my decreasing interest in the subject area that led me to resign from my position as a research associate in 1990.

Over a period of a year and half I was able to put together a composite of part-time positions that added up to "full-time work" at the University of Alberta. I had been afraid that I had no transferable skills or knowledge but I was pleased to discover that a PhD in biochemistry and many years as a research associate provided credentials and expertise I could employ elsewhere on campus.

I now teach two courses in women's studies as a sessional instructor, the introductory course and one called Women and Science. I spend part of each day in a research group in the Department of Medical Microbiology and Immunology preparing research reports, assisting with grant proposals and administrative tasks where my scientific knowledge is needed. I am the part-time coordinator of WISEST (Women in Scholarship, Engineering, Science, and Technology), a committee of the vice-president (research and external affairs), which has a mandate to increase the number of women wherever they are underrepresented at the University of Alberta. My responsibility is research and development: obtaining research funding, carrying out the projects we do, and supervising the part-time staff who coordinate our programs of conferences and summer jobs for young women interested in the sciences and engineering.

What I do in each of my roles is related to and facilitates my work in the others. Being present in a laboratory setting, for example, means that I remain current in my perception of how science is done in order to teach in women's studies. As I am in touch with science students, I can more easily contact volunteers to serve as role models and instructors for WISEST conferences. I also am readily available to female students in the lab who wonder if some of their experiences may be gender-related, and can respond to their questions out of my understanding of feminist theory that is deepened and refined as I continue to teach in women's studies.

My growing interest in women and the culture of science has reassured me that I do have the curiosity, ability, and commitment to carry out research, specifically on women in science and their careers (I have even used personal funds to cover some costs). I am intrigued to realize that my present work encompasses administration, research, and teaching, a mix similar to the mix of responsibilities of a full-time academic. Perhaps I have chosen coordinates rather than a matched suit, but I think I am well dressed!

A university is a large enough institution to offer more than one possibility, which is convenient for me because I don't have to travel across the city to go from job to job. Occupying different ranks simultaneously, working in different offices, and seeing the campus from more than one vantage point all contribute to a broader perspective on the university. This has worked well for me although I appreciate that these perceptions can be attained in other ways. I know from my own experience that treatment of sessionals, as regards salary levels and invitations to attend staff meetings, for example, is different in Biochemistry and Women's Studies, although in both cases I've been fortunate to have been given notice of teaching assignments well in advance.

My income is lower than it would have been had I continued in my full-time position, although the net amount is not drastically reduced. The major consequence of not being a full-time employee is the lack of benefits: I do not contribute to a pension plan, I pay my own health care premiums and have no dental insurance, and I pay fees to use facilities at the University of Alberta such as the physical education building. On the other hand, since I am not represented by either the academic or non-academic staff associations, I pay no association dues. It has been suggested that I could become a "full-time employee" by negotiating to be hired by one department and seconded to another, but I find I am really not interested in being fitted into a recognizable category in the institution, even one that is highly valued and rewarded. Funding for my research and travel to meetings to make presentations comes through WISEST, which simply means that my freedom to choose research topics is limited to work within the fairly broad mandate of WISEST. The funds we raise for WISEST projects must include my salary.

Have I sacrificed security and potential advancement for freedom and flexibility? I think it depends on how one defines security and advancement. Much of my security comes with the confidence that I can do a variety of things in a number of different places. Certainly more "external" security comes with tenured appointments, but since I have several positions, losing or leaving any one of them would cost me only some of my work and income. As for advancement, it is highly unlikely that I would be considered for a tenure-track position, should I ever change my mind and apply for one. I am sure, however, that the level and extent of my responsibilities have increased over the past seven years even though it is difficult to define what I do according to the university's classification system. I have met many new challenges and had opportunities to learn and grow, although these have not necessarily been reflected in increased pay or recognizable status. By not serving on committees in traditional roles I have few voting rights at the university, and I recognize that having indirect influence may be seen as taking a subordinate role. But I believe I do have other opportunities to make an impact on the thinking of staff and students.

My next frontier will be to extend my work into the world outside the university. I intend to find ways to use my knowledge and skills to benefit other members of the community more directly and immediately. The way my work is presently organized should make it relatively easy to spend some of my time away from the university while retaining most, if not all, of my connections. I am looking forward to a new stage in my adventure.

Happy People Have No Story?[1]

CÉCYLE TRÉPANIER

"Happy people have no story." According to this adage, perhaps I have nothing to say. But I know there are reasons for the satisfaction I get from my work. My happiness comes from who I am and how I live. I attribute it to luck, to the quality of certain people I have met along the way, to my modest ambitions, and to my freedom – although it has a price.

I chose a male discipline without knowing it. As I was somewhat timid by nature, my parents always gave me the impression that the world was mine. For them the key was education. We were an ordinary family with rural roots. I can still hear my mother scolding one of my uncles who maintained that education was not necessary for a girl. I was very lucky to have such open-minded and supportive parents.

In 1971, when I started my studies for a bachelor's degree in geography at the Université du Québec à Trois-Rivières (UQTR), the department head greeted my arrival with a "hurray." I didn't really understand why, until I realized that in a group of about forty new students there were only five girls. Even today I find it a bit surprising that none of the girls became a friend. In 1974, with the aid of a grant from the Canadian Mortgage and Housing Corporation (CMHC), I decided to do a master's degree at Université Laval in Quebec City. I was the only girl in my year, and there were only a handful in the whole geography graduate program but I didn't know any of them. All the professors were men. At the end of my studies in 1977, one of them, Dean Louder, offered me my first job in geography as a research assistant in Louisiana.

Professor Louder, a native of the United States, was taking a sabbatical year in Louisiana. He was moving his whole family, wife and four children, to a suburb of New Orleans. He offered me the chance to help him with his research, which had two main thrusts. The first entailed a study of residents of the Vieux-Carré, the historic district of New Orleans. The second was to develop and administer a questionnaire to the Cajuns living in an urban area, Westwego, a municipality on the "West Bank" of New Orleans, and in Lafayette, the official capital of contemporary French Louisiana. This Louisiana experience changed my life. First, it made me appreciate the special role of Quebec in North America and the difficulty of being francophone anywhere else on the North American continent. Next, it gave me the desire to continue my studies because now I had a taste of Louisiana. It also changed my research interests. From urban geography I moved over to cultural geography. The experience also made me realize the need to learn English if I wanted to be able to carry out my work and understand the point of view of people who could not express themselves in French. Finally, I discovered that it is an advantage to be a woman rather than a man when doing interviews. No one ever refused me an interview. A young male colleague, whom I was training to do interviews, occasionally encountered problems even though he was very kind and small in stature, thus non-threatening.

Once I had decided to continue my studies, it was Dean Louder who helped me choose the ideal university for me. So in 1979, I started studying with some of the great American cultural geographers, including Peirce Lewis and Wilbur Zelinsky, at Pennsylvania State University. It was located only one day's drive from Quebec. At Penn State all the twelve professors were men, but there were about twenty female graduate students, a third of them doing a PhD. They were a very convivial bunch. In fact, this spirit also extended to our male colleagues since five couples in the department got married. I was in this group. Neither my own thesis nor my husband's progressed as quickly as we would have wished. For my part, two summers of field work instead of one, the fact that I was working in English and the need for some extensive cartographic work delayed my graduation. My husband neglected his thesis more and more to become a computer wizard. Eventually he found a paying job that allowed us to live modestly even when my grant from the Quebec government was finished. When his work situation deteriorated in the winter of 1984–85, I decided to look for a job. I wrote first to my alma mater, Université Laval, to let them know my intentions. They advised me there would be no position open before the following year. At the meeting of the Association of American Geographers, I took the bull by the horns and introduced myself to Professor Zawatsky of the University of Manitoba, who had given a paper. I had applied to this university for a temporary position. He told me later that he was on the selection committee. I must have made a good impression for, after a telephone interview with the acting department head, Richard Foster, I was offered the job.

In August 1985, with an American husband and the first draft of my doctoral thesis in my pocket, I arrived at the University of Manitoba as an instructor for a year. It was a tremendous experience for me, since I had never lived in Canada outside of Quebec. As one always does during the first year of teaching, I worked like crazy. I taught three courses in each semester. There were a few female graduate students in the department and a female cartographer, but no woman professor. I was given a warm welcome and I fitted in easily. They even offered my husband a position in the Department's computer laboratory for the winter semester. Since geography is a multidisciplinary science, I never considered being married to a geographer a disadvantage. On the contrary, sharing a general geography culture but different working interests presents an ideal situation. I have very good memories of this year in the west.

The following spring a permanent position became available at Université Laval. I applied for it, went for an interview, and was offered the position. My husband had a job offer a few weeks later from a private company in Winnipeg, but since I had already accepted the job at Université Laval, we moved to Quebec.

In August 1986 I joined one of the largest geography departments in North America. Of twenty-seven professors, two of us were women. We are now three although the number of professors has dropped to twenty-four. This semester we have one woman and two men as instructors. Our department recently adopted an employment policy favourable to women. It should bear fruit when the next few positions open up.

As for me, I obtained my doctorate in 1988, partly thanks to Benoît Robitaille, department head at that time, and some of my colleagues in cultural geography. They gave me a reduced teaching load for the first year. I also benefited from the help and expertise of the employees of the cartographic laboratory in the design and completion of the maps I needed for my thesis. My colleagues in cultural geography, especially Dean Louder and Eric Waddell, included me right away in their research team and in their teaching. Also in 1988, I was awarded the "Globe Professor," a prize given by the undergraduate students in the department for quality of teaching and availability to students. The year 1988 was really great for me!

I obtained my tenure in 1991 without tears or gnashing of teeth. Although I was integrated into a research team, I made some personal grant applications to Quebec and Canadian funding agencies. My efforts were finally rewarded by the Social Sciences and Humanities Research Council of Canada (SSHRC) in 1992. This allowed me to do some new and intensive fieldwork during my sabbatical year in 1992–93. I studied Acadians in the Maritime Provinces, another corner of French North America, and with this work I was able to consolidate my reputation as a researcher. Since I am not skilled in political games, my professional ambitions are modest. They are limited to doing my best as a professor and researcher and above all to enjoying it to the best of my ability.

No fairy tale is perfect, however. An early menopause diagnosed in 1989 put an end to our dream of having children. A year later I was separated, and divorced in 1994. So I had a lot of time available for my work. I have enormous admiration for women who can successfully combine their roles of mother, teacher, researcher, and sometimes even administrator. I am impressed when I watch them. They appear blessed with an energy that I do not possess. I have been in love again since 1995 and consider myself a lucky and happy woman.

NOTE

1 I would like to thank Dr Alexander H. Paul, Department of Geography, University of Regina, for the English translation of my article.

And the Wisdom to Know the Difference

SUSAN M. TURNER

I begin this account of my experiences as a sessional in the Canadian philosophy market at a point when I have begun to consider employment outside the academy. Whether things will go better out there than they have in here is hard to say. One thing seems certain to me, however. They cannot possibly go worse. Perhaps this is naïve of me. But I don't think so.

For one thing, I would no longer have to do personal combat with so many post-pubescent "alpha" male students. This has been the most startling, treacherous, and soul destroying part of teaching. As a graduate student teacher, I never really noticed them among my pupils though in hindsight, they were there. In my first year of full-time professional teaching, where I was the first and only resident woman in the Philosophy Department of a small prairie university, one of my male students sent me dominatrix material by e-mail thinking I would be amused and after all, hadn't we become friends? He also asked, in front of a whole class, why I was not wearing any make-up when I had worn some the class before. That year, my office faced a large bulletin board in the hallway upon which some of the male honours students had posted a "joke" ad which promoted a logic tutorial called "Debbie Does Quodlibet." There were a number of criteria that one had to fulfill in order to receive the tutorial. For example, one had to have "well-hung proofs."

When one of the female students complained to the males, she was told that if I could post a notice on my office door announcing the formation of a women's reading group in philosophy, then he could post his porno ad on the department announcement board. I complained to the chair who said the board would be taken back for department business only. But that never happened while I was there. There was also the "joke" ad in the Philosophy Department general office to the effect that anyone sick and tired of our government sending money to countries where people are starving in order to help them out should instead donate money to an organization that would work to stop the government from doing that. After all, the ad urged, if these starving people are so badly off, why don't they just move? Instead, the ad continued, they prefer to whine and why should the rich help the poor anyway? We should stop being such suckers. I complained vigorously about this "notice" because I believed it constituted hate propaganda. WRONG. "It was only a joke." When I mentioned it to the chair and connected it with the "Debbie" notice in the hall, I was told that "boys will be boys" and that I had overreacted. I was not hired for a second year.

I did get another position, however, where the testosterone was more or less dripping down the classroom walls. I changed myself for this job – the way I dressed, did my hair, walked, talked – and so I was no longer free. I no longer wanted to be interpreted as "Susan the Warm" (read "available"). I was now Professor (or Dr) Turner the Cold (read "Authoritative"). The ratio of males to females was a lot higher here than it had been at my previous appointment. This gave the males an advantage that they began to press right away. With my new business-like persona, I was the enemy. I was regularly insulted, shouted at, and threatened by the department's male honours students both in class and in my office for almost four months. The firmer I became regarding these incidents, the worse they got. I finally had to take a two-week health leave but returned determined to get back on track. I believe I succeeded, and actually enjoyed the rest of the year, did well on teaching evaluations, and managed to get a book accepted for publication. I was not hired back at full time. An informant on the faculty said the reason for this decision was that I was not "interesting" enough.

The second thing driving me from the academy are the collateral effects of the nomadic nature of "sessionaling." Sessionaling assumes the unencumbered or well-serviced male. Women who have children and want work must live with constant moral anxiety not to mention physical exhaustion. The message is clear: Don't have your children until after you've got tenure. Yet I can't imagine a woman these days who wants to delay children until after she's got tenure since, for the vast majority, tenure never happens and, even for the lucky few, it takes a long time. And the "musical chairs" of sessionaling makes the already difficult situation of women as authoritative classroom figures worse. Women must face the challenge of appearing in charge by fighting their acculturation as available; as servants. The conditioning is deeply ingrained in us and it takes a great deal of courage to act against it. If, in addition, we have no reputation to back us up, no roots in the institution where we are teaching to help keep us on our mark, we are doubly vulnerable to attack. The psychological and emotional costs of maintaining our authority are high, sometimes too high, and women, who lack the legacy of authority that every man inherits just because he is a man, burn out more quickly than men do. The system thus selects men and thereby continues to exert pressures that we have otherwise come to regard as illegitimately discriminatory.

I have given these concerns a great deal of thought. Clearly, there are women who make it. But in my experience, short as it has been, I have learned that most of those who make it have done so for the most part because they've smiled with their mouths shut. Annette Baier, a highly respected and widely published professor emeritus in philosophy from Australia, advises up-and-coming female philosophers to keep their feminist thoughts and their complaints about the system strictly to themselves until they have tenure. Otherwise, they will be weeded out and it will hurt.

Silence, as Catharine MacKinnon points out over and over again, is women's voice. In the world of academia where "free expression" is tantamount to religious dogma, I have seen nothing to disturb her assessment. Silence, as we already know, is the free expression of all those with career goals and no job security. But it is especially the free expression of women in that situation. Nothing they do should draw attention to themselves as females. Given that everything women do has been construed by men, at one time or another, as just this sort of attention-getting and, given the invisibility that comes with part-time or temporary status, camouflage and stillness are women's presence. PhD virgins excepted, provided we publish canonical research like crazy, if we keep silent and invisible, we may be allowed in. But there are no guarantees. And just in case women should get the idea that there are sufficient conditions for entry, every once in a while, tenure is denied to a woman who has played it by the book. This is male supremacy at work in the academy. "See what we did to her? Don't go getting any ideas about who's calling the shots here."

In the midst of struggling to keep my own head above water in the sessional pool so that one day I might secure a tenured position, an excellent philosopher and dear mentor was denied tenure. The decision was eventually reversed, but the effect of the whole affair was deeply felt by untenured female colleagues and was unambiguous.

Is this what we have to look forward to? And so, I'm now looking outside the academy.

I bear, however, a feeling of guilt. For part of me experiences this redirection of my career goals as a betrayal. It seems partly a betrayal of my discipline, which I love beyond all else except my children. But more important, it seems a betrayal of women. Even if there is something going on here that ought to be accepted with serenity because it cannot be changed, we cannot know this now. So, on the off chance that deep changes can be made, women need to muster the courage to make them. The possibility of opening up the academy for women (to women as they are to women and not as they are to and for men) depends upon the relentless march of a vast number of female "heads of classrooms" (being themselves as they are to and for themselves) reshaping and diversifying the images of women with which young people, male as well as female, enter the "real world."

The grade schools we all go to as children are visibly dominated by women. By the time some reach the most exclusive centres of higher learning, the grade school ratio of women to men has been reversed. The greater an institution's power to exclude – university compared to grade school, for example – the harder it seems to maintain the ratio and the less likely women will be seen maintaining it. If women are not obvious in the "upper," or most prestigious positions in education or society, the reason is generally taken to be that, while they have what it takes to control boys, they do not have what it takes to professionally command the obedience of men. Thus, those women that do appear in prestigious positions are subject to special tests. Such women are seen as unusual and to the post-pubescent alpha male, unusualness in females is almost always sensed in sexual terms. She's hot for me or hot for us. Where there is no sexual interest, her unusualness signals that she is not a "real" woman at all. She's a dyke or an "ice queen," a Margaret Thatcher. Curiously, while male faculty place little or no value on student evaluations, when it comes to the male honours students' judgment of the "unusual" female professor, the worthless is suddenly valuable.

Unless women continue to struggle in academia and in even greater numbers than they are presently doing, we can know now that none of this will ever change. But it must be said that many of us will fall and that this may be the price of improvement. Each woman, then, must weigh her own self-interest, and in some cases the interests of her family, against the interests of women seen as part of a much bigger picture. While it may seem unfair to impose this sort of choice on us, it must also be admitted that members of other oppressed groups have faced the same choice. If they had not chosen to sacrifice themselves and their families for "the greater good," their causes would have disappeared under the crush of history. Knowing this makes my own choice to consider dropping out of the academic race problematic. I do not take it lightly.

Perhaps it is too early for me to see my fantasies of opting out of the academy as such a betrayal. Perhaps I will end up back on the professorial track; perhaps I will end up contributing to the greater good in some other way. Perhaps as I age I will acquire the costume of authority with less effort, less subterfuge. Perhaps the struggle for a boomimg voice and a formidable presence will become less hazardous, less threatening – less sexual. If the experience of other oppressed groups is any guide here, however, this is unlikely. For the most part, other groups have fared better only when they have determined their own cultural boundaries. Female academics outside of women's studies programs are unlikely to do this even under the tremendous pressure to draw a line in the dirt. Add to that the effects of backlash and the difficulty of overcoming the well-established cultural meme of women as a group subsumed by men under the koffee klatsch, the tupperware party, the gossip ring, and the chicken farm, and the odds against change are overwhelming.

Still, there is hope. There are males in the system who are sensitive to and even incensed by what they rightly perceive is the de facto weeding out of females by the selection process. They do not, in other words, regard their own successes as explained solely by their own achievements. That such men exist signals the possibility of recalibrating the entry and working conditions of the academy. Or perhaps of beginning new academies. I cannot help but think that the best future for women academics along with their sympathetic male colleagues is in this latter possibility. The virtue of this possibility for me is that it provides a ground for the reconciliation of my desire to get out of "the" academy and at the same time avoid betraying my discipline and my fellow footsoldiers. This sort of thing has happened before in the history of philosophy as well as in other disciplines. Interestingly, the flourishing of new schools has always been met with derision from the old, and often heralded new and exciting eras in thought, art, and invention. In the act of expressing this thought, my anxiety level rises.

There is a very old political question here: Can unjust basal traditions such as male supremacy be changed or must they and the institutions they give rise to be destroyed? Or if not destroyed, can either be quietly abandoned? Where might the "wisdom to know the difference" come from? Since women cannot rely on those traditions or institutions to point the way, I think the time has come for some of us to seriously consider the last approach and see what happens.

If You Are Dumped On, It Is Not All Bad

SWANI VETHAMANY-GLOBUS

It happened on a frigidly cold night; a tiny bird froze and fell to the ground. A cow passed by and dumped dung on the fallen bird. The warmth of the fresh dung revived the bird and it chirped. A fox came along, heard the chirping bird, and ate it. Thus, the moral of the story is: "If you are dumped on, it is not all bad, and when the going is good, you should keep your mouth shut." This parable (supposedly of Russian origin) was narrated to me by a senior administrator in the Faculty of Science at a crowded and noisy reception for new faculty, hosted jointly by the faculty association and the administration. I had just obtained a half-time faculty appointment in science (after a year of bitter grievance) and after working for fifteen years as a non-salaried research assistant professor in the Department of Biology, I was attending the reception as a new (old) faculty member.

I often think about my rather bizarre welcome and to this day I wonder what motivated that exchange. Perhaps there was a message for me in there somewhere. I will let the reader be the judge. Although this exchange stung me at the time, ten years later I view it philo-sophically. This may be due to my current stage of life. Having lived in both the Eastern and Western cultures and also having now entered my sixth decade on this planet, I have noticeably mellowed and greyed. As a result, I find myself seeing a lot of grey rather than black and white in many life-situations. In the face of limited choices, there comes a certain acceptance of life's uneven dealings. More important, I have gained the resolve to do my best under given circumstances. My Indian mother and my great-aunt, both teachers in their time, taught me this very early on. Furthermore, one also runs out of the finite energy to be swimming against the current all the time. I can well relate to the exhaustion of migrating salmon as it reaches the end of its journey. A lot of them never even reach their destination!

I am a Canadian-trained scientist with a PhD in developmental biology from the University of Toronto. I held two subsequent postdoctoral positions with prominent scientists at Brandeis University. I spent my first twenty-seven years in India, my motherland, and the next (more mature) thirty-seven years in the West, in my adopted country, Canada, with close ties to my colleagues and friends in the United States. My Eastern beginnings followed by an immersion in the Western culture give me a unique but chimeric perspective on life. In 1972 I married my fellow graduate student, Morton Globus, a Canadian from Montreal, and we became an academic couple of mixed ethnic background. We did collaborative research in the field of limb regeneration and made a synergistic, innovative, and productive academic team. Our research, which was often ground-breaking, received international recognition.

When two hearts lock in the euphoria of romance, practical considerations as to its effects on the careers of the partners invariably take a back seat. With academic couples, this casual attitude generally affects the wife's career more than that of the husband. Nor was I aware that my identity as a *bona fide* scientist would be difficult to establish among my colleagues and that I would forever fight the image of the wife coming to the laboratory to clean glassware and assist her husband in her spare time, while raising her children.

In 1972 I accompanied my spouse to Waterloo where he was hired as a Developmental Biologist. As my biological clock was fast ticking toward the limit of my child-bearing age, we started on our family right away. The call to motherhood was very strong for me; Morton and I were ecstatic when Julie was born in 1973 and when Brian joined us in 1975. Although I was offered a faculty position in the University of Guelph (twenty minutes' drive from Waterloo), I opted to take the research assistant professorship, though unsalaried, in the same department as that of my husband, while I raised my young family. Our joint decision to turn down the offer at Guelph later proved to have been career suicide. Sharing the laboratory with my husband, I set out to be an independent researcher. I held my own NSERC (Natural Sciences Engineering Research Council) operating grant for many years, published in refereed journals, presented papers in conferences, and supervised graduate students. In spite of all this, I had to fight an uphill battle to establish my identity and independence as a scientist in my own right.

In fact I soon discovered a double standard with regard to collaborations. While collaborations and joint publications among unrelated colleagues were acceptable, worthy of credit and even encouraged, a husband-wife research team was not looked upon favorably. It was ludicrous that the independence issue was played against both of us, whenever one of us came up for tenure, promotion, or appointment consideration. It was truly a no-win situation. My own sense is that, since self-interests and mutual gains largely govern collaborations and since husband and wife teams tend to be more self-contained, they are not given the recognition that is freely given to other collaborations.

I had hoped that keeping up my scholarship would place me at an advantage for a faculty position when my family responsibilities eased. Wrong! I faced an extraordinary resistance in getting my research position converted to a regular full-time faculty position, even after putting in fourteen years of (unsalaried) service in the department.

To fuel my fire, I was passed over in 1985 when the government of Ontario introduced the Excellence Fund program to rectify gender imbalance within the institution. In fact, in hiring for this program, the department looked outside and hired three women from the White dominant group. Until this point, I thought I was fighting the perception that I was the wife of a faculty member and not a scientist in my own merit. However, at this juncture, I became afraid that I was perhaps facing yet another form of discrimination, that of a woman belonging to a visible minority group, clad in a sari! After a year-long grievance, I was begrudgingly offered a half-time, definite-term faculty position at the assistant professor level, instead of the full-time associate professor's position for which I had applied.

In the midst of all this, I was hit by an iceberg: NSERC suddenly withdrew its support after supporting my research for well over fifteen years. Denial of NSERC research funding, at the crucial moment when I had just obtained a regular faculty position was the biggest blow I had to endure professionally. Talk about winning the battle and losing the war! I prided myself as a creative scientist, having made original and significant contributions in my field which were recognized internationally, and I was poised to make further new findings. The fact that I had tried to keep research going against all odds without a salary for fourteen years was totally ignored by the Grant Selection Committee members. This still remains an irreconcilable injustice in my mind and a total disregard on the part of NSERC to my past, present, and potential future contributions to science.

The practice of science, I realize now, is not above politics, gender bias, or racial discrimination. Science in Canada remains almost the exclusive domain of the privileged and the powerful and is unsympathetic to women who combine career with child-rearing and to women of colour. We often talk about a glass ceiling for women. For women of colour, this ceiling seems to be made up of impenetrable steel. The careers of male and, more recently, female graduates of the White dominant group are often more enthusiastically supported and promoted by their supervisors. On the other hand, mentors for women of colour seem nonexistent.

In this context, I heard a caller in one of Anne Petri's shows on CBC television (when she was interviewing the author of *White Lies*) saying that "the chief beneficiaries of affirmative action in Canada are White women." Although I have plenty of company in the margin with members of the privileged group, I find myself pondering this statement. During the last decade I have watched with anticipation, hope, and optimism the attempts within the academy to improve social justice for traditionally marginalized groups, especially women. The rescue helicopters do come after a lot of hue and cry, but some of us never get on them and are left behind, untouched by the winds of reform. Why? I ask. Who are these discards? The term "women of colour" is an imposed Canadian label I had to endure in the struggle for equity. No one asked me whether or not I wanted to be identified this way and it is even humiliating that I am simply left holding this awful tag without reaping any benefits whatsoever. Thus, some of us have not one but multiple strikes against us, namely: being a woman, combining motherhood with career, being a member of an academic couple team, and being a "woman of colour."

For the past twelve years, I have held one half of a regular faculty position, finally salaried, albeit at the lowest salary for my rank, qualifications, and years of service. My request for conversion to a full-time position has been totally ignored even though there has been new hiring. (Ironically, I recently served on a selection committee for hiring a new physiologist.) I am the only untenured faculty member in the department with many years of service, and my pension is meagre. My career path is considered so bizarre that I tend to throw my women activist colleagues into total shock with my story; the only way they get out of their mental paralysis is to dismiss it as an anomaly. Can any one blame them? I have stopped telling my story.

Witnessing on a daily basis her mother's struggles as a woman scientist, my daughter, in spite of her excellent academic potential, shunned the academic life altogether. This has happened with the daughters of several of my women friends who have had similar career paths. Concerted efforts may be mounted to attract young women into the sciences and other non-traditional fields. But daughters who have experienced the unsupportive nature of the terrain first-hand through their academic mothers will resist them. If we want to convince our daughters that survival is possible in the tundra, we need to treat their mothers right.

After my personal experience of exclusion, I threw myself into equity issues and social justice and I have grown enormously through this process. I have come to realize that there is life after a rejection from NSERC's granting committees. I got involved in the faculty association, served on the university senate and the board of governors, and gained invaluable insight into the inner workings of academe. Through my activities with the Status of Women and other equity-related committees, I have met some remarkable equity-conscious women and men, both in my institution and nationally and internationally. I hope that this book, a product of such involvement, connects women within Canada and beyond in a special way. (I am grateful for the added bonus of forming a precious three-way friendship with the other two co-editors in the process.) I have taken on more administrative duties within the department and the faculty, advising and acting as a mentor for undergraduate students, which I find extremely rewarding.

Time fortunately moves on, and healing is taking place both within and around me. New actors are on the scene. There is a new-found recognition and support within the department and outside that brings a smile to my face as I begin my day. That is progress indeed!

Now, coming back to the latter half of the saying, "When the going is good, keep your mouth shut," I never could keep my mouth shut. When it came to matters of equity I risked being eaten on more than one occasion. I paid for speaking out by being sidelined in the game of academic politics. It is a myth that the academy nurtures free speech and debate. If you rock the boat, you will be thrown overboard! Will I be labelled a mere dreamer if I wish for the new millennium that the habit of loyal collusion in the upper echelons of governance and the silencing of dissenting voices would change toward more openness, social justice, compassion, and equity?

There never was any question in my mind whether I belonged in the academy in spite of its harsh unsupportive terrain. My life journey brought me to the Canadian academic world. As I reflect at the twilight of my academic life, I feel that I have run a hard race against the chilly arctic winds and contributed in my own way to warming the climate.

My story has a touch of triumph amid the adversity that I faced in the academic tundra. The fact that I managed to even subsist in this inhospitable land without hitting the dust and vanishing could be attributed to my tender beginnings in India, where my dear parents gave me the necessary tools of wilderness survival. In addition, my deep commitment to my calling as an academic, my adaptability, tenacity, and inner strength; strong support and a sense of justice from three vice-president academics and provosts; in addition a supportive dean, a humane chair, and many friends often from outside the department; and above all, the unwavering support of my life/academic partner and my two children sustained me.

After thirty-five years of living in this land, I may be just beginning to fathom what lies behind the Canadian psyche. It signifies to me that mere survival itself is something to celebrate in this harsh but beautiful land. I suppose I must feel content to be a survivor of sorts in this landscape, the Canadian Academic Tundra, although my dreams were once of thriving in it.

Science and Business:
Two Working Lives Compared

IRENE WANKE AND PETER BOWAL

"All animals are equal, but some animals are more equal than others."
George Orwell, *Animal Farm*

This phrase was coined by Orwell to relate his story of pigs that controlled the government. Their proclaimed equality for all was in fact only equality for the pigs. It did not yield true equality across society. This phrase has since been popularly adapted, and well understood. In the same way, former US President Gerald Ford's slip of the tongue that "things are more like they are now than they've ever been" resonates with meaning. Some departments may have come very far toward fostering equality of treatment, but other departments in the same institution may do little to ensure actual equality.

This is the true comparison of a wife and husband who started at approximately the same time to work at the same Canadian university. We recount this contrast of working life in the same household, in the same occupation, in the same university in the spirit that it is better to light one little candle than to curse the darkness in isolation. The husband's story and circumstances begin this comparison to establish a benchmark. This is a tale not so much about disparate treatment between men and women *per se* by an academic institution, as about the extraordinarily disparate treatment of spouses *between two faculties* that are both historically male dominant. Ultimately, the outcomes are even more pronounced and impossible to overlook when the discrepancy happens in the same family.

PETER'S STORY

I was unable to convert even short-term full-time sessional work, and some respectable research publications, into any secure academic job.

In 1989 I was not even told my position would not be renewed at my last university. I was replaced by graduate students, most or all being less educationally qualified women. Nevertheless, such are the vagaries of sessional status, and I recall believing that, already into my thirties with no established academic career, my chances of ever getting one were by then microscopic.

Obtaining a secure academic position is a "hit or miss" proposition in Canada. Judgments are rendered early after graduation as to one's academic fitness and prospects. If one is passed over then, it is difficult to recover in time to get a tenurable position. Woe be to the aspirant who did not give adequate attention to cultivating credentials and contacts in the window of prime time that quickly closes.

I was therefore, at thirty-four years of age, grateful to be hired on the tenure track at the business school in the summer of 1991. My training is in law, and I had been "sessionaling" and practising law for eight consecutive years. In this new job I was offered heaps more salary (all "hard money," which means that I did not have to raise it myself each year) than I had expected, and was appointed at associate professor level.

There was a $5,000 research account set up in my name when I arrived, as well as opportunity to compete for more summer research projects. My office was great, in a modern state-of-the-art building. We were served with a high performance computer and printer with bells and whistles, and all the personalized support of which most academics can only dream. We did not have to be overly concerned about long-distance calls, clerical support, faxes, photocopies, couriers, or supplies. We were handed generous travel allowances to present papers, on top of the university-level grant programs. Some academic members in the social sciences can thrive as prodigious researchers without having to raise substantial, or any, funds from outside sources for that purpose. My new faculty was then in an expansion stage and had recently raised money from the business community and government.

We were spoiled and remain so. While there have been cutbacks, they have had little tangible impact on my work life and we remain blessed. I must add that we very actively recruit women and members of minority groups, but remain for now, like most business schools, a professional discipline dominated by men. However, my colleagues who are women enjoy the same good life described here. We all should be slow to complain. I enjoy my work so much that I can only wish that happiness upon everyone else.

In Canadian business schools, new junior faculty are often hired ABD ("all but dissertation) soon after they pass their candidacy examinations. This has been the lay of the land in business disciplines for decades. There are always academic positions for new business school graduates even well before they have the PhD in hand. New recruits are often given course and service releases for their first few terms in order to enable them to finish their dissertations on the new business school employer's dime. The scenario, however, is much different for science academics, as in the case of my wife, which we describe below. In science, one may toil for two to ten years in a post-doctoral position in someone else's laboratory at minimum wage before even being considered for an academic post.

As a young boy taught to work hard as I grew up on a small farm, I have always had little sympathy for feminism. I had to break out of humble rural roots, develop some sense of self-confidence, and put myself through eight years of university with no support from home. I believed that there was equality of opportunity for everyone in Canada if they applied themselves and make some choices that involve sacrifice.

Now we turn to my wife. She is far more qualified than I am, and much more of a "pure research scholar." Her story about toiling in the trenches of science raises doubts, indeed concerns, about treatment across academic disciplines in Canada.

IRENE'S STORY

After I got my MD, I interned and became qualified as a physician. I then completed a residency in internal medicine and ultimately a sub-specialty in endocrinology. Bench research tweaked my interest, so I earned a PhD in medical sciences in 1989.

Science is an important field for research and study, and we often hear that women do not venture into it in sufficient numbers. Today, however, it is a field cluttered with PhDs and underemployment. Unlike the case in business studies, funding is primarily dependent on governments and, to a much lesser extent, a few industry sources such as drug companies.

Freshly-minted PhDs can rarely embark on a research career by getting a position in any post-secondary environment today. They must "postdoc" for years, often away from where they got their doc-torate, and certainly away from where they want to ultimately settle. For too many, they end up with a "career" as a postdoc, often work-ing for a salary in the low to mid-$30,000s, with meagre benefits or none. They suffer low wages, few benefits, no security, and are not protected by the university, but remain entirely dependent on the good faith and generosity of their supervisor, who usually engages them on "soft" research grant money.

Once one has survived this apprenticeship, one may be "invited to apply" for a tenure-track position when one opens up in the Faculty of Medicine. Being eventually chosen for the position really means that one is then allowed, by faculty sponsorship, to submit scholarship applications to the few granting agencies in Canada that competitively fund salaries for medical researchers.

Not only does one need to submit applications for salary funding in order to obtain the position but additional grant applications are required to entirely fund the operation of the science laboratory, right down to paper clips and photocopies. Each of these two components is considered separately for funding. It even occurs that one can obtain a grant to run the lab but not for one's salary, or vice versa. In such a case, one would not get the university position. The application takes months to prepare and must be preceded by robust accomplishment in the field as evidenced by numerous publications in the top journals. Original letters of reference must be solicited and forwarded, and a comprehensive, detailed research proposal must be tightly knit together. One must, furthermore, demonstrate one's "independence" from any previous doctoral or postdoctoral supervisor, who inevitably will insist on his or her name being on all work that commenced in that lab.

This grant-writing cycle must be repeated every two to five years. It is very stressful and conducive to pursuing a strategy of "quick wins." Researchers can be refused funding, or one type of funding, on any application. The process has little respect for seniority or childbirth. University tenure is, likewise, a misnomer in the Faculty of Medicine for the many individuals required to generate their own salary. The university only supplies lab and office space and the benefit plan if one is successful at raising one's salary from outside grants. Even with tenure, no grant, no job.

The three- to four-year funding cycle makes it very difficult to plan. It is even difficult to plan for sabbatical leaves, something other academic members take for granted. After Year 3, three years being the minimum service credit for sabbatical eligibility, I do not technically even "have a job" for the next sabbatical year, although the granting agencies often extend one year of grace if one is unsuccessful in obtaining new funding. I generally have to wait until my grant is renewed before I can apply for sabbatical leave. In this way, I lose at least one or two years of service credit, since I would apply in my fourth year to go on sabbatical leave in Year 5.

All of what has been described here is, of course, no different for men than it is for women. We all share the rigours of the "soft money" model. While I was single and without children, there was no gender disadvantage. This convergence is borne out in the absence of a wage gap among young single men and women. The various differences began to appear after marriage and pregnancy. For example, before I met Peter I had won a considerable grant to study in Texas at a prestigious medical research centre. That would have been my "BTA" ("been to America") credential. After Peter and I met and married, we decided to follow and take up his position in Calgary, and I reluctantly passed on the Texas grant. Many women, for various reasons, including career vulnerability in the child-bearing years, choose to follow their husbands' career locations. I believe that the resulting lack of the BTA degree, and the characterization of me as a "locally trained" scientist will always constitute a brake on my career. The impact of gender was manifested in subtle forms, but they were palpable.

After serving my endocrine research fellowship, I was fortunate to be "invited to apply" for a position, despite marriage restricting my mobility. Simply everything must be promising about the candidate to get to that point: academic record and potential, certainly, but also the personal profile and all the variables this encompasses. After some predictable concerns about independence, my grant application was successful for both salary and lab expenses. One cannot over-state the fierce, and shrinking, international market for elusive research grants in which medical and basic scientists must compete. I began as an assistant professor in 1995, at slightly under my hus-band's starting salary. The position comes with clinical obligations at the university's health science centre. No clinical service, no job.

When I enrolled in the university benefit plan four years after my husband, I was told that academic spouses could not "top up" the benefits if their spouse was already enrolled. This meant, for exam-ple, that my husband was already getting 80 percent coverage for extended health and dental benefits. With my same plan, I could not top that up to 100 percent. In other words, I would enjoy none of these benefits, apart from my husband. Curiously, two married uni-versity staff members could top up, but not academic spouses. I dispatched a letter to the president and employment equity officer, invoking the language of the oppressed. This policy was changed and the penalty on the "second academic spouse to be hired" was removed, the policy rescinded.

We decided to start our family right away. Within the year, I applied for a maternity leave from the granting body. Until that year, they never had a maternity leave policy. My maternity leave (with twins) was the first; my salary grant was extended for six months and I was grateful. We went on to have two more children, and while maternity leaves are available, they still do not represent a full actual leave from all the various responsibilities of one's academic work.

Maternity leaves do not release one from the clinical responsibilities of patient coverage. One's referral base is not maintained and clinical income is lost. The scientific reviewers, governed by fixed funding cycles and inertia, still do not account for loss of productivity during maternity leave, much less over a longer career period. I have served on recruiting committees and at numerous meetings for that purpose. When a female candidate's dossier is discussed, where she clearly has taken time for maternity and child care, no consideration whatsoever is given to what role that fact may have played in her academic record to date. All candidates of both genders are on the same Adam Smith–like playing field.

Some of the major funding agencies, most of which are government-based, still do not ask for information regarding pregnancy leave. When it is pointed out, their evaluations of an application make no mention of its having even been a factor in the evaluation. Presumably, the agencies and their reviewers do not take into account the leave, the decreased research productivity on resumption of service, the need to catch up on the new scientific literature, and the expected increased child care responsibilities in the home at that time in one's life. When the husband works, the wife is unable to devote as much time and effort to science on weekends and evenings as she could when she was single and childless. The wife is under greater hardship to travel to academic conferences with infant children.

Funding is essential to our employment and careers in science. Can there be any wonder why this is such an unattractive option for young Canadian women? We do not know how many women quietly withdraw from science each year.

The merit assessment process at the university level in my faculty also does not account for maternity leave. After a year of one baby and six strong articles, I was awarded a much less than average increment, with a "satisfactory" appraisal. There was no discernible recognition that half the year was maternity leave, or that I discharged all teaching and some clinical obligations while on maternity leave. It has been suggested to me that I cannot be serious about science in view of the one maternity leave I have taken since joining the faculty.

Like most female academics, I do not expect a free ride or preferences over men. Neutrality in assessment, which is to say, a level playing field would be enough. I simply look forward to the day that I am not punished or made worse off in the workplace for having children.

Institutional equity across academic disciplines is a good enough reason to rethink the structure of scientific research. The law is another. There is no doubt that the employment equity advisors and

Human Rights Commissions would be interested in the "adverse impact" and systematic effect that such official university research practice has on the numbers of women in science and their long-term success. The Alberta *Human Rights, Citizenship and Multiculturalism Act*, R.S.A. 1980, c. H-11.7, section 38(2) states: "Whenever this Act protects a person from being adversely dealt with on the basis of gender, the protection includes, without limitation, protection of a female from being adversely dealt with on the basis of pregnancy."

This personal story highlights the challenges that exist today for women in the world of scientific research in Canada. It contrasts with the career conditions of a different field, that of business, also male-dominated, at the same university at the same time. The "free market" approach that government and its funding agencies passed on to Canadian universities creates a great divide in working conditions at the same university. The "live or die" research-funding approach presents virtually insurmountable obstacles for women hoping to thrive in Canadian science research. The "winner takes all" trend is expressing itself today in international mega-labs run by men who are in no danger of asking for maternity leaves and allowances for child care. The available research funding will be diverted to them as if to a vacuum. They can work around the clock and leverage legions of inexpensive postdocs to conduct the research under their tutelage to provide the only deliverable that counts, publications. It is an industry where more is simply better, and the biggest labs able to structure themselves to best exploit the funding structure will dominate.

I love nothing more in my life's work than to be able to read, think, design experiments, and carry them out for the love of knowledge and the advancement of science. The structural obstacles to me, as a women, in the itinerant three-year research funding cycle encourage me to gaze wistfully at an academic career in … well, the business school. I hear that there are scores of job openings, and conditions are better there.

Largesse: Gains and Losses in the Classroom

DEBORAH WILLS

The image on the classroom wall looks like the drawings of naked ladies I used to find in the margins of grade-school readers and library books; it evokes that same instantaneous crash of shock and repudiation. Like those marginal drawings, it is repellent as much for the evident hatred it betrays as for its familiar elements of design: the swollen breasts, bulbous spread thighs, the body hair scribbled in with such ferocity it's hard not to imagine the paper tearing beneath the pen. It used to come like a blow to the stomach every time, like a dirty joke with your name as the punch line. Even now it's not easy to look at. It's Graffiti Woman, generic object of lust and derision, pictured in a thousand variations on a thousand surfaces. This time it's projected on an overhead screen. This time I put it there: larger than life.

This scene unfolds in a class on the "carnivalesque body," part of a senior undergraduate course in literary theory. Perhaps because I teach theory and gender issues and cultural studies, "the body" always seems to follow me into classrooms, like a pet I'm fond of but can be embarrassed by. This week, we've been talking about cultural representations of femininity, about the insistent binaries that link the masculine with reason, intelligence, and spirit and the feminine with emotion, carnality, flesh. This particular incarnation of Graffiti Woman is from a 1919 Polish drawing; an obscene, spraddle-legged giantess in a gaping soldier's uniform looms over terrified troops, the fleeing men marked by the exaggerated expressions of horror and loathing stamped on their faces. Her tunic is open, her soldier's puttees lowered to reveal a forest of pubic hair in which whole platoons could flounder, nipples so pointed and protuberant they bring to mind the kinds of careless missiles our mothers used to warn us could put out an eye. She is a weapon, all right, and every woman in the class knows how sharply edged.

My greatest fear in my first years of teaching was that I would walk into a class one day and find something like this on the board: some iconic representation of a contempt so encompassing it could never be answered; some image that would drag me away from the familiar realm of the mind and force a recognition that I was a body, too, and a woman's body at that; something that would attack me in the one way that seemed irrefutable. To wait for that moment is to be always braced against the same sense of abrupt violation that used to come with finding Graffiti Woman, yet again, in the margins of a book. This was insult and injury both, to find in books – those welcoming havens of words and ideas – that vitriolic reminder that even these places were permeable, penetrable by such violent renditions of the body, my body, drawn beyond redemption. Mine is a big body, hard to overlook, and the fact of its largeness, even more than the fact of its materiality, seemed to make it somehow essentially more feminine, in all the ways that Graffiti Woman most embodies: more exaggerated, more grotesque, more out of control.

I know that this imagined, uneasily anticipated attack – finding a rude drawing, overhearing a crude remark – could happen whatever my body shape and size; being biologically female is enough to warrant it. I have thin friends whom I used to envy, thinking, as I did in high school, that they were safe in their normality (I believed there was such a thing, then); I thought that they would be professionally valued in ways I imagined I could not. These same friends have time and again been fiercely attacked in their teaching. Their authority has been challenged, their taste in clothes critiqued, the grades they have awarded countered with chants of "bitch" conducted by anonymous voices at just-audible levels. The fact that I have never knowingly experienced such an attack strikes me as incidental; it is the waiting for it, the bracing against it, that leaves its mark.

Often, of course, what happens is more subtle than such an overt assault. Most women are aware of the kind of blithe, accidental discourtesy that we can be subjected to simply because we occupy a space that is still not ours by right, because a woman in authority still creates unease, because a public woman is still a woman who opens herself to attack by virtue of invading public space. The public woman, the argument runs, like the socially suspect nineteenth-century actress, takes her body willingly onto a stage and thus shouldn't complain if things get thrown at it. Perhaps I have been spared the more overt offensives because it seems impossible to see a fat woman as a sexual object, and sexuality is never very far from most kinds of assault. Perhaps my size, the very thing that makes me most visibly a female body, also distracts attention from it, in the way that our eyes slide away from something messily dead on the road: we look, and then we look away. What draws the attention is sometimes what deflects it. And a university is a particularly good place for not looking: the silent standard of the academy is the exaltation of the mind at the expense of the body. The silent aesthetic of the academy is a body that is as close to gone as possible.

The thin body is a rigorous, disciplined body, a body successfully under the rule of the mind. That's why it is the academy's unspoken ideal. It is a body that is regimented and reliable: durable enough to stay up late working and survive on irregular sustenance; controlled enough not to crack under pressure; contained enough not to risk embarrassing eruptions of any kind. The body is there to serve, and not to interfere with, the mind. When you've got a big body, a body that's undeniably *there*, you represent in your very bones – or rather, in the flesh upon your bones – the embarrassing failure of that ideal. You're a body that takes on too much, demands too much, and the evidence of this is visible. Your body materially challenges the idea that the mind is all there is. It liberally illustrates the whole, suspect concept of "more." And gradually I've come to think that it can offer more, too. Perhaps because I do what I do against every inner and external voice that tells me I take up too much public space, too much space to be public, I've come to see my professional life as brave and necessary. As for any woman, taking that first step onto the stage is challenging; I just make a bigger target. But I also make a bigger model: easier to see, visible from the back rows. Larger than life. I've come to accept these risks and to enjoy the pleasures. There are a lot of smart young women in those back rows, watching and listening.

This is a success story, but unlike the success stories in magazines and diet books, it is not bound up with loss. It is, instead, about gain. It is about healing that harsh division between the mind and body, about seeing the two as part of an intricate and rewarding and extraordinarily diverse dance. This is a well-worn metaphor, but how can I say it otherwise: it is like a dance. The metaphor is surprising, too, since I am in many ways physically cumbrous. That's one of the things weight does: it encumbers you. But it also gives ballast, balance, presence. The air moves when I walk, giving way before me. My students hear my footsteps as I walk down the hall towards them. I don't think I am wrong when I speculate that many of them hear this sound with pleasure. They know I am coming to give them a good portion, to give them whatever I have to spare. And that's quite a lot.

Losing weight is hard, but not nearly so hard as losing self-contempt. When you've done that, you have made such gains that you are happy to share them. In my mind, I sail down the hall like Lady Bountiful, my arms as full as my head. The halls of the university are narrow, but I widen them as I pass. And in the classroom, I am full of grace – not the most easily recognized kind, perhaps, but grace nonetheless. In that grace, deeply encrypted in the choreography of give and take that is teaching, is a secret message to all the young women in the room: see, you can do this. I can do this; so can you. See how full of delight this can be? See how light I am on my feet? It is true that the way I now think about my body is inseparable from the way I think about my teaching. Both are places of complex pleasure, of plenitude, of benevolent overflow. They go beyond expectation, beyond necessity: with both, I am able to run the joyful risks of offering more than the meagre minimum. All my excesses are pleasing ones. They are by nature sites of a large and generous practice, a self-reflexive gift: always offering a little bit more than I'm asked for, a little bit more than you need.

"To Everything There Is a Season"

SUSAN WILSON

Autumn, Keats's "season of mists and mellow fruitfulness"; it's a clear, crisp afternoon in early November, an afternoon that presents me with a variety of options as to how I'll pass the time. Shall I mark another ten or fifteen of the ninety-odd essays stacked on the floor next to the bookcase in my kitchen? Shall I reread, for the umpteenth time, the next few chapters I'm to teach from Michael Ondaatje's sumptuous novel *The English Patient*? Shall I leave all pedagogical pursuits aside on this, my last weekend of comparative freedom before the onslaught of the end-of-term workload, and venture outdoors to plant the bulbs that will lie dormant as dreams throughout the wet Westcoast winter, to emerge in a blaze of glory next spring? Choices. There are always choices. In this instance, I savour the act of choosing, enjoying the relative simplicity of these choices compared to the prolonged deliberation that has led up to the more significant decision I've arrived at this weekend, to close the chapter on my life as a Canadian academic after twenty-two years as both a scholar and instructor.

In the end these ruminations lead me back from the window onto my garden to the article taking shape on the lined pages before me, then inward, to poetry. The words of Robert Frost's "The Road Not Taken" echo in memory and seem well suited to the preoccupations of this afternoon. I first discovered the poem in an anthology my grandfather gave me for my twelfth Christmas. The collection still sits among the other works that crowd the shelves in my office. "Two roads diverged in a yellow wood, and sorry I could not travel both and be one traveler, long I stood and looked down one as far as I could to where it bent in the undergrowth; then took the other, as just as fair, and having perhaps the better claim, because it was grassy and wanted wear" (Frost, 1916). Perhaps I resurrect this childhood relic precisely because it is such a deceptively simple, straightforward poem, yet like all Frost's works, one pregnant with meaning: a poem about choices.

The act of choosing can, in and of itself, become merely another form of procrastination, an attempt to suspend time, to avoid the inevitable (or at least the wrong choice), to abrogate responsibility. Heaven knows I've watched my students agonize endlessly over choices – which topic to write on, which course to take – to the point that the act of arriving at a decisive course of action is invested with more energy than the alternative they are trying to avoid. Surely "choosing" ranks among the top five on the hit list of ultimate avoidance techniques! Thus, while I celebrate choice and believe in the right to choose, I also believe in action, for therein lies the essence of responsibility. Empowerment: my choices are my own, and choosing allows, however illusory, a sense of control over my destiny, an involvement in the direction my life takes, a faith in individual initiative and human endeavour that lends credence to the cliché that there are no mistakes, only choices and the lessons that are incumbent on those choices. Perhaps this explains in part the "how" and the "why" of my pursuit of an academic career. In the end it has always been about choice and the pursuit of knowledge, about the idealistic aspiration to belong to a generous community of learners whose knowledge and experience "give something back" to the world in general, and to their students and colleagues in particular. The great Elizabethan essayist, Sir Francis Bacon, once wrote, "A man must make his opportunity, as oft as find it." Despite the inherent gender bias on the part of a courtier who served one of England's greatest monarchs (and a woman at that), I share his philosophy. Having measured my professional idealism against the reality of experience, I stand on the threshold of change, yet how do I sum up that experience?

Further choices arise; the truth is not always pleasant. When I began my academic career, at York University's Glendon College at barely seventeen years of age, my professors smoked during their lectures and "political correctness" and "edutainment" were catchphrases yet to influence the academic landscape. Obviously, much has changed in the interim, but sadly many of the changes have been merely cosmetic: in the end, much has remained the same, at least as far as the female academic experience is concerned. I've certainly seen my fair share of the declining academic standards, the moral ambiguity, the inequalities, and the profound lack of mentorship or collegiality which run rampant in the halls of Canadian academe. These have contributed, in no small measure, to my desire for change and ultimately to my debate over leaving a tenured position with a college located in one of the most beautiful parts of our country.

What are some of the negative truths of my experience? I hesitate to elaborate, for fear of sounding embittered, for fear of reprisal, yet how else can change be possible? It is a fact that at every level of my university education, I have been harassed in one manner or another by a male professor or administrator in a position of power and authority, capable of influencing my academic career. As recently as two years ago, I felt incredible rage at the irony that as I lectured my students on academic ethics and the perils of plagiarism, I had a female student in my class who admitted to me that she had had sex with one of my colleagues to ensure a final "A" grade. Worse still, she was one of several such women who had participated in this abuse of the student-instructor relationship, a fact that was common knowledge among the student body on campus. Somehow the immorality of succumbing to the unacknowledged use of another's words or ideas paled in comparison with the bartering of sexual favours to ensure a modicum of academic success. Things have changed? I think not.

Equality? I frequently wondered how it was that the ratio of men to women in the average post-graduate English program was so disproportionate to their respective representation as departmental faculty. Or how was it that when I and another female colleague applied for the position of department coordinator, the selection process suddenly came to involve an oral presentation and subsequent question period, when this had never been required of the four previous coordinators, who happened to be men? Interestingly, when I mentioned this inequity to an older "feminist" colleague, she replied that this was required of us because we were younger faculty members and many in the department might not be familiar with us. Ageism? Sexism? Having been associated with the department for nine years, I could only conclude that it is as common for women to endorse a double standard for their co-workers as it is for men. Perhaps only the motivation differs. The glass ceiling is steadfastly in place, and women as well as men have played their part in erecting it. Enough of these truths: I grow angry even as I write. I know what I leave behind, what I will not miss. I would rather turn to the strengths that have made it possible to survive twenty-odd years in a challenging and often toxic environment.

I am enormously proud of my fortitude and staying power, that I have not allowed experience to compromise my values, that my thirst for knowledge has yet to be quenched. What have I achieved? I was one of the youngest students ever granted admission to York University; I have received numerous scholarships at both the undergraduate and graduate levels; I have studied abroad, as well as here in Canada; I have had the privilege of being mentored by several brilliant international scholars who have also been wonderful human beings; and I have managed to juggle two and sometimes three jobs while carrying a full academic load. My calibre as an instructor has been such that I was granted a faculty position at my college before I had completed my graduate degree. I have survived serious illness that resulted in the loss of my ability to have children; I have weathered the disintegration of my marriage, yet managed to persevere, to rebuild my life emotionally and financially while keeping my career intact. I have always tried to deal with my students with honesty and respect and endeavoured to inspire them to trust themselves and to continue their quests for knowledge and truth.

Perhaps one of the most ironic choices of my teaching career involved a contract assignment I recently took on for my college, an entrepreneurial activity that netted my division an additional $18,000.00, a tidy little sum for a fiscally strained institution. I volunteered to teach two courses in technical communications at the Canadian Forces Fleet School in Esquimalt. My students? Marine Engineers, more commonly known in the Navy as "Stokers." Given all the negative press the armed forces have received in the last few years, one would have thought I was walking into the last unofficial bastion of Canadian sexism. Nonetheless, despite the fact that a male instructor would probably have seemed the most obvious choice for such an assignment, my time at the Fleet School was a sheer delight, an unqualified success. The environment was predominantly male, yet I never felt at a disadvantage because of being a woman. I was always treated with respect and courtesy. Indeed, military personnel and civilian instructors alike went out of their way to help provide any information or assistance I required. My students were intelligent, articulate, and committed. The result? I developed two course packages that will serve as the Fleet School's templates for future technical communications courses, and in appreciation of my instruction, my students collectively presented me with a $100.00 gift certificate to be used towards the purchase of my first electric drill. Sometimes life's lessons are learned in the most unlikely places, under the most unforeseen circumstances. The satisfaction that arises from such a success is part of what gives me the courage to contemplate a change in direction, to choose another path.

There are numerous things I will take on my new journey: the memory of a Cree student's invitation to participate in the sweet grass ceremony she would use to prepare her spiritually for her final exams; the mug inscribed with my name featuring Raven, the bird of knowledge, a gift from my students in the Native Indian Teacher Education Program; the wonderful card beginning, "All I Need to Know About Life I Learned From My English Teacher"; the string of cobalt blue glass beads from a young student who needed to find an anchor in an overwhelming academic environment; the print of an eagle perched atop a Westcoast totem. These are the tangible treasures that are part of a greater store of things shared with my students, those who have really counted in all of this. In choosing to leave my position at my college, I turn my face to the future and head to foreign shores, down a road "less traveled" (Frost 19), one which may or may not lead to a PhD. Unlike the speaker of Frost's poem, however, I shall not be "telling this with a sigh/Somewhere ages and ages hence:"(16–17), for the future holds nothing but promise. I have followed one road for twenty-two years. It's time to take another.[1]

NOTE

1 Susan Wilson continues to teach part time at Camosun College. A diagnosis of insulin-dependent diabetes mellitus in April 1998 has precluded her making any major life changes for the time being. Susan has been struggling to stabilize her health in order that she may return to teaching full-time.

Postgraduate Journal: Blood, Sweat, and Tears

N. ROCHELLE YAMAGISHI

My story is fraught with tension. I feel as if I am walking a tightrope between academe and home, between fulfilling my dreams and meeting the needs of my family. It seems that I have to choose between my children (produced from my body) and my studies (produced from my mind) to achieve a spiritual end. That they are also body, mind, and spirit is the saving grace.

My agenda is to complete an advanced degree while at the same time maintaining my role in a traditional family. (I have been warned by more than one academic that separating from your family is dangerous to the stability of relationships.) Academic structures generally are not amenable to the part-time nature of married women's attentions. However, through what sometimes seems to be a small miracle, I have somehow managed to transform myself, a third generation Japanese-Canadian from working class roots in Southern Alberta, into a doctoral student in the most venerable educational institution in Alberta. I have been able (with the help of an advisor who was recommended to me as "a fine human being") to manoeuver around the complexities and realities of attending university in a city some 350 miles from my home to try to work out compromises at both ends. This means that I arrive in Edmonton Tuesdays around noon and leave for home in Lethbridge on Thursday evening or Friday morning. (The cooperation of an understanding professor and classmates has enabled me to make Thursdays the rule from the middle of October.)

This evening on the phone I was so glad to be able to reassure my ten-year-old daughter, who will always be my "baby," that there will only be one more of these weeks when I will spend three nights away from home. "But I miss you, Mommy!" was her plaintive response. The feeling of helplessness is the epitome of tension.

I heard the cries and questions of very young children in the hall-ways of the Education Building this morning as I sat in my office struggling through the rhetoric of critical pedagogy, and while my first response was, "What are little kids doing here?" I quickly checked myself: "What is education all about, if not kids?" My third response was, "What about my kids? Where are they now? What are they doing? How are they managing without me?"

Giving up maternal duties and relinquishing them to my husband and older daughter is emancipating in many ways, but again tension-producing. For decades I have been conditioned to the mothering role. Society tells me that I must make the best choices for my children. I must constantly monitor my behaviour, ensuring that it is good for my children's welfare. I rationalize that I am becoming a better person, therefore will be a better mother: I am providing a positive role model for my children, and I am allowing my children, aged 16, 13, and 10, to develop a special relationship with their father. Deep down inside, I have a lot of questions. If this is so good, why is it so difficult? Am I afraid that they will learn to get along just fine without me, and that if I am not successful in obtaining this degree, I will also have failed as a mother in the process?

In a feminist article I was reading today regarding academic achievement of women of colour, the questions were raised: "Are personal advancement and social mobility the only ends that we seek? Do we seek more money? Greater influence? To what end?" (Wilkerson, 1983, cited in Sleeter, 1991, 7). These succinctly echo my questions and those of others around me. Why am I doing this? I know that my parents advocated education and that I come from a family of achievers. And I know that my mother probably would have gone into teaching if the evacuation of people of Japanese origin from the west coast during World War II had not cut off that career opportunity for her. Am I living out my mother's dreams? My answers are like the ones I read that were given to the above questions: "need and desire for personal advancement while connecting ... with a collective effort to improve the quality of life for many."

I feel fortunate that I am in a time and space where I can consider such questions and answers. I can legitimately give voice to the quandary of female education. In the 1800s, higher education for females was thought to be irrelevant. Critical theorists tell us that

women have been coopted into education to carry out further nur-
turing duties (Grumet, 1988). While this is perhaps not as true for me
as a postsecondary educator as it would be for a primary teacher,
perhaps there is still more than a grain of truth to it. These analysts
would put the responsibility for critical pedagogy squarely on the
shoulders of teachers. Teachers must save the world. However, teachers and parents, both female and male, must nurture children; they
both have a potentially healing role.

When I arrived at the University of Alberta last May, I was struck
by the oldness of the place. The residence, Pembina Hall, originally
a residence for women only, was one of the first structures built on
the campus in the early 1900s. To think that they would have a whole
residence just for women that early in the century is rather surprising
in view of the fact that the suffragettes were not successful in their
bid to have women recognized as "persons" until 1929. (Who were
all the non-persons who inhabited these rooms?)

An inscription, literally carved in stone, over one of the outside
doors reads, *Payuk uche Kukeyow*. I hadn't taken much notice of it
until a friend who was assistant to the dean of women in the 1970s
informed me that the Cree meaning is "All for one, one for all" and
that the residents practised a Native ceremony in which they handed
a piece of firewood from one "person" to another and into the fire,
symbolizing their oneness and togetherness.

Although the residence is now co-ed and there is no longer a dean
of women calling each of us into her office individually to inquire
whether she can be of any assistance to us, I am happy to say that I
am feeling a togetherness with other students. Although students here
come from various walks of life and differ widely in age, experience,
colour, cultural background, and ableness, I find them generally
friendly, open, and helpful. I have the feeling that we are all genuinely
in this together! My connection with other people of colour has been
particularly gratifying. In particular, I am indebted to Iris,[1] a Native
woman, to whom I was initially drawn in a gender class, by her side
comment about a lack of identity with White women's issues. She
urged me to seek out my elders and was thereby instrumental in leading me to a watershed experience in which I came face to face with
my own epistemic violence toward myself. I realized that in trying to
deny my own ethnicity while growing up in the "melting pot" of the
1960s, I was not only trying to achieve the impossible by trying to
pass as White, but I was missing out on a sense of belonging with
what I should call "my people." I walked the halls in something of a
daze, on the verge of tears, for many days. One day, when I happened
to meet Robert, an African from one of my earliest classes, he sincerely

asked me how I was, and I realized that I could not lie to an African. I could not say the culturally correct, "Fine," but had to tell him how I *really* was. He understood instantly, and encouraged me by stating quite matter-of-factly that he felt himself to be considered "the lowest of the low," someone thought to be quite stupid by many Whites. He advised me not to let it get the best of me, but to press on: "If you fail, no one will care." He offered a listening ear whenever I might need one. I greatly value this connection with other people of colour. Rarely do they misunderstand concerns about racism.

When I arrived at Pembina Hall in May, the wide balustrades on either side of the double stairway leading into the residence were bare grey cement. As the days and weeks passed, they gradually became covered with Virginia Creeper. By June, a veritable cavalcade of greenery covered the balustrade on one side only. It connected with more leaves in abundance travelling up the height of the stately brick building. It was a lovely sight to behold; almost day by day there was discernible growth as the larger, delicate leaves accompanied by dainty tendrils reached out for a grasping place. When I returned in the fall, after being away from the campus during the summer months, the growth was even more magnificent, arrestingly beautiful on all sides of the building. The scarlet leaves clung to the wall, appearing in some places like rivulets of blood.

Women walking between two worlds are the main vine; I am among them, clinging to the ivory tower, but my children are clinging to me. We climb. We change colours with the seasons. We sweat blood. We carry on.

NOTE

1 Pseudonyms have been used.

Postscript

The personal narratives in this anthology dramatically illustrate the barriers that, still today, stand in the way of many academic women's success. Overcoming the pressures for discretion, the writers have recounted their experiences as they rose to the challenges of the chilly university climate, with its endemic prejudice, androcentricity, and patriarchal structures. We thank them. Their voices provide a powerful collective testimony to the strength and courage of women in the Canadian Academic Tundra.

Although considerable research and soul-searching have taken place in recent years, much more remains to be done both at the academic investigational level and in the attitudinal and behavioural realms. The field is still wide open for research projects and comparative studies among disciplines, regions, and universities. Topics abound within these pages. The inequity inherent in the concentration of women in the lower ranks of academia, which has been so vigorously underscored throughout this book, still demands particular attention.

We hope that the voices of the academic women showcased here will be heard in concert with those of others who are working toward change, so that future generations of women will be enabled to contribute their full measure to the quest for knowledge without sacrificing family, health, or selfhood.

Elena Hannah
Linda Paul
Swani Vethamany-Globus

Contributors

JENNIFER BANKIER is a professor of law at Dalhousie Law School. She has been active in union and equity issues at the local and national level (including four years as chair of the CAUT Status of Women Committee), and her areas of expertise include torts, women and law, equity and academic freedom issues, university governance, and intellectual property and technology law.

SUZAN BANOUB-BADDOUR is an associate professor at the School of Nursing at Memorial University of Newfoundland. Her research interests include health promotion for mothers and infants, the benefits of breastfeeding and children diagnosed with cancer and their families. She is also involved in accessibility of health information to the francophone community.

PETER BOWAL is a professor of law in the Faculty of Management at the University of Calgary. His research interests include public legal education, employment, corporate government and real estate property. He is a Presiding Justice of the Peace in Alberta, as well as a Fulbright Fellow (1998) and a Killam Research Award recipient (1999). He is currently serving as the Judicial Fellow in the Administrative Office of the Chief Justice at the United States Supreme Court.

HELEN BRESLAUER, who now has her own research and consulting business, taught at the University of Toronto, and spent sixteen years as Senior Research Officer for the Ontario Confederation of University Faculty Associations (OCUFA). In 1992 she received CAUT's Sarah Shorten Award "in recognition of an outstanding contribution to the advancement of the status of women in Canadian universities."

DIANNE L. COMMON at the time of the preparation of this book was the vice-president academic at the University of Regina. Her fields of specialty include Educational Administration and University Management. As well, Dianne has been heavily involved in administrative roles. She has been a participant of the University of Regina's project on gender equity in Chinese schools.

LILLIAN EVA DYCK is a professor in the Neuropsychiatry Research Unit, Department of Psychiatry at the University of Saskatchewan. Her field of specialty is biological psychiatry. In addition, she has played an active role in equity issues at the university. Lillian's mother, Eva Quan, was from the Gordon's Reserve in Saskatchewan and her father, Yok Leen Quan, was from Hoiping, Canton, China.

ELLEN E. FACEY is the regional chair and program coordinator at the University of Northern British Columbia in Quesnel BC where she teaches anthropology and women's studies. Her research interests focus on identity, political ideology, and change. Ellen has been developing research projects on the current state of gender equity, the lives and finances of older women, and the potential of the Internet in the education of disadvantaged groups.

WENDY FELDBERG taught English as a second language at the University of Ottawa from 1970 to 2000, fifteen years full-time and fifteen years part-time. She worked on university committees, union activities, and community projects throughout her career. Her (mostly-female) work unit closed at the end of the 2000–2001 academic year. While Wendy continues to publish in the field, she no longer teaches.

SHANNON GADBOIS is currently in a three year full-time position in the Psychology Department at Brandon University. Her latest research is on sports participation as it relates to self-esteem. She has a strong interest in women's issues and is a member of the Status of Women Review Committee at Brandon University. She is also involved in examining the impact of social policy on women's unpaid work.

JANE GORDON teaches in the Department of Sociology and Anthropology at Mount St Vincent University. In addition, she has been closely involved in women's studies programs. She has served as the chair of the Status of Women Committee at CAUT and of the Nova Scotia Confederation of Faculty Associations. She has also worked with women's groups in the community on reproductive health issues and on violence against women.

FYRE JEAN GRAVELINE is a Métis scholar who is associate professor and director of the First Nations and Aboriginal Counselling Degree Program at Brandon University. She has worked in the fields of education and social work for the last twenty-five years. Fyre Jean is also a therapist, community organizer, consultant, and ceremonial leader.

JOYCE GREEN is an associate professor of political science at the University of Regina. She specializes in Canadian politics, and has particular interests in citizenship theory, aboriginal-state relations, and feminist theory and analysis.

MARY RUCKLOS HAMPTON received her EdD in Counseling and Consulting Psychology at Harvard University, after which she taught at the University of Alaska in Fairbanks. Currently she is an Associate Professor of Psychology at Luther College, University of Regina. Her research interests include feminist psychology, and community and cross-cultural psychology.

ELENA HANNAH teaches in the Psychology Department at Memorial University of Newfoundland. Her areas are developmental, personality, and social psychology, sexual behaviour, and gender. Her research has been primarily in social and health psychology. Her expertise in women's reproductive health issues makes her a frequently invited public speaker.

LESLEY D. HARMAN is an associate professor of sociology at King's College, University of Western Ontario. She has published on gender, deviance, poverty, qualitative methods, and social theory. Lesley has three young children. Juggling parenting and career inspired the study upon which her contribution to this volume is based.

ALISON HAYFORD graduated from Barnard College in 1968 and completed her doctorate in geography at the University of Michigan in 1981. She has been a member of the Department of Sociology and Social Studies at the University of Regina since 1978.

DIANE HUBERMAN-ARNOLD, a recipient of the CAUT Sarah Shorten Award (1998), is currently teaching in the philosophy department, Carleton University. Diane's research interests are in applied ethics: bioethics, business ethics, and feminist ethics.

MARTHA (MARTY) KENISTON LAURENCE is a professor of social work at Wilfrid Laurier University. Her research and teaching focus on women and change, learning and mental/social health, clinical, organizational, and community practice. Her excellence in teaching has been recognized by the 1997 OCUFA Teaching Award as well as by Laurier's 1998 Outstanding Teacher Award.

ANNE M. LAVACK is an associate professor in the Faculty of Administration at the University of Regina. She spent ten years working in the advertising and marketing field prior to obtaining a PhD in marketing from the University of British Columbia. Her research is focused on social marketing and tobacco advertising.

BLUMA LITNER is associate professor in the Department of Applied Human Sciences at Concordia University, Montreal. In recent years, Bluma has received a national 3M Teaching Fellowship for excellence in university teaching and leadership in education, as well as two other teaching awards. Her research interests centre on processes of empowerment for marginalized groups, inclusive education, and organizational change.

JEANETTE LYNES is an associate professor of English at St Francis Xavier University. Her research interests centre around the collection of poems by women, and she has published several books. She is active in women's issues and is past Chair of the CAUT Status of Women Committee.

HARRIET D. LYONS is an associate professor of anthropology at the University of Waterloo, where she has also taught women's studies. Her research interests include the anthropology of religion and psychological anthropology, and she has worked on joint projects with her husband on mass communications in Benin City, Nigeria, and on the history of anthropologists' accounts of sexuality.

GERALDINE (JODY) MACDONALD is a contractual teacher in the Community Health Nursing program of the Faculty of Nursing at the University of Toronto. Her research interests focus on health promotion directed at parents and, in particular, on creating a culture of peace. She is an active member of Voice of Women, a non-governmental organization.

JENNIFER MATHER is a professor in the Department of Psychology at the University of Lethbridge. Her teaching interests include perception, developmental and abnormal psychology, and aging. Her research focuses on the behaviour of cephalopod molluscs. She is on the board of the Lethbridge Alzheimer's Society and has been active on equity issues in the faculty association locally as well as nationally.

DENISE S. McCONNEY (Naapiaaki/Moonias) teaches courses in the departments of Native Studies and English, both on campus and at distance sites, including English courses on reserve for the Thunderchild Plains Cree First Nation. Her PhD English Field exams in Native literatures, the first at the University of Saskatchewan, were completed in December 2000. Denise was awarded a SSHRC doctoral fellowship in March 2001.

SUSAN McCORQUODALE, a professor at Memorial University of Newfoundland, taught political science for thirty-five years. Susan survived childhood polio, and proved to be an achiever in spite of being physically challenged. She won the Lieutenant-Governor's 1994 award for excellence in public administration. Susan was admired and loved by all who came in contact with her. She died suddenly in January 1999 while holidaying in Vancouver, BC.

SHAHRZAD MOJAB is associate professor in the Department of Adult Education, Community Development, and Counselling Psychology, The Ontario Institute for the Studies in Education at the University of Toronto. Her specialties include educational policy studies with a focus on policies affecting the access and academic life of marginalized groups in universities and colleges.

PATRICIA A. MONTURE-ANGUS, a Mohawk lawyer originally from the Six Nations Territory near Brantford, Ontario, is a professor at the University of Saskatchewan, Department of Native Studies, Saskatoon. She has been involved in politics and activism, advocating for the rights of Aboriginal women and Aboriginal prisoners.

ANNE MORGAN, who is a biologist, was an assistant professor in the Department of Biology at the University of Waterloo where she carried out collaborative research with her husband. Anne interrupted her academic career to raise her two children. Currently she is a Master Gardener and volunteers to educate community groups on environmental issues.

MAXINE C. MOTT is currently dean of community and health studies in Kwantlen University College, Surrey, BC, and was previously dean of Page Campus, Coconico Community College, in Arizona. She has been an advocate for gender equity throughout her career.

ANDREA O'REILLY is an Assistant Professor in the School of Women's Studies at York University. She was the recipient of the 1998 University-Wide Teaching Award at York University. She is founding president of the Association for Research on Mothering (ARM) and managing editor of the ARM journal, and she has edited several books on motherhood and feminism.

MARIANNE D. PARSONS teaches as a contractual part-time faculty member at Dalhousie University, Mount Saint Vincent University, and Saint Mary's University. She is completing her doctoral dissertation, examining gender and the casualization of university teaching, at York University. Addressing equity issues has been a key focus in her activist work.

LINDA JOAN PAUL is a geographer primarily interested in human geography with special emphasis on geography and literature, gender, culture, and urban and political geography. Currently an instructor at the University of Regina, Linda is a passionate champion of the causes of part-timers/session-als and is active locally and nationally through CAUT in improving working conditions for women in the Canadian academy.

PETRA REMY co-authored with Lesley Harman the article in this collection "Life Gets in the Way of Life." Petra completed her Master's degree in Sociology under the supervision of Lesley Harman. She is currently working with Canada Trust.

AMY ROWAT is a graduate of Mt Allison University (BSc Honours Physics, BA Asian Studies, French, and Mathematics). She is currently living in Copenhagen and pursuing her PhD in Biophysics at the Department of Chemistry, Technical University of Denmark.

JOAN SCOTT, recently retired, taught biology and women's studies at Memorial University of Newfoundland. Her interests are in qualitative research on the careers of academic women and men in the biological sciences. Joan has been active in equity issues at the local as well as the national level.

STEVI (M.E.) STEPHENS earned her PhD in anthropology while a single parent. She has taught at colleges and universities in Georgia, North Carolina, British Columbia, and Alberta. Her expertise is in the areas of archaeology, paleontology, and cultural anthropology. She is currently on her first non-limited term teaching contract at the College of the Rockies at Cranbrook, BC.

CAROL ALEXIS STOS is an assistant professor of Spanish language, literature, and culture, and former chair of the Department of Modern Languages and vice-dean of Humanities and Social Sciences at Laurentian University. She is particularly interested in the works of Emilia Pardo Bazán (1851–1921), Luso-Hispanic humour, the work of Spanish and Latina women writers and women in academia.

MARILYN TAYLOR is a professor in the Department of Applied Human Sciences at Concordia University. She has been active in equity issues both at the local and the national level. She is a member of the SSHRC-funded women's research network team and has published on equity initiatives in Canadian universities.

DOROTHY TOVELL, a biochemist, is currently working part-time at the University of Alberta as an administrative assistant in the Department of Medical Microbiology and Immunology and as a sessional instructor in women's studies. She recently started her own business as a health information provider.

CÉCYLE TRÉPANIER est professeure au Département de géographie de l'Université Laval dans la ville de Québec. Sa recherche s'inscrit dans le champ de la géographie culturelle et concerne principalement la francophonie nord-américaine. Cécyle is a professor at the Department of Geography at Laval University in Quebec City. She is currently teaching cultural and regional geography and conducts her research in these areas, pertaining primarily to French North America.

SUSAN M. TURNER, a single parent of three, has taught philosophy at the University of Lethbridge, the University of Victoria, and Athabasca University. Her area of scholarly specialization is moral, social, and political philosophy and, she is also a practising philosophical counsellor.

SWANI VETHAMANY-GLOBUS is an associate professor (50% fractional load) in the Department of Biology at the University of Waterloo. Her research interests include salamander limb regeneration, and she teaches embryology and histology. In addition to carrying her undergraduate student advising duties, she has been active in the UW Senate, the Faculty Association board and numerous equity-related committees.

IRENE WANKE is currently an assistant professor in the Faculty of Medicine at the University of Calgary. Her research interests are on the effects of diabetes mellitus on gene expression and gene therapy in the treatment of diabetes. Irene has co-authored the article in this book with her husband, Peter Bowal, comparing their career paths as members of an academic couple.

DEBORAH WILLS works in the English Department of Mount Allison University, where she teaches courses in literary theory, cultural studies, genre, and postmodernism. She has published or presented papers on, most recently, novelists Joanna Russ, Larissa Lai, Angela Carte, and the pseudonymous writers of the Black Lace series.

SUSAN WILSON continues to teach part-time at Camosun College and is working on her PhD in English at the University of Victoria. In addition to her academic pursuits, she has travelled extensively, and enjoys pen and ink drawing and working in water colours.

ROCHELLE YAMAGISHI completed a PhD in sociology of education at the University of Alberta in 1997. She works as an elementary school counsellor, teaches intermittently at the University of Lethbridge in the Sociology Department and the Faculty of Education, and at the University of Calgary Faculty of Social Work. Recently she became an individualized study tutor for Athabasca University. She has won awards for her writings.

References

Adler, N.J. 1997. Global leaders: A dialogue with future history, *Management International*, vol. 1, no. 2, 21–33.

Astin, A. 1985. *Achieving Academic Excellence*. San Francisco: Jossey-Bass Publishers.

Bacon, F. In *Collins Dictionary of Quotations*. 1978 ed. New York: Collins.

Baker-Miller, J.B. 1986. *Toward a New Psychology of Women*. Boston: Beacon Press.

Bateson, M.C. 1990. *Composing a Life*. New York: Plume.

Berardo, D.N., Shehen, C.L., and Leslie, G.R. 1987. A residue of tradition: jobs, careers, and spouses' time in housework. *Journal of Marriage and the Family*, 49: 381–90.

Berk, L. 2000. *Child Development*. 5th Ed. Boston, MA: Allyn and Bacon.

Boyer, E.L. 1990. *Scholarship Reconsidered: Priorities of the Professoriate*. Princeton, NJ: The Carnegie Foundation for the Advancement of Teaching.

Brayfield, A.A. 1992. Employment resources and housework in Canada. *Journal of Marriage and the Family*, 54: 19–30.

Burton, R.C. 1987. *The Academic Life, Small Worlds, Different Worlds*. Princeton, NJ: The Carnegie Foundation for the Advancement of Teaching.

Canadian Association of University Teachers. 1993. CAUT Status of Women Supplement.

Caplan, P.J. 1994. *Lifting a Ton of Feathers: A Woman's Guide to Surviving in the Academic World*. Toronto: University of Toronto Press.

Cohen, A., and Gutek, B. 1991. Sex differences in the Career Experiences of Members of Two APA Divisions. *American Psychologist*, 46 (12): 1291–8.

Committee G. (Nov./Dec., 1992). On the status of non-tenure-track faculty. *Academe* vol. 78, no. 6: 39–49.

Concordia University, Office of the Status of Women. 1991. *Inequity in the Classroom*. Montreal: Concordia University.

Corcoran, M., Duncan, G.J., and Ponza, M. 1984. Work experience, job segregation and wages. In B. Reskin (ed.), *Sex Segregation in the Workplace: Trends, Explanations, Remedies*. Washington: National Academy of Sciences.

Daly, M. 1973. *Beyond God the Father: Toward a Philosophy of Women's Liberation*. Boston: Beacon Press.

Devereaux, M.S. 1993. Time use of Canadians in 1992. *Canadian Social Trends*, Autumn: 13–35.

Desserud, D. Women in New Brunswick politics: Waiting for the third wave. In Arscott, J. and L. Trimble, eds. 1997. *In the Presence of Women*. Toronto: Harcourt Brace Canada.

Douthitt, R.A. 1989. The division of labour within the home: have gender roles changed? *Sex Roles*, 20: 693–704.

Drakich, J. and Stewart, P. April 1998. A profile of women faculty in Canada: rank, discipline and age, 1957–1994. *Status of Women Supplement*. CAUT *Bulletin*. vol. 45, no. 4: 7.

Eagly, A.H. and Chaiken, S. 1993. *The Psychology of Attitudes*. Fort Worth, Texas: Harcourt, Brace, Jovanovich.

Eichenbaum, L. and Orbach, S. 1989. *Between Women: Love, Envy and Competition in Women's Friendships*. New York: Penguin Books.

Eisenstein, Z.R. 1988. *The Female Body and the Law*. Berkeley: University of California Press.

Frost, R. 1920. "The Road Not Taken," *Mountain Interval*. New York: Henry Holt.

Gappa, J.M. 1987. The Stress-Producing Working Conditions of Part-time Faculty, *New Directions for Teaching and Learning*, no. 29 (Spring): 33–42.

Gardner, S. 1993. "What's a nice working-class girl like you doing in a place like this?." In M. Tokarczyk and E. Fay. (eds.), *Working-class Women in the Academy, Laborers in the Knowledge Factory*. Amherst: University of Massachusetts Press, 49–72.

Greer, G. 1991. *The Change: Women, Aging and the Menopause*. Toronto: Alfred A. Knopf.

Grumet, M.R. 1988. *Bitter Milk: Women and Teaching*. Amherst: The University of Massachusetts Press.

Hamilton, A.C. and Sinclair, C.M. 1991. *Report of the Aboriginal Justice Inquiry of Manitoba: The Justice System and Aboriginal People*. Winnipeg: Queen's Printer, 85–8, 109–13, and 658–9.

Hochschild, A. 1989. *The Second Shift: Working Parents and the Revolution at Home*. New York: Viking.

Holden, K. and Hanson, W.L. 1987. Part–time work, full–time work, and occupational segregation. In Brown, C. and Pechman, J. eds. *Gender in the Workplace*. Washington: Brookings Institution.

Hornosty, J. M. 1998. Balancing child care and work. In Stalker, J. and Prentice, S. eds., *The Illusion of Inclusion*. Halifax, NS: Fernwood Publishing, 180–93.

Jackson, M. 1992. *The Mother Zone: Love, Sex and Laundry in the Modern Family.* Toronto: Macfarlane, Walter & Ross, 5.

Jewson, N. and D. Mason. 1992. "Race," equal opportunities, policies and employment practice: Reflections on the 1980s, prospects for the 1990's, *New Community*, 19(1): 99–112: 108.

Kelly, J. 1998. *Under the Gaze: Learning to Be Black in a White Society.* Halifax: Fernwood.

Kettle, J. 1996. Good practices, bad attitudes: An examination of the factors influencing women's academic careers. In Morley, L. and Walsh, V. (eds.), *Breaking Boundaries: Women in Higher Education*. London: Taylor & Francis Ltd.

LaRocque, E. 1996. The colonization of a nature woman scholar. In C. Miller and P. Chuchryk (eds.), *Women of the First Nations: Power, Wisdom, and Strength*. Winnipeg: University of Manitoba Press.

LaRocque, E. 1999. Native writers resisting colonizing practices in Canadian historiography. Unpublished dissertation. University of Manitoba.

Laurence, M.K. 1989. Role models – Importance and availability. In Filteau, C. (ed.): *Proceedings of a Conference on Women in Graduate Studies in Ontario*. Toronto: Ontario Council on Graduate Studies: 60–7.

Laurence M.K. 1996. Women's conceptualization of their place in the university. Presented at the International Interdisciplinary Congress on Women. Adelaide, Australia.

Laurence M.K. 1998. Surviving and thriving as a feminist change agent in the university. In: *Proceedings of the 11ᵗʰ Annual International Conference on Women in Higher Education*. El Paso, TX: University of Texas at El Paso.

Laurence M.K. 1999. A three-part collision: my negotiated passage in a patriarchal organization. In Malmo and Laidlaw (eds.), *Consciousness Raising: Women's Theories of Connection and Transformation*. Charlottetown: Gynergy Books.

Lee, Diane M. 1998. Learning to listen and listening to learn, *Women in Higher Education*, June 1998: 19–20.

Lerner, H.G. 1985. *The Dance of Anger*. New York: Harper & Row.

Lynn, M. and Todoroff, M. 1998. Women's work and family lives. In Mandell, N. *Feminist Issues: Race, Class and Sexuality.* Scarborough, ON: Prentice Hall Allyn and Bacon Canada.

Maccoby, E. 1980. *Social development*. New York: Harcourt Brace Jovanovich.

Macdonald, G. 1996. *Sustaining Energy for Caring: The Experience of Mothers who are Nurses*. Unpublished doctoral dissertation. Toronto: University of Toronto.

Macguire, P. 1987. *Doing Feminist Research: A Feminist Approach*. Amherst, MASS: Center for International Education.

Moss Kantor, R. 1977. *Men and Women of the Corporation*. New York: Basic Books.

Mulligen, A. 1989. Women's Studies and Tenure Still Don't Mix. *American Association of University Women, 83,*(4).

Ng, R. 1999. Sexism and racism in the university: analyzing a personal experience. In Amin, Beer et al. (eds.), *Canadian Woman Studies: An Introductory Reader*. Toronto: Inanna Publications.

Ondaatje, M. 1992. *The English Patient*. New York: Vintage Books.

Ornstein, M., P. Stewart, and J. Drakich. 1998. The status of women faculty in Canadian universities. *Education Quarterly Review.* Statistics Canada, Cat. no. 81–003, vol. 5, no. 2.

Overall, C. 1998. *A Feminist I: Reflections from Academia*. Peterborough: Broadview Press.

Paul, L.J. April 1998. Dilemmas and solutions for part-timers, CAUT Supplement, *The Bulletin*, vol. 45, no. 4: 3, 10.

Rajagopal, I. and W.D. Farr. 1992. Hidden academics: the part-time faculty in Canada. *Higher Education*, vol. 24, no. 3: 317–331.

Rajagopal, I. and W.D. Farr. 1999. The political economy of part-time academic work in Canada. *Higher Education* vol. 18, no. 3: 267–85.

Razack, S. 1998. Looking White People in the Eye: Gender, Race, and Culture in Courtrooms and Classrooms. Toronto: University of Toronto Press.

Redekop, C. and U. Bender. 1988. *Who am I? What am I?* Grand Rapids, MI: Academie Books-Zondervan.

Reynolds, C. 1994. The educational system. In Mandell, N. (ed.), *Feminist Issues: Gender, Race and Sexuality.* Toronto: Prentice-Hall, 272–93

Reynolds, C. and B. Young. 1995. *Women and Leadership in Canadian Education*. Calgary, AB: Detselig Enterprises Ltd.

Richard Ivey School of Business. 1998. *Women in Management*, Editorial, What are the Organizational Policy Trends for Women Walking the Tightrope?, 9, no. 1, Sept./October: 1–3.

Rosenblum, G. and B.R. Rosenblum. 1990. Segmented Labor Markets in Institutions of Higher Learning, *Sociology of Education* 63 (July): 151–164.

Rosenblum, G. and B.R. Rosenblum. 1994. Academic Labor Markets: Perspectives from Ontario, *The Canadian Journal of Higher Education* XXIV, 1: 48–71.

Royal Commission of Aboriginal Peoples. 1994. Statistics Infobase. *The Legacy Interim CD-ROM Report* [Pilot Version].

Rupp, J. 1988. *Praying Our Goodbyes*, New York: Ivy Books.

Schiebinger, L. 1999. *Has Feminism Changed Science?* Cambridge: Harvard University Press.

Schwartz, F. 1992. *Breaking with Tradition: Women and Work, the New Facts of Life*. New York: Warner Books.

Sharff, J.W. and J. Lessinger. 1994. The academic sweatshop: Changes in the capitalist infrastructure and the part-time academic. *Anthropology of Work Review* XV, 1 (Spring): 2–11.

Sleeter. C.E. 1991. Introduction: Multicultural education and empowerment. In *Empowerment Through Multicultural Education*. New York: SUNY Press, 1–23.

Spain, D. and S.M. Bianchi. 1996. *Balancing Act: Motherhood, Marriage, and Employment among American Women*. New York: Russell Sage Foundation.

Stalker, J. and S. Prentice (eds.) 1998. *The Illusion of Inclusion: Women in Post–Secondary Education*. Halifax: Fernwood Publishing.

The Economist. August 1996. Women in American Boardrooms: Through the Glass Darkly, 50–1.

Thompson, K. Nov./Dec. 1992. Recognizing mutual interests, *Academe* 78, 6.

Tittle, C.K. 1986. Gender research and education. *American Psychologist*, 1161–8.

Tudiver, N. 1999. *Universities for Sale: Resisting Corporate Control over Higher Education*. Toronto: James Lorimer.

Turk, J.L. (ed.) 2000. *The Corporate Campus: Commercialization and the Dangers to Canada's Colleges and Universities*. Toronto: James Lorimer.

Tzu, L. 1990. (ca 1 CE) *Tao Teh Ching*. (Trans. John C.H. Wu). Boston and London: Shambhala, 32–3.

University of Alaska. 1991. *College of Rural Alaska Newsletter*, 7.

Valdes, F., J.M. Culp, and A.P. Harris (eds.) 2001. *Crossroads, Directions, and a New Critical Race Theory*. Chicago: Temple University Press.

Warme, B. and K. Lundy. 1986. Part-time faculty: institutional needs and career dilemmas. In Lundy and Warme, *Work in the Canadian Context: Continuity Despite Change*. Toronto: Butterworths, 132–48.

Weaver, L.H. 1993. A Mennonite "hard worker" moves from the working class and the religious/ethnic community to the academy: A conflict between two definitions of "work." In Tokarczyk, M. and E. Fay eds. *Working-class Women in the Academy, Laborers in the Knowledge Factory*, Amherst: University of Massachusetts Press, 112–25.

Yeatman, A. 1993. The gendered management of equity-oriented change in higher education. In D. Barber and M. Fogarty (eds.), *A Gendered Culture*, Wellington: Victoria University of Wellington, 24.